START YOUR OWN

airbnb
Business

HOW TO MAKE MONEY
WITH SHORT-TERM RENTALS

Entrepreneur. STARTUP ⠿

START YOUR OWN

airbnb Business

HOW TO MAKE MONEY WITH SHORT-TERM RENTALS

**THE STAFF OF ENTREPRENEUR MEDIA
AND JASON R. RICH**

Entrepreneur Press, Publisher

Cover Design: Andrew Welyczko
Production and Composition: Alan Barnett Design

Library of Congress Cataloging-in-Publication Data

Names: Rich, Jason R., author. | Entrepreneur Media, LLC, issuing body.
Title: Start your own Airbnb business : how to make money with short-term
    rentals / by The Staff of Entrepreneur Media and Jason R. Rich.
Description: Irvine, CA : Entrepreneur Press, [2024] | Series: Start you
    own | Includes index. | Summary: "Start Your Own Airbnb Business is your
    step-by-step guide to illuminate your property's assets and maximize
    your earning potential through the Airbnb platform"—Provided by publisher.
Identifiers: LCCN 2023015590 (print) | LCCN 2023015591 (ebook) | ISBN
    9781642011616 (paperback) | ISBN 9781613084724 (epub)
Subjects: LCSH: Airbnb (Firm) | Rental housing. | Hospitality industry.
Classification: LCC HD1394 .R53 2024 (print) | LCC HD1394 (ebook) | DDC
    333.33/8--dc23/eng/20230707
LC record available at https://lccn.loc.gov/2023015590
LC ebook record available at https://lccn.loc.gov/2023015591

Table of Contents

Acknowledgments

Thanks to the folks at Entrepreneur, including Sean Strain, for inviting me to work on this book. I'd also like to thank all the Airbnb hosts and Superhosts who agreed to be interviewed for this book, and who were willing to share their experiences and advice.

About the Author

Jason R. Rich (www.JasonRich.com) has written more than a dozen books for Entrepreneur covering topics related to entrepreneurship, operating a successful e-commerce business, and using the internet and technology to effectively market/promote a business. One of his most recent books is *The Remote Worker's Handbook: How to Effectively Work from Anywhere,* which is now available from bookstores, Amazon, B&N, and the Entrepreneur Bookstore (www.entrepreneur.com/bookstore).

In addition, he has worked full-time as a consumer technology writer for Forbes Vetted (www.forbes.com/vetted) and continues to contribute technology-related articles to *AARP the Magazine, AARP Bulletin*, and a variety of other publications and websites. Throughout the year, he also serves as an enrichment lecturer aboard cruise ships. He lectures to passengers about digital photography, smartphones, tablets, internet security, social media, online privacy, and how everyday people can easily incorporate technology and smart devices into their daily lives.

Please follow Jason R. Rich on Instagram (@JasonRich7), Twitter (@JasonRich7), Facebook (www.facebook.com/JasonRich7), and LinkedIn (www.linkedin.com/in/jasonrich7).

Preface

Airbnb (www.airbnb.com) was originally founded in 2008. Its popularity among travelers around the world has allowed the company to experience tremendous success and growth since then. This has also allowed the 2.9 million hosts on Airbnb (as of early 2023) to generate revenue by making their property available for short-term rental. In fact, according to Stratosjets.com, in 2022 there were upwards of seven million listings on Airbnb around the world, with 14,000 new hosts joining the platform every month. This collection of Airbnb hosts extends throughout 220 countries (encompassing more than 100,000 cities) around the world. In the United States. Airbnb reported there were more than 660,000 property listings on the Airbnb platform in early 2023.

So, yes, becoming a host on the Airbnb platform has proven to be a viable income-generating opportunity—but becoming a successful host is not without its challenges. The goal of this book is to help you overcome those challenges, outperform your competition, and generate the highest revenue possible from your short-term rental property by listing it on Airbnb.

Unfortunately, COVID-19 (which officially became a pandemic in 2020) had a dramatic and negative impact on the moneymaking opportunities available to Airbnb hosts. In early 2023, however, hosts started to recover when vacation- and business-related travel started picking up. This uptick in business began in the first quarter of 2022. During this period, Airbnb reported more than 100 million bookings and an increased revenue of $1.5 billion. This was a dramatic 80 percent increase compared to the first quarter of 2019 (according to Stratosjets.com).

With the proper planning, approach, and dedication, you, too, can become a successful Airbnb host, Superhost, and/or Airbnb Experience provider and then enjoy a reasonably steady income from your efforts—provided you have realistic expectations. Today, Airbnb offers a range of different accommodation options to travelers, including the "classic" Airbnb Experience, Airbnb for Work, Airbnb Plus, and Airbnb Luxe. The most common option for hosts is to provide a classic experience, which means renting out an entire property, a single private room within a property (with spaces shared with the property owner and potentially other guests), or a shared room (where multiple people potentially share the same bedroom and bathroom, for example).

Since its inception, Airbnb has been an online marketplace for travelers who are looking for affordable accommodations. However, the service's offerings and focus have changed rather dramatically to keep up with changing demands. Airbnb's core business model still involves connecting travelers with Airbnb hosts who choose to rent out a portion of their home, apartment, or other type of property (or an entire property) to people seeking out temporary housing accommodations or, in some cases, unique and memorable experiences—often for less than what traditional hotel accommodations cost.

Beyond just offering a classic Airbnb Experience, some hosts cater to people traveling for work or who are looking for a remote work location. There are also hosts who have earned the Superhost designation and who provide superior classic accommodations to travelers. For hosts able to provide a truly unique and upscale experience for their guests, it's possible to have a property listed in the Airbnb Luxe database, but out of the seven million total Airbnb listings, the number of Airbnb Luxe listings is less than 5,000 (as of early 2023). Currently on Airbnb, the fastest growing type of short-term rental listing is for unique types of accommodations—from remote cabins in the woods, to tiny homes, upscale RVs, castles, lighthouses, yurts, treehouses, private islands, and even igloos.

For example, as of early 2023, there were more than 288 treehouse listings throughout the world on Airbnb, along with upwards of 252 nicely furnished accommodations within caves, 140+ igloos, 300+ lighthouses, 292+ accommodations on vineyards or wineries, and more than 264 houseboats available for short-term rental.

While most travelers who use Airbnb are looking to save money, compared to staying at a traditional hotel or motel, there's a growing percentage of travelers willing to pay a premium for truly unique accommodations and experiences. It's because of this evolution and expansion of Airbnb's offerings that the service has been able to help more than one billion travelers find accommodations to meet their demands and budget since the company's inception.

With all that said, if you have a home or apartment with one or more extra bedrooms, or an entire property that you could offer as a short-term rental to earn extra income, you, too, can become an Airbnb host. However, it's important to understand that your revenue potential will depend a lot on the property's location, demand, competition, what's being offered, your reputation as a host, and what you charge. It's also important to understand the types of people who frequently use Airbnb to find and book accommodations. For example, according to Stratosjets.com, 36 percent of Airbnb users are between the ages of 25 and 35, while 23 precent are between the ages of 36 and 44. About 15 percent are between the ages of 18 and 24, and 14 percent are between the ages of 45 and 54. It's the senior population (people over the age of 55), however, that's currently Airbnb's fastest growing group of customers.

Beyond just the type of accommodations travelers are seeking through Airbnb, the amenities and services travelers are looking for from their hosts have also changed. For example, according to TheRealist.io, the most searched amenities travelers were looking for in 2022, in order of demand, were pets allowed, swimming pool, Wi-Fi, kitchen, and free parking. Back in 2019, the five most searched amenities (in order of popularity) were swimming pool, Wi-Fi, kitchen, air-conditioning, and pets allowed. As of early 2023, Airbnb reported a more than 55 percent increase in demand for pet-friendly accommodations, while the demand for laptop-friendly workspaces was up 73 percent (indicating that more and more travelers want or need to work remotely during their stay).

Listing your property as a short-term rental on Airbnb allows people like you to become a travel host. If this type of part-time, moneymaking business opportunity seems appealing, or you want to learn more about it, *Start Your Own Airbnb Business* offers a comprehensive, independent, unbiased, and informative how-to resource you need to read! Airbnb allows travel hosts (people like you), from all walks of life, to list their extra bedroom(s), or their entire home, condo, or apartment, as a short-term rental option for travelers. Airbnb helps to match up travelers quickly, securely, and conveniently with hosts—and then handles virtually all of the related financial transactions and reservation management responsibilities.

As you're about to discover, depending on your geographic location, as well as local laws and ordinances, what type of property you have to offer, the level of commitment you want to make as a host, and a variety of other factors, there are multiple things to consider prior to becoming a travel host.

First and foremost, *Start Your Own Airbnb Business* will help you make intelligent decisions, take appropriate actions and precautions, and deal with realistic expectations, while protecting yourself, your property, and your personal belongings as much as possible once you become a host. This book will also help you quickly acquire the core knowledge you need to become a successful travel host and help you maximize your revenue, while avoiding the most common pitfalls and mistakes that are often made by first-time hosts. You'll discover a variety of optional tools and resources at your disposal that will make handling your responsibilities as a travel host easier and less time consuming, while helping you increase your revenue and dramatically improving your chances for success.

In addition to providing detailed "how-to" and "step-by-step" information related to becoming a successful host with Airbnb, this book offers in-depth and exclusive interviews with a handful of successful hosts and veteran Airbnb Superhosts. These hosts each share their firsthand experiences and advice. From these interviews, you'll discover what works, what pitfalls to avoid, and how to make the most out of your hosting experience from a personal and financial standpoint. You'll also gain valuable insight about how to interact with your guests, earn the best possible ratings and reviews, and at the same time, avoid common mistakes made by new hosts.

How Much the Average Host Earns Per Year

While this varies greatly by location, according to Airbnb, in 2022 the average host earned $924 per month ($11,088 per year), although many hosts earned a six-figure income from managing one or more properties offered for short-term rental through the service. Meanwhile, iProperty Management reported that, on average, a host received $185 per night, the average booking length was 4.3 nights, and a host's property had an average occupancy rate of 48 percent. In some U.S. cities, these stats were much higher. AirDNA reported that, in 2022, the average occupancy rate for an Airbnb property was 59.8 percent. About 45 percent of bookings were for one week or longer, as travelers booking through Airbnb typically stay 2.4 times longer in their chosen accommodations than they would at a traditional hotel or motel.

Before moving any further, the thing you need to understand is that, these days, most travelers who use Airbnb are looking for clean, safe, and comfortable accommodations, superior customer service, and a hassle-free stay at the accommodations they ultimate choose. According to the *Dream Big Travel Far* blog, more than half of Airbnb's customers choose Airbnb for accommodations to save money compared to a traditional hotel or motel. And a growing number of travelers who use Airbnb to find accommodations are looking for someplace to stay that's unique. If you're not willing or able to provide this, you should seek out an alternate income-generating opportunity.

CHAPTER 1

Airbnb: Changing the Way People Travel

Do you have a clean and comfortable spare room in your apartment or home where your friends and family enjoy staying when they visit? Perhaps you have a second apartment or vacation home that you don't use as often as you'd like, so it sits vacant for much of the year. Well, without making any long-term commitments, thanks to online-based travel hosting services like Airbnb, it's possible to share extra living spaces with other people, on a short-term basis, and generate some extra income in the process.

The focus of this book is to teach you the ins and outs of being a successful Airbnb host, so that you're able to avoid the pitfalls, generate the highest revenue possible, and earn the best possible reviews and ratings from your guests.

Beyond Airbnb, there are other platforms that offer similar services, like Vrbo, Homestay, and Booking.com. However, the focus of this book is exclusively on Airbnb. Before becoming a host on this service, consider investing time to do your own research to determine—based on your own preferences and what you're offering—which other service(s), in addition to or instead of Airbnb, might offer the best opportunity for you as a travel host. At first glance, the concept behind Airbnb and similar services is rather straightforward and simple. You provide guests with a place to stay, and they pay a nightly fee.

However, before you opt to become a travel host, there are a handful of important factors you'll need to consider, misconceptions you'll need to overcome, preparations you'll need to make, and expenses you'll need to factor into your budget. There are also local and state laws you'll need to abide by, insurance to acquire (beyond basic homeowner's insurance), and plenty of additional planning to do.

It's important to understand, right from the start, that becoming an Airbnb host is not a get-rich-quick scheme, nor is it a viable moneymaking opportunity for everyone. Many factors, which you'll learn about shortly, go into whether you'll be able to consistently generate enough revenue as a host to make this opportunity worthwhile. However, if you make all the right moves, as a property owner, you can be successful. For example, out of the more than 2.9 million Airbnb hosts worldwide, some are making consistent money, continue to meet awesome new people, and absolutely love the opportunities that Airbnb provides.

From the relatively small amount of time spent fielding traveler inquiries and coordinating the cleaning and maintenance of their property, owners (hosts) use the money they earn to pay off their mortgage, upgrade and renovate their property, fund their everyday living expenses, and save for retirement. There are also a growing number of Airbnb hosts who choose to invest in multiple properties that they use exclusively for short-term rental income. This is a business model we'll take a closer look at within Chapter 11, "Ways to Make Being an Airbnb Host Your Full-Time Career."

Be aware, however, that there are many other hosts who have had to deal with a wide range of problems and frustrations, such as inconsiderate guests, unexpected fines, and, in some cases, fraud or crime, resulting in financial losses. There could also be issues with the property manager or cleaning service you choose to hire, or technical issues with the smart technology you use to control door locks and alarm/video surveillance systems, for example.

Discover Airbnb and What So Many Travelers Are Raving About

Founded in August 2008, Airbnb has evolved into a massive online community and marketplace that allows travelers from all walks of life to discover, book, and pay for short-term, nightly accommodations almost anywhere in the world. The

Airbnb Experience starts online, by visiting the Airbnb website (www.airbnb
.com) or utilizing the official Airbnb mobile app from any smartphone or tablet
that has internet access.

Types of Accommodations That Can Be Offered on Airbnb

Airbnb allows hosts to offer a private guestroom or shared rooms (within a
home, condo, or apartment, for example), an entire apartment, or an entire
home (or condo living space) to guests. Accommodations should include a
private or shared bathroom, as well as other amenities and options, such as
use of a kitchen, in-home Wi-Fi, laundry facilities, and private or nearby parking.

When a private or shared guestroom is offered, this typically means that the
property's host is living on-site. Based on space available, additional Airbnb
guests may also be sharing the property. However, when a traveler books an
entire apartment or home, this means they are reserving the entire place for
themselves (and their travel companions). The host will initially greet them (in
person or remotely) and be available during the guest's stay, but not living/
staying on the actual premises.

Airbnb also offers unique or unusual places for travelers to stay, including
historic castles, lakefront cottages, ski chalets, or even treehouses (that can be
lived in). Another type of accommodation that's quickly becoming popular
on Airbnb is experiential, a topic we'll cover more in Chapter 2, "Get Started as
an Airbnb Host."

Instead of offering traditional, full-service hotel rooms, bed-and-breakfast
accommodations, timeshare opportunities, or resort accommodations, for example, the entire focus of Airbnb is to provide travelers with a fast, easy, and a relatively low-cost way to stay in someone's guestroom, apartment, entire home,
or even a castle. That said, Airbnb has also evolved over time to allow hosts to
include premium-level accommodations at higher rates, remote work-friendly
accommodations, family-friendly accommodations, pet-friendly accommodations, and unique vacation experiences that go well beyond just offering a place
for guests to sleep.

Currently when travelers visit Airbnb, they'll discover more than seven million different places to stay, offered by Airbnb hosts in more than 100,000 cities (within more than 220 countries) around the world.

Most people who become Airbnb hosts are not full-time hospitality professionals or real estate investors. Instead, they're ordinary people, from all walks of life, with a vast assortment of backgrounds. These people choose to invite travelers to stay with them so they can earn some extra income and meet new people (potentially from around the world).

For travelers, Airbnb is attractive for several reasons, including:

- Accommodations offer a less commercial, homier alternative to chain hotels/motels and traditional accommodations.

- The nightly cost to stay at an Airbnb property is typically somewhat less than a traditional hotel/motel in that same area. As you'll discover, nightly pricing offered on Airbnb is based on a handful of criteria, but rates are ultimately set or agreed to by the host.

- Finding and booking a reservation is all done online, via the Airbnb.com website or mobile app.

- Travelers can quickly learn about a place to stay by reading its description, viewing the provided property photos, reading the host's profile, and reviewing the ratings and reviews that the property and host have received from past Airbnb guests.

- Travelers can get their questions answered and their concerns addressed before making and prepaying for their booking by contacting a prospective host via the Airbnb website or mobile app. (Hosts are expected to respond extremely quickly, so as a host, this will be one of your day-to-day responsibilities.)

For Airbnb hosts, this service is attractive for several reasons, including:

- Hosts determine exactly what they're offering in terms of accommodations and/or experiences. They can target their accommodations to a specific type of traveler or vacationer, or welcome anyone interested in staying at their property.

- Using the scheduling tool built into the Airbnb platform, hosts can determine on what dates they want to make their property available. Airbnb does not set a minimum or maximum number of nights per month or year that the property needs to be available.

- Hosts can communicate with and approve a guest before the reservation is made, unless the host turns on Airbnb's Instant Book feature. (New hosts should keep this feature turned off for reasons that will be explained in Chapter 2.)

- Hosts set their own nightly pricing. (Airbnb charges a small percent as a host service fee on each reservation, which is one way the service itself makes money.)

- Hosts can meet, interact with, and, in some cases, socialize with their guests and make new friends.

- Airbnb offers a way to generate extra revenue, requiring a relatively low time commitment.

- The Airbnb platform generates guest referrals, handles all the reservation processing, and manages all the financial transactions between the travelers and hosts. The host, however, can (and should) do their own marketing to generate a higher occupancy rate throughout the year and maximize their revenue. Be sure to read Chapter 10, "10 Ways to Promote Your Airbnb Property," for insight into how you should promote your property online and in the real world to attract the types of guests you want staying at your property. For example, a savvy host uses social media to its utmost advantage.

 **WARNING**

Local laws, or apartment/condo/homeowner's association bylaws, often have their own rules and regulations pertaining to tenants and property owners who want to use their home, condo, or apartment to host paid guests via a service such as Airbnb. Failure to adhere to these laws/regulations could lead to hefty fines or eviction. In certain places, a property owner must either register as a short-term rental with local government or obtain a special license.

In Santa Monica, California, Airbnb hosts must register for a business license and collect an occupancy tax, which gets paid to the city. In New York City, Airbnb hosts can only list one property at a time and cannot rent out an entire apartment for less than 30 days. Meanwhile, 26 U.S. states have taxing agreements for Airbnb that hosts are responsible for.

10 Important Factors to Consider before Becoming a Host

Just as with any business opportunity, there are a handful of prerequisites that will help lead to your success as an Airbnb host. Each of the following factors and considerations will be explained in much greater detail later within this book. However, as you first begin contemplating whether to become an Airbnb host, it's important to have a clear understanding of what you're signing up for.

The following are 10 important factors to consider *before* you register to become an Airbnb host and begin having guests stay in your home or property.

1. Determine if local laws and/or the bylaws of your apartment complex, co-op board, or homeowner's association prevent you from utilizing your home or apartment to host paid guests via short-term rentals.

WARNING

Airbnb has begun working with apartment buildings across the United States to allow for Airbnb short-term rentals. If your apartment complex is not part of this program, proceed with caution as you could wind up being in violation of your apartment/condo bylaws. For apartment complexes that participate in this program, however, as the property owner, you're often required to live at that property for a specific amount of time each year. To learn more about this Airbnb-Friendly Apartments program, visit www.airbnb.com/airbnb-friendly.

2. Determine if you have the personality, time, wherewithal, and willingness to interact with and manage guests (strangers) who will be staying at your home or property.

3. You're able to consistently provide a clean, comfortable, well-located, and desirable place for people to stay.

4. Your lifestyle and schedule allow you to be available to your guests and have people staying in your home. If you have young children or unfriendly pets, for example, this could be problematic. If you're not going to be readily available, are you willing to pay a property manager to oversee your Airbnb rental(s)? This would deduct from your potential profits.

5. You're willing to set competitive nightly pricing, based on what you're offering, competition, and demand in your geographic area.

6. You understand that as a host, customer service is an important key to your success. This will require an ongoing time commitment and effort on your part. Successful Airbnb hosts consistently receive positive feedback and great reviews from their guests. Earning anything less than stellar reviews and ratings will have a lasting and negative impact on your future success as a host.

7. Prior to having guests pay to stay with you, it's necessary to sign up to become a host with Airbnb. This requires you to create a detailed, accurate, and well-written profile that conveys information about yourself and what you're offering. You'll also need to take and share professional-quality photos of your property. For the best results, seriously consider hiring a professional real estate photographer to take and edit your property images.

8. Before each guest checks in, it is necessary to prepare your property. This means both cleaning it and providing a selection of amenities that will make guests feel more comfortable and welcome. As a result of COVID-19, guests now expect a thorough cleaning and disinfecting of the property in between stays. Adherence to Airbnb's five-step enhanced cleaning process (described here: www.airbnb.com/help/article/2809) is an absolute must. In 2023, and moving forward indefinitely, hosts must also follow Airbnb's

COVID-19 safety practices (described here: www.airbnb.com/help /article/2839), which change as new guidance is provided by the World Health Organization and Centers for Disease Control and Prevention within the United States (www.cdc.gov).

9. Protect your own property and belongings. In addition to having adequate insurance (that covers you having paying guests stay in your home), make sure that any expensive décor (antiques, art, etc.), home electronics, and furnishings will remain safe, even with guests staying in your home. Through AirCover (www.airbnb.com/aircover-for-hosts) from Airbnb, hosts receive $3 million in damage protection (caused by guests to your home), but make sure your homeowner's or renter's insurance covers you serving as an Airbnb host and that you have ample liability insurance (beyond what's provided by Airbnb) if someone gets injured on your property, for example. This is something you should discuss, in advance, with your insurance broker.

10. Develop a comprehensive list of "House Rules" that your guests will need to abide by. These rules need to be spelled out and clearly communicated to guests, and then enforced, but also be fair. The rules you set will help determine the types of guests who stay with you. For example, your House Rules can include: no smoking, no pets, no kids, no parties, no noise after 11 p.m., and/or no utilizing or accessing certain areas of your home or property. Guidelines for setting House Rules are offered within Chapter 6, "Responding to Broken Rules."

Ultimately, how successful you can be as an Airbnb host depends on several key factors, including the location of your property, the type of accommodations you're able to offer, timing, and the overall experience you can offer to your guests. For example, offering a single bedroom within your home with a shared bathroom, which is in a rural area and not close to any major tourist attractions or local events and only offered on weekdays (as opposed to weekends and holidays), will generate a much lower income than an entire home or apartment that's within a major city or that's close to popular tourist attractions, and that's available during holiday or popular vacation periods. How much you can charge for your accommodations will also depend heavily on local competition.

In Chapter 3, "Planning for Profit and Setting Your Rates," you'll learn about services and tools that will help you determine the value and income potential of your property when it comes to short-term rentals. Before investing too much time and effort in becoming a host and listing your property, do research to ensure you'll be able to earn enough income to make your efforts financially worthwhile.

Meanwhile, if you plan to offer experiences as an "Experience Host" (www .airbnb.com/help/article/1581), want to earn the title "Superhost" (www.airbnb .com/help/article/829#section-heading-2-0), or hope to offer an Airbnb Luxe property or one that caters to business travelers, there are additional guidelines from Airbnb you'll need to abide by. Be sure to familiarize yourself with these requirements in advance.

After considering each of the factors discussed thus far, if you still believe you have what it takes to be a successful Airbnb host, and you have a guestroom, apartment, home, or an unusual place for guests to stay, then you may have stumbled upon an opportunity that will allow you to earn extra revenue. Being a travel host will also allow you to meet new people and better utilize your property in a way that offsets your property-related costs/expenses—and maybe even generate a profit.

Here's a Quick Reality Check

Chances are, you're not the first potential host to learn about this opportunity in your geographic area. Based on where you live, and what you're offering in terms of guest accommodations, you may have intense competition from local hotels, motels, B&Bs, resorts, timeshare properties, and other Airbnb hosts.

If you set your nightly pricing too high, based on what you're offering, potential guests will simply seek out alternate accommodations. However, if you set competitive nightly pricing that's much lower than your competition, you may determine that being a host is not financially rewarding after all. Plus, if your rates are much lower than your competition, potential guests may be leery about booking with you, because they'll assume your accommodations are subpar. Setting the most desirable nightly price for your potential guests, based on what you're offering and your location, as well as other factors, will be a key factor in your financial success as a host. This topic is covered in much greater detail within Chapter 3, "Planning for Profit and Setting Your Rates."

As you'll soon discover, the most successful Airbnb hosts offer:

- Affordable, clean, safe, and comfortable accommodations that cost less than the competition (local hotels, for example).

- Accommodations in or near a highly desirable location that's close to public transportation, nearby attractions, or where guests will want to visit. (On-site or nearby parking is also available.)

- Extra amenities, beyond clean sheets and towels, are provided by the host to help set their accommodations apart from the competition. How to choose the best selection of amenities to offer is also covered within Chapter 5, "Preparing Your Property."

- A truly unique or unusual accommodation experience that guests are willing to pay a premium for provides a way for travel hosts to charge higher rates.

Understand Airbnb Property Categories

In May 2022, Airbnb introduced a new way for travelers to seek out special accommodations using the Airbnb website or mobile app. Near the very top of the main Airbnb website homepage, for example, is a list of property categories. This list allows someone looking for a unique place to stay to quickly find what they're looking for within a selected region.

As of early 2023, there are more than 30 categories listed. These range from OMG! listings, to mansions, luxe properties, lakefront homes, or castles, to private islands, barns, properties containing a chef's kitchen, windmills, or lighthouses that people can stay in. Offering some type of unique or unusual property as a short-term rental will set you apart from the local competition and allow you to charge premium nighty rates.

Being Readily Accessible as a Host Is a Must

When your Airbnb listing catches someone's attention, the potential guest will contact you via the website or app. It's important that you, as the host, respond promptly and accurately to inquiries, always maintaining a friendly and professional attitude. This communication is done through the Airbnb website or mobile app, so you're not tied to your desktop computer if you have an internet-connected smartphone or tablet, for example. Ultimately, however, it'll be up to your property's text-based description, its list of amenities, and its photos to initially capture a potential guest's attention. You can also solicit interest in your Airbnb property by promoting it yourself using social media, word-of-mouth, referrals, paid advertising, and other tools at your disposal. We'll focus on these options within Chapter 10, "10 Ways to Promote Your Airbnb Property."

Once the reservation is made, as the host, it's your responsibility to clean and prepare the accommodations for each guest's arrival. Everything should be set up and waiting for them before they arrive. It's essential that the description of the property that you provided on the Airbnb platform, and the amenities you say are included, are all accurate and ready for your guests.

After you've agreed to an arrival time with your guest, you (or an approved representative) will typically need to be on hand to welcome the guest, present them with the keys, review the House Rules, provide a tour, and get them settled in. Some hosts handle these tasks remotely.

 **WARNING**

If you opt to charge an extra cleaning fee, which is your prerogative as a host with Airbnb, your guests will expect professionally cleaned accommodations that go above and beyond just meeting Airbnb's guidelines.

As a Host, Stay in Touch with Your Guests

As the host, it's your responsibility to check in with your guests periodically during their stay and make sure they have everything they need. Also, be sure you're available to answer their questions, address their concerns, and ensure their overall experience is as positive as possible.

Keep in mind that when it comes to writing reviews and ratings, guests who have something bad to say are more apt to post a review and rating than someone who has something positive to say based on their overall experience staying with you. The ratings and reviews you receive as a host are very important! It's essential you take steps to ensure the best possible reactions from your guests.

During your guest's stay, it's up to you and them to determine how much interaction you have. As you'll learn, some hosts opt to socialize with their guests, share meals, take on the role of tour guide, and have a lot of day-to-day interaction with their guests. Others remain available in person, by phone, email, or text message, but give their guests lots of freedom and autonomy. Your involvement and level of interaction with your guests will be based on your own personal preference, as well as the wants and needs of your guests.

Depending on the type of accommodations you're offering, your geographic location, competition, demand, and seasonal trends, for example, you may find that you're able to keep your accommodations booked night after night, with short-term, mid-term, or even long-term guests. This means that for every night one or more people are staying at your property, you'll be earning money.

More realistically, especially for new Airbnb hosts in geographic areas that are not popular tourist or vacation destinations, you can expect guests to book your accommodations less often. This might mean you'll have guests sporadically throughout each month.

Based on your goals, this book will demonstrate many proven strategies for attracting the attention of guests using the Airbnb platform. However, if you're offering accommodations in an undesirable geographic location, or what you're offering does not meet the needs of most Airbnb travelers, don't expect to receive consistent bookings, even if you have top-notch reviews and ratings.

One thing you can be sure about, however, is that if you start receiving negative feedback and ratings from your guests, it will become harder and harder for you as a host to generate bookings, as guests who are savvy using the Airbnb service will know to seek out accommodations that have received better reviews and ratings from past guests.

As a Host, You Need to Meet or Exceed the Expectations of Your Guests

Throughout this book, and within the interviews with successful travel hosts, the concept of offering a clean, comfortable, and safe place to stay is emphasized heavily and repeatedly. As a prospective Airbnb host, if you're unwilling or unable to offer this, don't bother to become a host. It's that simple. Offering dirty, uncomfortable, or otherwise uninhabitable accommodations will lead to bad reviews and ratings, which will deter future guests from booking with you.

As you create your profile and property listing on Airbnb, be positive, but be brutally honest. Back up the description of your property with clear, detailed, and professional-looking photographs. It's important that you set realistic expectations for your guests, based on what you're offering and how much you're charging. Total accuracy within your online profile and property listing is essential. This includes your list of amenities and your description of what the property offers. Many potential guests are not as interested in hotel-style amenities as they are in safety-related amenities and House Rules that are not overly strict.

First and foremost, guests want a clean place to stay! This means that the bedrooms and bathroom(s) should be spotless, fully functional, and comfortable. The bedding (sheets, blankets, pillows, etc.), as well as the towels that you provide, should also be all clean, odor free, freshly laundered, and stain free.

Depending on how much you're charging, and the expectations you create within your Airbnb profile and property listing, guests will expect their accommodations to be cleaned and prepared prior to their arrival. For example, if they're being offered access to a kitchen, the dishes, countertops, and appliances should be clean and ready to use. The beds should be made (with clean bedding), and the bathroom should have clean towels, toilet paper, and other necessities (hand soap and perhaps shampoo) available and ready to use.

Most guests will understand that they're saving money by staying in a private residence, as opposed to a hotel with professional and on-call housekeepers and front desk personnel. However, these same guests will also have basic expectations that become your obligation as a host to meet or exceed. This relates to the actual accommodations you're providing, as well as your attitude, friendliness, and helpfulness that you offer as a host before and during each guest's stay with you. That said, if you wind up becoming a Superhost or your property earns the Airbnb Plus designation, expectations of guests are much higher.

So, lesson one for being a successful Airbnb host is to set realistic expectations for your guests, set a fair nightly price based on what you're offering, and then do whatever is in your power as the host to meet or exceed the expectations you've set via your online profile and property listing.

Some Airbnb hosts generate enough money to cover some or all of their mortgage payment or monthly rent, as well as extras, like utility bills and real estate taxes. There are also some people who have been able to earn enough money to support themselves exclusively as an Airbnb host.

But realistically, becoming an Airbnb host is *not* a continuous and reliable revenue stream that you should count on, at least initially. However, based on what you're offering and your personal experience as an Airbnb host, you could eventually achieve a high occupancy rate and steady income. For most Airbnb hosts, having guests stay at their property offers a secondary and sporadic revenue stream that gives them extra money to help cover their bills or improve their lifestyle.

Don't Be Impulsive!

When you visit Airbnb's website, you're encouraged to immediately start setting up your profile so you can become a host. Before taking this step, however, finish reading this book, learn more about what you're getting involved in, and most importantly, make sure you're legally allowed to serve as a host based on where you live.

A growing number of cities around the world no longer allow private home, apartment, or condo owners to participate on these services or allow paid guests to stay within privately owned homes. Thus, it's illegal to have paying guests for fewer than 30 days, unless the property is locally licensed as a hotel or bed-and-breakfast, for example.

Some cities that allow home, apartment, or condo owners to utilize their property for short-term rentals, or accommodate paying nightly guests, require hosts to acquire a special permit or business license. Failure to comply with local laws could result in hefty fines.

Meanwhile, if you're not hindered by local laws or regulations, you may discover that your homeowner's association, co-op board, or landlord forbids participation in this type of service as a host. Many apartment leases, for example, do not permit short-term rentals or sublets of any kind, and a violation of the lease could lead to eviction by the landlord. Check with your landlord, homeowner's association, or co-op board before you register and start offering your apartment, home, or condo as a short-term rental or allow paying guests to stay at your property.

If you live in rent-controlled or subsidized housing, there will likely be limitations on what you're allowed to do in terms of participation as a host on Airbnb. Check with your property manager, and carefully review your lease or rental agreement.

The Airbnb website offers a section that covers legal requirements and restrictions in about 50 U.S. cities (see www.airbnb.com/help/article/1376/responsible -hosting-in-the-united-states). However, it's ultimately your responsibility to determine what's legal and permissible in your local city or community. One way to do this is to check with the state or local government. For example, check with your city or town hall, the city's zoning board, and/or the local housing authority.

If from a legal standpoint you're able to become a host with Airbnb, because you are earning money from this activity, you're expected to pay federal and state income taxes on this income. In some cases, you may also be required to pay a hotel/transient occupancy tax or sales tax. It's a good idea to have a conversation with your accountant to determine what tax implications becoming a host will have for you personally and how this additional income will impact your tax-filing procedures.

Once you determine that being an Airbnb host is permissible, also have a discussion with your insurance provider. Make sure that you have the necessary insurance coverage related to liability and property protection. Do not simply rely on promises made by Airbnb that state that its hosts, the host's family members, their pets, as well as their property and belongings, are fully covered and insured. In certain situations, this may *not* be the case, despite what hosts are led to believe.

Use Common Sense to Avoid Potential Problems

Every business opportunity attracts its share of scam artists and criminals. Overall, Airbnb offers a credible and viable way for hosts to earn money by inviting guests to stay on their property for a nightly fee. Out of all the transactions between hosts and guests that take place around the world daily, a very small percentage involves guests (or in some cases, hosts) perpetuating some type of scam or illegal activity.

Throughout this book, you'll discover tips and strategies for identifying and avoiding potentially problematic guests. However, as a host, it's a good idea to stay informed about the types of scams being perpetrated. This is not something that Airbnb will necessarily advise you of or protect you against.

One way to find out about these scams, and how they're evolving over time, is simply to access any internet search engine, and within the search field, type "Airbnb scams." Then, click on the search results from credible sources, such as news agencies you know.

As you'll discover, simply by using common sense and taking a few basic steps to protect yourself, your family, your pets, your belongings, and your property, chances are you'll be able to avoid problems as a host.

Airbnb Is Evolving as a Travel Service

Originally, the Airbnb.com online service and mobile apps were simply used to help travelers find and book interesting places to stay. In November 2016, however, Airbnb started to evolve into a full-service travel site that focuses on allowing travelers to learn about and book travel experiences—not just accommodations.

Airbnb users can now choose a travel destination, find accommodations, and at the same time, learn about (and make reservations for) unique experiences.

An Airbnb Experience is classified as an in-person or online activity that's hosted by inspiring local experts. It's not a traditional class or tour. The host shares their expertise in a way that allows the guest to immerse themselves in an experience for several hours. An experience can also include behind-the-scenes access to a unique location. Experiences that tend to be popular evolve around food, culture, history, nature, wellness, photography, art, hands-on activities, or unique tours.

What's possible is limited only by your imagination and the need for the experiences to adhere to Airbnb's guidelines. To learn more about what's allowed and what's not when developing an Airbnb Experience, be sure to visit the Airbnb Experiences Standards and Requirements web page (www.airbnb.com/help/article /1451) and read the "Create Your Unique Experience Offering" section in Chapter 2, "Get Started as An Airbnb Host."

Meet Airbnb Superhosts Zev and Melissa Forrest

This husband-and-wife team currently operate 11 Airbnb short-term rental units and have been doing this since 2018. Within months after getting started, their work ethic and attention to cleanliness, customer service, and detail allowed them to earn the Airbnb Superhost designation.

How did you initially get started with Airbnb?

Zev Forrest: "We attended a free workshop about five years ago, before my wife and I got married. After attending the workshop, we tested the waters by approaching my mother, who used to rent out her backhouse to long-term tenants. I shared all the information we learned and began offering her accommodations as a short-term rental through Airbnb. It quickly became a profitable endeavor. When Melissa and I went on to buy our own house, we knew we loved the hospitality industry and decided to offer rooms in our home through Airbnb. Over time, we expanded our portfolio to 11 units, and now operate them as our full-time jobs. We have 10 separate properties, and one of them is a single property with two listings. All are located within Southern California."

When selecting your properties, what did you look for to help ensure they'd be profitable for short-term rental through Airbnb?

Zev Forrest: "First, I researched the location's short-term rental ordinance to make sure the property could be used as a short-term rental property via Airbnb. Our other criteria is constantly evolving, since our goals are changing based on how we see our company's brand. At first, we looked at single-family homes that could fit 8 to 10 people. Later, we started looking at one- or two-bedroom apartments as well that could accommodate traveling couples or corporate professionals. Now, our focus has been on mid-to-high-level luxe, single-family home properties located along the coast.

"My wife handles the day-to-day operation of our short-term rental business. I work full-time analyzing real estate deals so we can expand our portfolio. When I first look at a property, I always use the AirDNA [www.airdna.co] service to acquire a detailed analysis in terms of its profit potential as a short-term rental property. This service can be a bit pricey, but we have found it's well worth the investment. If that report comes back favorable, I then look at Airbnb itself and search for similar listings to the property we're interested in acquiring that are in the same geographic area. I seek out geographic areas that have at least 10 different Airbnb properties with at least 40 reviews each.

"If the reviews are above 4.6, generally I consider this to be a good area to acquire a property. I also look at the occupancy rate of these other nearby properties and believe a 60 percent occupancy rate or higher is favorable. Then, depending on the size of the property, I look at the income potential, compared to what the mortgage and operating costs for that property will be, in relation to what we calculate will be the average nightly rate we could charge for that property. For a single-family home, after crunching the numbers before purchasing the property, I am seeking out at least a 30 percent return on the investment. If we're subleasing a home and using rental arbitrage, we're looking to earn between 1.5 to 2 times the lease payment that we'd be paying." [What rental arbitrage is and how to utilize it to grow your short-term rental business is covered later in this book.]

"Aesthetically, when I look at a property, I am interested in only B+ or higher neighborhoods, because we want to attract a higher caliber of guests. I start by driving around the neighborhood within a 5-to-10-minute radius of the potential property and look for things like a convenience store that someone could walk to. I also want a location where someone will feel comfortable walking their dog around at night.

"For the home itself, ideally, I look for the kitchen and bathrooms of a potential property to be up to date. I also look at the age of the property and what the life expectancy of things like the roof are before major repairs would be required. If we plan to lease the property, I pay careful attention to how well the property owner maintains it. After all, if we lease a property that we will ultimately manage as an Airbnb property, we're basically becoming a partner with that property owner. When we are running a hospitality business out of someone else's property, we need major or minor repairs to be handled immediately and for everything inside and outside to be properly maintained, or it will reflect negatively on our short-term rental business.

"Being in Southern California, we insist that all our short-term rental properties all have air-conditioning and central heating. We also look at the quality of the water. If the area has hard water, this can generate rust stains in the toilets and showers, which take away from the appearance of the property, even though it's been cleaned very well. Hard water also tastes funny, which guests often perceive as a negative. We also seek out properties with at least one full bathroom for every two bedrooms, so a three-bedroom with just one bathroom will not work for us. We don't want unrelated guests to share a bathroom and potentially wait for other guests to shower.

"We also want our properties to have close and convenient parking, especially if the local community is very tight on parking. While not necessary, we also try to include a washer and dryer within each property. We have found this to be an amenity people want and it helps to increase our occupancy rate. Having a washer and dryer will also allow the property to be used for mid-term [three to seven nights] or long-term rentals [30 nights or longer]."

When you first got started with your short-term rental business, how much capital did you originally have and how did you quickly expand the business to include 11 units?

Zev Forrest: "The first property we started with was one we purchased for 10 percent down via a conventional loan. Speak with a mortgage broker or real estate attorney to figure out the lowest amount of money you can put down for an investment property, and the type of loan you should seek out. The property was priced around $370,000, but after the closing costs and other fees, this was another $60,000. After that, we spent about $12,000 to furnish and decorate the three-bedroom, 1,500-square-foot home. After acquiring this investment property, we did not have the funds to purchase others right away, so we began leasing additional properties and taking advantage of rental arbitrage. This is when you rent someone else's property for a long-term and then sublease it out and manage it as a short-term rental property with the landlord's permission. So, if we are spending $2,000 per month for the long-term lease of a property, we aim to earn $4,000 per month using it for short-term rentals through Airbnb. We then earn that $2,000 spread. Through rental arbitrage, we were able to scale our business very quickly, because we were able to show the various landlords our proof of funds to support the long-term leases."

Now that you operate 11 short-term rental units, do you rely on property managers to help you manage them?

Melissa Forrest: "For the first few years, I managed the day-to-day operation of the properties and managed the cleaners and maintenance people. More recently, we have built a team that's comprised of virtual assistants that I have trained to handle the day-to-day operations involving the guests and the cleaners. The virtual assistants can make financial decisions up to a certain limit before getting me or my husband involved if there's an emergency. Because they are virtual assistants, this keeps our costs low. Rounding out the team, we have a reliable cleaning service and a maintenance service that is local to each unit. I initially find these services on TaskRabbit or Thumbtack, and then build up a relationship with them. For example, the cleaning service or maintenance service will also act as a runner, so if a guest calls and says they need extra towels, for example, the runner will quickly deliver them to the property. The virtual assistants handle all the communications with the guests.

"For new Airbnb hosts, I recommend having a list of 24-hour plumbers and electricians on call in case an emergency happens. For cleaning services, I originally used a professional cleaning company, but that was a nightmare. They sent out different cleaners to the properties each time, so there was a huge lack of consistency. We found it is much more economical to hire independent contractors as our cleaners, and they've turned out to be much more reliable and consistent. We often find cleaners through referrals and through social media. We can train them to clean and prepare each property for guests exactly how we want it done. The cleaners get to know the ins and outs of the property and how to maintain consistency when preparing and staging each property for each guest. The service called Turno [https://turno.com] can also be used for finding reliable cleaners, for example."

How did you choose the type of mattresses, pillows, linens, and towels, for example, that you use within each of your properties and how often do you replace them?

Melissa Forrest: "This has evolved a lot. We started using synthetic and low-cost sheets, for example, but the guests didn't like them, so we quickly shifted to 100 percent cotton sheets and linens. After much research, the linen brand I like the most is California Design Den [www.californiadesignden.com]. We only use white linens and towels. Using white is luxurious and shows more transparency in terms of our cleanliness.

"White sheets and linens can also be bleached to disinfect them. The cotton towel brand we rely on is called Charisma, which we purchase from Costco. They're luxurious, affordable, and durable. We replace sheets, linens, and towels when the cleaners notice that they no longer look new. For the past five years, we have also worked with a mattress wholesaler to provide all our mattresses. This saves us money. Within all our properties, we only offer king-size beds. As for pillows, we offer guests a selection of four pillows per bed, two of which are down filled and two use memory foam. On the beds, we provide a duvet with a luxurious and easy-to-clean cover."

What are the most important amenities you offer to your guests that they seem to really appreciate?

Melissa Forrest: "A coffee machine with a wide variety of coffee and tea selections, as well as a choice of milk, creams, sugar, and sugar substitutes. We also provide a dispenser in each shower that includes a high-quality body wash and shampoo. We provide disposable toothbrushes and travel-size amenities, like toothpaste, mouthwash, and dental floss, because if a guest flies in and their luggage gets lost, they show up to our property needing these toiletries."

Zev Forrest: "For our guests that arrive with young babies or toddlers, we offer pack-and-plays, strollers, and high chairs. One policy we have found that goes a long way when it comes to customer service is that if a guest has a reasonable request for an amenity we do not offer, we will go out and buy it right away and have it delivered to the property as quickly as possible. We consider these purchases to be an investment in the property. We put our guests' experience first and foremost and refuse to nickel-and-dime on things.

"It's most important that we offer a top-quality guest experience. In addition to welcoming families with kids, in almost all our properties we welcome pets as well. We have found that Airbnb hosts are really leaving a lot of money on the table if they don't open their properties up to pets. This is an amenity that's in demand and that helps us stay competitive. We do not charge guests a refundable deposit, since we rely on AirCover [www.airbnb.com/aircover-for-hosts] in case there is damage to the property caused by guests. We have found that guests do not appreciate a lot of extra fees added to their booking."

What strategy do you use to set your nightly rates?

Melissa Forrest: "We look at comparable Airbnb properties in the area and pay attention to what the highest rated and most successful properties are charging. I take this information and then use a dynamic pricing tool, called PriceLabs [https://hello.pricelabs.co], to help us set a base nightly price. We then set a minimum price, which is the lowest rate we're willing to go for each unit. The dynamic pricing tool helps us set the optimal price, based on a wide range of factors. This service updates our pricing daily for each property. We believe using a dynamic pricing tool, like PriceLabs, is an absolute necessity for all Airbnb hosts. Not using a tool like this leaves a lot of money on the table."

What strategies have you adopted to create attention-grabbing property listings on Airbnb?

Melissa Forrest: "We put a lot of emphasis on design, cleanliness, and comfort. I believe design is important. I try to use a luxury, attention-grabbing design to help our properties stand out. If you don't have an eye for interior design, we recommend hiring a professional designer who will work within your budget. The design of a property impacts the type of guest you'll attract, your ability to charge a higher nightly rate, your occupancy level, and the attention your property listing will get. Design is not something an Airbnb host should cheap out on."

Zev Forrest: "Featuring professional photography within your Airbnb property listing, in our opinion, is an absolute must. When someone looks at images of our properties, we want them to think they're luxurious, spa-like, comfortable, clean, and relaxing. We focus on an aesthetic that offers these qualities for each of our properties, but the décor of each property is different."

What are the most essential House Rules you recommend all hosts implement?

Melissa Forrest: "No parties or events, no outside guests, no smoking inside the property, and quiet hours between 9 p.m. and 8 a.m. We also note that any costs associated with damage caused to the property, especially if it impacts the next guest's reservation, will be charged to them. This includes lost income if we need to cancel the next reservation to fix the damage. We also note there is a $500 violation fee if someone smokes inside the property. If someone breaks a rule or term, and there is a fee associated with breaking that rule, it's easier to get Airbnb to collect these fees on your behalf from the guest. However, for anything covered by AirCover, the host needs to keep detailed records and take photos of the damage to file a claim."

Are You Ready to Proceed?

Now that you have a basic understanding of what's involved in becoming a travel host, let's take a closer look at how to get started as a host with Airbnb. This is the focus of Chapter 2, "Get Started as an Airbnb Host."

Get Started as an Airbnb Host

One of the first steps required when joining Airbnb is to create a personal profile and a listing for your property on the website. Before you can effectively promote your service, it's important to do an honest self-assessment and a thorough analysis of your property. Your property's listing is your primary opportunity to promote what you have to offer and showcase (through text and photos) why potential guests should stay with you.

What It's Like Being an Airbnb Host

Airbnb is often referred to as a "peer-to-peer short-term rental service," meaning that you, as the host, will work directly with your potential and actual guests. Initially this will happen through the Airbnb website or mobile app, but once someone books a reservation and arrives at your property, at least some interaction will likely be done in person—face-to-face. Most people who use Airbnb to book their accommodations are looking for an experience that's more home-like, as opposed to staying at a hotel or motel. Some are seeking a unique experience in addition to lodging.

As a host, what this means for you is that offering your property as a short-term rental through Airbnb will allow you to earn a passive income while having the opportunity to meet and socialize with other people from your home country or potentially from around the world. For people who enjoy this socialization, hosting can be a highly rewarding experience. It's important to understand that, depending on how you set up your property listing on the Airbnb platform, you may or may not get final approval over the people who will be staying at your property.

While there is a social component to being an Airbnb host, there are certain responsibilities you need to take on—from providing a clean and comfortable place for guests to stay, to creating and maintaining an accurate property listing on the Airbnb platform, and then managing your bookings (reservations). The Airbnb platform utilizes its own, proprietary reservation system and handles all the financial transactions between you and your guests. This certainly makes your job as a host a bit easier.

However, you'll occasionally have to deal with rude guests, the threat of theft or damage to your property, the possibility of complaints from your neighbors, potentially higher utility bills, the cost to properly clean your property between guests, and paying for the amenities you choose to provide to your guests. If your guest will be staying at your personal residence, you'll also need to secure your valuables and any sentimental items you don't want your guests to have access to. Airbnb does offer some insurance to its hosts, but it's important you have your own insurance as well, and to use common sense when protecting your belongings.

As a host, you need to put serious thought into the décor of your property. You want to create a clean, comfortable, and aesthetically pleasing environment for your guests that somehow reflects your personality (while trying to avoid the stale and generic look of a hotel room). You don't want to invest in overly expensive furnishings, appliances, or décor that could easily be damaged or that can't withstand the wear and tear imposed on it by guests. That said, some hosts do extremely well by integrating a unique theme throughout their property that is initially expensive to create. When you visit Airbnb, click on the OMG! property category to see some of these often over-the-top, short-term rental properties.

Expect things to occasionally be broken or disappear. For example, if someone decides to grab some silverware or dishes from the kitchen so they can enjoy a snack while you're out and about, they may forget to return it or not want to deal with the hassle of carrying around dirty items for the rest of the day, so they'll simply discard them. Yes, this is rude, but it does happen. Likewise, if a guest accidentally breaks a lamp or tears a blanket, they may try to hide the damage by getting rid of the evidence, hoping you won't notice it until after they've gone. It's minor inconveniences like these that you need to be prepared to deal with. You may also need to replace broken items or do minor home repairs before your next guest arrives. Even if you get reimbursed for these expenses by AirCover or your own insurance, it's still an added hassle you'll have to deal with.

 TIP

> Refrain from displaying expensive artwork or antiques within your property, leaving your jewelry lying around in "public" areas, and giving your guests access to extremely expensive consumer electronics. For hosts who plan to rent out space within their own residence, installing separate locks on your bedroom door, storing valuables within a safe, and not leaving personal documents where guests can see them are a few precautions you'll want to take.

The chance of you being in personal danger from your guests is very low, especially if you opt to only accept guests who have completed Airbnb's Verified ID process, and who have earned glowing ratings and reviews from previous hosts. As you create your property listing, you also have the option of procuring a refundable security deposit that you can use to recuperate any loses from a guest causing minor damage to your property or belongings, or the need for you to pay for a more elaborate cleaning (to remove a pet stain from the carpet or the smell of cigarette smoke from a bedroom, where smoking is not permitted, for example).

If you choose to pursue being an Airbnb host for the money, and you live within the United States, research conducted by Airbnb in 2021 revealed that properties in California, Florida, Texas, New York, Georgia, North Carolina, Tennessee, Arizona, Colorado, and Pennsylvania were the most in demand. And as you'd expect, the busiest times of year (in terms of booked reservations) are Labor Day weekend, Memorial Day weekend, Fourth of July, Thanksgiving, during the fall season (in certain areas), during peak summer travel periods, and around Christmas.

Thus, to capitalize on these higher demand periods, you'll need to make your property (and yourself as a host) available. This could impact your own personal travel or vacation plans unless you hire a trusted and responsible property manager to handle the responsibilities of being an Airbnb host for your property while you're away.

As an Airbnb host, managing your short-term rental property should operate smoothly, especially if you follow the advice in this book and that's provided by Airbnb. However, you need to be ready to deal with the unexpected. Have a plan in place if your property's electricity goes out, the toilet overflows, an appliance breaks, or there's a problem with the heat or air-conditioning, for example.

Regardless of your actual experience with guests, it's essential to keep the relationship as positive as possible. Most of your guests will likely cause no problem whatsoever and could wind up becoming a friend. Remember, your long-term success as a host relies on receiving positive feedback and ratings from guests on the Airbnb platform. You also want guests to provide positive referrals to their family, friends, coworkers, and online friends. Favorable word-of-mouth advertising from past guests will play a future role in receiving new bookings. And, of course, you want to encourage repeat visits from previous guests.

Determine Exactly What You Have to Offer to Your Future Guests

It's important to establish what you're willing to offer related to your property. Your options may include:

- A single private room within your home
- A shared room within your home
- Your entire home or apartment

- A special type of property, such as a guesthouse, cabin, ski chalet, tree-house, castle, studio apartment, multi-floor apartment, finished basement, private island, oceanfront villa, loft, townhouse, boat/yacht, or bungalow

Next, determine why people will want to stay with you and what you can promote within your property listing to get their attention. In addition to promoting that you offer a clean, safe, and comfortable living space (which is typically the bare minimum of what potential guests look for), figure out what exactly you're able to offer that will make your property appealing and unique.

 TIP

Look at other property listings (and photos) on Airbnb to determine what aspect of each listing catches your attention and why. What is it about each listing that would make you want to stay there? If something turns you off about a property, determine what that is. Don't make the same mistake when creating your own listing.

Get Acquainted with Airbnb Hosting Best Practices

The Resource Center of the Airbnb website provides a vast amount of information to make the job of a host as easy, stress free, and lucrative as possible. Proper planning and developing your own routine as a host will serve you well. As for best practices, Airbnb recommends keeping your space clean, developing a smooth check-in process for your guests, being on hand to welcome guests (in person or remotely), and making yourself readily available during their stay (even if you're not at the actual property where the guest is staying).

Many Airbnb hosts have also discovered the benefit of hiring a property manager or co-host to help them manage their property and interact with guests. They also use a professional cleaning service or hired cleaner to properly clean the property in between guests, and have a maintenance person they're able to call to handle emergency repairs or maintenance issues—days, nights, on weekends, and during holidays. Yes, these services cost extra and reduce your revenue, but they're legitimate business expenses and can make your life as a host much easier.

Other important best practices include responding to inquiries or booking requests within hours (not days). It's also important for hosts to develop House Rules for guests. As a new host, it makes sense to turn on the ID verification as part of your reservation requirements and to turn off the Instant Book feature. Doing this allows you to decline a reservation request you're not comfortable with, based on the potential guest's profile or initial communications. Once a reservation is booked, guests and the Airbnb platform look very unkindly to hosts making last-minute cancellations.

We'll go into more details pertaining to best practices as a host in each chapter of this book. However, you can also access Airbnb's *Discover the World of Hosting* guide online at www.airbnb.com/resources/hosting-homes/g/discovering -the-world-of-hosting-2.

Do Your Research and Determine Why Superhosts Have Become Successful

Before you start creating your own personal profile and property listing on Airbnb, investigate your competition. Carefully read the profiles and property listings created by already successful Airbnb hosts and Superhosts in your geographic area and elsewhere. You can easily find the successful hosts by looking at the number of positive ratings they've received and by looking for the Superhost badge that accompanies their profile and property listing.

A Superhost is an experienced Airbnb host who has hosted at least 10 separate guests (or 3 reservations that total at least 100 nights) within the past year; at least 80 percent of their reviews are 5 stars; their response rate when it comes to communicating with potential guests is 90 percent or higher; and, as a host, they honor their confirmed reservations (with very few or no cancellations). A Superhost also maintains an overall rating of at least 4.8 (out of 5). Once a host earns the Superhost title, it's their job to continue meeting Airbnb's Superhost requirements to keep it.

When looking for accommodations, some of the key things potential guests often look at include:

- *Your geographic location.* How close is your property to popular tourist attractions, landmarks, a beach, a ski slope, the waterfront, special events happening in your area, and/or public transportation? What's most desirable about the location?

- *Available value-added services.* Things like on-site or nearby parking, laundry facilities, or being within walking distance to local shopping or restaurants are always a plus.

- *Amenities you offer.* Being able to offer your guests a private, clean, and fully functional bathroom (as opposed to a shared bathroom) is sought after by potential guests. There are countless other amenities you should offer, as well as additional and optional amenities that your guests will likely appreciate. Choosing the best selection of amenities is covered a bit later. For now, understand that your offerings are among the factors that will attract potential guests to select your property when they're choosing a place to stay.

- *Your commitment as a host.* Are you willing to prepare meals for or dine with your guests, act as a tour guide, or socialize with your guests? Beyond the bare minimums of what's expected from a host, what else can you offer?

- *The experience you're able to provide.* A growing percentage of people who book accommodations through Airbnb are looking for a unique experience, not just a place to sleep. If a potential guest falls into this category, they're looking to enjoy some type of activity or experience they can't get elsewhere. And for this, they're willing to pay extra.

In short, ask yourself, what makes your property special or unique? Why will people want to stay with you? These are two of the most important questions you'll need to address, promote, and showcase within your Airbnb property listing, photos, and personal profile.

Beyond Accommodations: Types of Experiences You Can Offer

In addition to providing accommodations, a growing number of hosts are choosing to provide experiences to their guests through the Airbnb Experiences program. Providing an experience that allows you to tap and showcase your expertise or benefit from a unique setting, for example, allows you, as the host, to charge a premium.

Before you're able to begin hosting experiences, you must apply to become an Airbnb Experiences host, which is a more elaborate process than simply becoming an Airbnb host. You must come up with a fun and unique experience, demonstrate to Airbnb that you have the expertise and knowledge needed to provide that experience, and meet the standards and requirements of an experience host (which you can find described here: www.airbnb.com/help/article/1451).

A typical Airbnb Experience is designed to last several hours on average and provide the guest with access to your specialized knowledge and experience. It might also include special access to unique places, or a hands-on activity that the guest can't easily experience elsewhere. The types of Airbnb Experiences that are currently offered are extremely diverse. Before pitching your own potential experience, become acquainted with what's already being offered and the types of experiences that Airbnb has already approved. You can find the latest Airbnb Experience listings here: www.airbnb.com/s/experiences.

As you'll discover, a wide range of unique Airbnb Experiences are already offered. You can apply to host a similar experience or something entirely new and unique that meets Airbnb's standards and requirements. Priced between $30 and $300 per person, here are just a few examples of popular Airbnb Experiences available within the United States:

1. Pasta-making classes with an Italian

2. Explore Salem, MA, with a local

3. Private photo shoot in Time Square (New York City)

4. Hands on with miniature horses

5. Make a handblown glass object

6. Master sushi making with a professional sushi chef

7. Hands-on dairy farm tour

8. Llama/alpaca hike and farm experience

9. Wacky and whimsical scavenger hunt adventure

10. Snowshoe tour up a mountain (with champagne)

11. Making Chinese dumplings with a chef

12. Graffiti workshop in Brooklyn

13. Craft a diamond ring with a jeweler

14. Lighthouse bike tour

15. Sculptural candle-making workshop

16. Art studio paint party

17. Weave a wabi-sabi tapestry

18. Fossil hunting with a scientist

19. LED neon sign making in an art studio

20. Create your own perfume class

21. Adirondack metal detecting adventure

22. Pottery class: Learn to wheel throw

23. Scenic snowmobile rental with guided two-hour tour

24. Afro fusion dinner and cooking class

25. Guided scenic kayak excursion

26. Coffee with a psychic

27. Harbor seal and boat tour (Cape Cod)

28. Chocolate mousse-making class in a chocolate factory

29. Japanese flower arranging

30. Knit a hat in an afternoon

Create Your Unique Experience Offering

The Airbnb website (www.airbnb.com/help/article/1555) will guide you through pitching, creating, pricing, and hosting an Airbnb Experience. To create a proposal, be prepared to provide the following information to Airbnb for consideration:

- The title for your experience

- A description of what you plan to offer

- The location(s) where you'll provide the experience

- Details about what equipment, tools, or special clothing you'll provide and what your guests will need to bring

- At least seven professional-quality photos of people engaging in your experience (with you as a host/guide/teacher)

- The minimum age requirements for guests

- The level of guest activity and skill that's required for the experience

- The maximum group size (Airbnb recommends groups less than 10 people)

- The start time and length of the experience (Airbnb recommends keeping it to less than three hours, but this varies)

- The price per guest for the experience

- A detailed profile of yourself and your skill set that explains why you're qualified to host the experience

In conjunction with your experience application, you'll need to go through Airbnb's Identification Verification process. If any special licenses or insurance is required to provide the experience, you must provide verification to Airbnb that you already possess what's legally required. Once your application is approved, it will get listed on the Airbnb website. Depending on the experience, it can include accommodations (with you as the Airbnb host), or you can host a stand-alone experience for people visiting your area.

Don't Guess: Get the Online Help You Need Every Step of the Way

Especially if you're first getting started as a short-term rental host, the process can be a bit confusing. Plus, the requirements and guidelines are constantly changing. In addition to what's outlined in this book, make sure you access the up-to-date information that's provided by Airbnb's online-based Help Center (www.airbnb .com/help/all-topics). To meet and interact with experienced Airbnb hosts online, visit and become active within the Airbnb Community Center (https://community .withairbnb.com/t5/Community-Center/ct-p/community-center).

In 2022, Airbnb introduced additional features to help first-time hosts. For example, you can get one-to-one guidance from a Superhost via phone call or video chat, interact with experienced Airbnb guests to get help managing your first bookings, and receive specialized support directly from Airbnb's Community Support agents.

 TIP

> To get matched up with a Superhost for guidance, visit www.airbnb .com/host/homes, scroll down to the Still Have Questions? heading, and click on the Match with a Superhost option. If you don't yet have an Airbnb account, you'll be prompted to create one for free.

Your Airbnb Personal Profile and Property Listing Should Reveal a Lot about You

One of the key reasons why Airbnb works as an online community is because hosts and guests alike are asked to create their own personal profile, which is publicly displayed on the service. Potential guests can look at a host's profile, in addition to their property listing(s), to help make a more educated decision about where to stay.

Meanwhile, hosts can review the profile of each potential guest before deciding whether to accept a requested booking (unless the Instant Booking feature is turned on by the host). Your online presence with Airbnb has the following important components:

- Your personal profile
- One or more photographs of you
- Your property listing
- Photographs that showcase your property
- Your personal ratings/reviews
- Your property's ratings/reviews

Your personal profile introduces you as a person to potential guests. It includes a list of identification/contact-related details that have been verified by Airbnb. After Airbnb verifies your identity, your profile will automatically receive and display a "Verified" badge. This helps to enhance your credibility on the platform.

As a host, the contact information you provide (such as your phone number, email address, and social media listings) is *not* revealed to potential guests until *after* they've booked and paid for a reservation to stay with you. The driver's license information you provide to Airbnb when creating your profile is never revealed to others but is listed as a form of "Verified ID" that Airbnb has received.

Your profile page also includes photos of you, details about where you're from, how long you've been a member of Airbnb, and a summary of your reviews. The About Me section of your profile can include additional, at-a-glance information about you, such as where you went to school, what you do for work, what languages you speak, as well as information about your interests and hobbies. Ideally, the information you provide can make you come across as more appealing to potential guests who share things in common with you.

As a host based in the United States, if you're fluent in French, for example, promote this within your profile so travelers visiting the United States from France may be more inclined to stay with you because you speak their language.

Keep in mind that every piece of information that's requested by Airbnb to include in your personal profile or property listing can help you showcase yourself and your property in a positive way, based on the information you choose to provide. While you always have the option to refrain from sharing certain pieces of requested information, the more forthcoming you are, the easier it will be for potential guests to virtually get to know you, so you can begin building credibility and trust even before you begin communicating with or meet potential guests.

 **WARNING**

> Your profile page includes a summary of both the reviews you have received as a host, as well as those you have received as a guest during your own travels. Someone can use information offered by both sets of reviews to draw conclusions about you. If you're rude, messy, and unreliable as a guest, once you become a host, these reviews will be viewable by your potential guests.

Acquaint Yourself with the Airbnb Website and Mobile App Right Away

As a host, it's essential that you become acquainted with the online-based tools offered to you by Airbnb's website and mobile app. This is information that's covered within Chapter 4, "How to Use the Airbnb Website and Mobile App." While it's easier to create and update your profile and property listing(s), manage reservations, and communicate with potential and paid guests via the website, when you're out and about enjoying your own life, the communications and host-related tools offered by the mobile app will certainly come in handy.

The Airbnb mobile app is available from the App Store for iPhone and iPad (https://apps.apple.com/us/app/airbnb/id401626263), or the Google Play Store (https://play.google.com/store/apps/details?id=com.airbnb.android) for Android-based mobile devices. The Airbnb website (www.airbnb.com) can be accessed from your internet-connected desktop or laptop computer, using your favorite web browser.

Create Your Airbnb Account

There are three main tasks involved in establishing an Airbnb host account:

1. Sign up for the service.

2. Create a profile.

3. Create a property listing.

These are discussed in the following sections. Once you complete these steps, you can expand your profile to include additional information, plus create a detailed property listing for each of your properties (one at a time).

The remainder of the chapter will walk you through the process of creating a personal profile and then a property listing on Airbnb. However, keep in mind that the Airbnb website and mobile app are constantly evolving, so the order in which information is requested, and the steps involved in creating the profile and property listing(s), may vary when you do this. As you go through this process, be sure to provide the information that's requested in a succinct and accurate way. Keep in mind, if you plan to offer two separate areas within your home to separate guests, this will require you to create a separate listing on Airbnb for each room or living space.

Sign Up for the Airbnb Service

Signing up for free needs to be done only once. The process takes just a few minutes to complete, but plan on spending much more time when creating and fine-tuning your profile and property listing.

1. Go to www.airbnb.com, click on the empty profile icon in the top-right corner of the web browser window, and select the Sign Up option. If you're using an iPhone or iPad (or an Android-based smartphone or tablet), download the app to your device, launch the app, and from the opening screen, tap on the Create Account button to begin creating your personal profile.

2. The Log In or Sign Up pop-up window will appear. Start by selecting your country/region from the pull-down menu and then entering your mobile phone number. Click the Continue button to proceed. Alternatively, you can

sign up using your preexisting Facebook, Google, or Apple account, or enter your email address. If you enter your mobile phone number, Airbnb will send you a onetime use verification code via text message. Enter it into the website's Confirm Your Number field to finalize the account setup process.

3. If you choose Facebook, Google, or Apple, you'll need to grant permission to Airbnb so it can access the appropriate account information.

4. If you choose the Sign Up with Email option, you'll be prompted to enter your email address and then click on the Continue button.

5. When prompted, enter your First Name, Last Name, and Date of Birth, and then create a password for your account. Click on the Agree and Continue button to proceed.

 TIP

Your Airbnb account password cannot include your name or email address. However, it must include at least eight characters and at least one number or symbol.

6. Click on the Get Started button to continue. You'll next be asked to click on the Agree and Continue button that's associated with the Airbnb community guidelines.

7. Regardless of which sign-up option you choose, once the free sign-up process is complete, you'll see the "Welcome to Airbnb" message. Click on the Continue button to proceed. You'll be prompted to begin creating your account profile.

Create Your Airbnb Account Profile

In the future, you simply need to log in to the website (or mobile app) using the email or cell phone number and password you just used to set up your account. Alternatively, you'll use your Facebook, Google, or Apple account details to log in.

The first step in creating your profile is to add your mobile phone number to your account and verify it. Keep in mind that this is the phone number that will ultimately be provided to the hosts you opt to stay with as a guest, as well as to your guests with a paid reservation once you become a host. The phone number is not publicly displayed as part of your profile. When Airbnb needs to send you text messages, this will be the phone number that's used (unless you change it later by updating your profile). Next, you'll be asked to provide a profile photo.

Add Photos

When prompted to add a profile photo to your account, upload a digital photo you have of yourself that's stored on your computer or that you've previously published on Facebook. Select the Upload Photo or Use Facebook Photo option, and then follow the on-screen prompts to add your personal photo to the account. Alternatively, the Airbnb website will prompt you to use your computer's webcam to take a photo of yourself.

 TIP

> Select personal photos for your profile where you are smiling and look friendly. After all, the photo(s) people see in your profile will be their first impression of you. It's important to select and use photos in your personal profile that clearly show your face. Choose a headshot (a close-up of your upper body, not a full-body photo).

Populate Your Profile

To begin populating your account profile, click on the profile icon that's displayed in the top-right corner of the web browser window and select the Account option. This menu screen displays nine boxes. Start by clicking on the Personal Info box.

When the Personal Info screen appears, click on the Edit option displayed to the right of each field to fill in the appropriate information. You'll be asked for your Legal Name, Gender, Email Address, Phone Number(s), Government ID, Address, and for an Emergency Contact.

After entering and saving this information, return to the Account menu screen and click on the Login & Security option. After providing the information requested, again return to the Account screen, and proceed to the next box. Ultimately, you'll need to provide information related to the Personal Info, Login & Security, Payments & Payouts, Notifications, Privacy & Sharing, Global Preferences, Travel for Work, Professional Hosting Tools, and Referral Credit & Coupon options. Not all the options, however, will immediately apply to you, so only fill in what's required, based on your situation.

Verification ID

During the account setup process, you'll be asked to upload a copy of your government-issued ID to participate in Airbnb's Verified ID process. This requires you to share a copy of your driver's license, passport, or government-issued identity card with Airbnb, plus link your personal social media accounts (such as your Facebook, Google, and/or LinkedIn accounts) with your Airbnb profile in a way that allows Airbnb to verify this information. You can quickly jump to the Verified ID section of the Airbnb website by pointing your web browser to www.airbnb.com/account-fov.

 **WARNING**

Honesty is important. If you're caught falsifying information within your profile, people who write reviews about you in the future will point this out, and your credibility will be tarnished.

Verifying your ID only needs to be done once and then a Verified ID badge will be displayed as part of your personal profile once you complete the process. The more verifications you have listed on your profile, the more credible you appear.

Many hosts require their guests to have a Verified ID with Airbnb prior to accepting a reservation. As a host, however, having a Verified ID is ultimately a requirement. Again, the more pieces of information that Airbnb can verify, the better this will look when someone views your profile. While the verified information itself is not shared, your profile will say that your driver's license, phone number, email address, Facebook page, and/or your LinkedIn account, for example, have been verified.

Once you begin using Airbnb as a traveler or host, the ratings and reviews you receive will automatically be added to your profile. Note that potential guests will appreciate one additional piece of information in your personal profile: optional references.

Create Your Airbnb Property Listing

After you've created your Airbnb personal profile, the next step is to create a listing for your property. To do this, return to the Airbnb website, sign into your account, and click on the Airbnb Your Home button that's located near the top-right corner of the web browser window. Next, click on the Airbnb Setup button that appears near the top-right corner of the web browser window. This process is broken up into three steps:

1. **Tell Us about Your Place**—You provide basic information about your property, including where it's located and how many guests it can accommodate.

2. **Make It Stand Out**—You'll be prompted to upload at least five photos of your property (including its interior and exterior), plus compose a title and description for your listing.

3. **Finish Up and Publish**—Answer a few additional questions about your property, set your nightly rate, determine when it's available, adjust your

reservation requirements, and then publish your listing. You can also compose and add a Host Guidebook to your listing. This explains some of the points of interest, restaurants, and activities that are close to your property that potential guests might be interested in.

 TIP

You may ultimately need to create and manage multiple property listings on Airbnb if you'll be renting out more than one separate bedroom within your property (potentially to different guests) or if you have multiple properties to promote.

Step 1: Provide Your Basic Information

Select the type of property you're listing. Your options include Entire Place, Private Room, or Shared Room, for example. Choose the option that best describes what you'll be offering as a host. The following are some of the additional questions you'll be asked about your property:

- *How many guests can your place accommodate?* Enter how many beds you have to offer, the types of beds they are, and the total number of guests that can stay at once.

- *How many bathrooms?* Enter the number of bathrooms your property contains and whether the bathrooms are private or shared.

Keep Your Profile and Property Listing Up to Date

Once you create and publish your property listing, you can always go back onto the Airbnb website to tweak or fine-tune the listing, based on feedback you receive from guests or improvements you've made to the property, for example. If you've purchased a new mattress or brand-new bedding, or have begun offering additional amenities, these are definite reasons to update your property listing.

It's a good strategy to get into the habit of updating your property listing at least once every month, to ensure it's up to date and describes the most compelling reasons why potential guests should stay with you.

- *Where's your place located?* Provide your complete address, including the house and/or apartment number, as appropriate. Only confirmed guests, with a prepaid reservation, will receive your exact address. This information is *not* displayed as part of your public profile or listing. On the map that's displayed, if necessary, drag the virtual pushpin to the exact location of your property. Based on the address you entered, the Google Map that's displayed should be able to pinpoint your address rather accurately, however.

- *What amenities do you offer?* From the list that's provided, check the box for each amenity listing that applies. You'll have the opportunity to describe other amenities later.

- *What spaces can guests use?* Based on all the rooms/areas included within your property, check the boxes associated with which area(s) your guests will be able to freely utilize. Your options include Kitchen, Laundry (washer/dryer), Parking, Elevator, Pool, Hot Tub, and Gym. You'll be able to describe other areas within your property that guests will have access to later, if applicable.

Property Photo Tips

Taking proper photos is a time-consuming and detail-oriented task. Be sure to clean and prepare your property *before* photographing it. Remember, you can always click on the Remind Me Later option, finish composing your listing, and then go back and spend the time needed to take and edit your photos before publishing your property listing online.

While you can use the camera that's built into your smartphone or tablet to snap some photos, you will likely achieve more professional-quality results if you use a higher-end, high-resolution digital camera. Many hosts opt to hire a professional photographer to take their property photos to ensure they'll wind up with professional-looking, clear, and well-lit results that will make their property look its absolute best. A professional photographer, especially one that specializes in real estate, will also be able to create a virtual walk-through of your property and/or incorporate drone footage to help you best showcase your property and its surroundings.

Step 2: Share Photos and Add a Descriptive Title

Take photos of your property and the room(s) where your guests will be staying. Show as much detail as possible and try to make your photos as professional looking as possible. Thus, proper lighting is important. See the section "Strategies for Adding Attention-Grabbing Photos to Your Listing" for more information about taking and editing digital photos that properly showcase your property.

Now, create your property description. When prompted, fill in the following fields:

- *My place is close to.* Enter any points of interest, tourist attractions, or other geographic locations that your potential guests may find appealing. For example, if you're within walking distance to public transportation, or a beach, list this.

- *You'll love my place because of.* Type the most important reasons why someone will want to stay at your property. This might include a brief description of the ambience or something special that your property offers that hasn't been listed elsewhere. In addition to typing text into the provided field, you can choose from these options: the Views, the Location, the People, the Ambience, or the Outdoor Space.

- *My place is good for.* Check each box that applies to the type of traveler who will enjoy and be comfortable staying at your property. Your options include: Couples, Solo Adventurers, Business Travelers, Families (with Kids), Big Groups, and Pet-Friendly.

Strategies for Adding Attention-Grabbing Photos to Your Listing

What you say within your listing is important; however, the visual images of your property (the photos) that you showcase will ultimately play a huge role in the decision-making process for your prospective guests. Thus, it's essential that your photos truly showcase your property in the best way possible. In other words, your property photos are extremely important.

 TIP

> While your prospective guests might spend a few minutes reading your personal profile and property listing, it'll be the photos of your property (and your personal profile photos) that play a major role in their decision to book a reservation to stay at your property.

You've probably heard the saying that a picture is worth a thousand words. When it comes to photos within your Airbnb property listing, this is a very true statement. Offer prospective guests a collection of photos that truly showcases all aspects of your property. Show them the outside as well as specific areas within the property they'll be utilizing, such as the bedroom(s), bathroom(s), kitchen, patio, parking, and/or living room area.

Remember, you want to communicate visually that your property is clean and comfortable, so stage and capture your property in a way that showcases this in the best possible way. The following are a few tips for taking the best possible photos:

- *Use the highest-resolution camera you can.* If you're using a smartphone or tablet's built-in camera, use the rear-facing camera, which typically allows you to take higher-resolution photos.

- *Use natural lighting.* Shine as much natural light into each room as possible. Try to avoid using the camera's flash. Capturing natural, ambient light will make the property look more appealing.

- *Clean up before taking your photos.* Showcase photos that present your property exactly how guests will discover it when they arrive. Remove personal items or clutter from each room before taking your pictures.

- *Showcase what's unique or special about your property.* Be sure to highlight any special or appealing amenities, such as a big-screen TV, hot tub, kitchen, or patio that your guests will enjoy using.

- *Include a selection of both interior and exterior shots.* If you live in an area that experiences distinct seasons, update your photos in the future to showcase the current season.

- *Study what others have done.* In addition to reviewing photos presented in other Airbnb property listings, look at photos of homes/apartments being sold. Notice how each room is "staged" to look clean, uncluttered, and home-like. Try to replicate this approach to visually convey as much information about your property as possible within your photos.

- *Determine the best order in which your photos get displayed on the Airbnb website and mobile app.* Showcase the most appealing aspects of your property first, keeping in mind that guests want to see where they'll be sleeping and spending most of their time while staying with you.

- *Showcase the bedrooms.* Make the beds, and highlight the clean pillows, sheets, and blankets you offer. Also be sure that other furniture in the room is presented nicely, including nightstands, dressers, etc. Ideally, you want to include at least three photos of each room or area of your home.

- *Showcase the bathroom.* Make sure the shower/bathtub, toilet, and sink areas are all visible and appear very clean. Towels should be folded and presented neatly on a shelf or on a towel rack within the photo(s). No mold, mildew, soap scum, or dirty laundry should appear in these photos. Your potential guests will want to see a clean and sanitary bathroom that will provide them with privacy when it's in use.

Again, consider hiring a professional photographer to photograph your property. Yes, you may need to pay for photography services up front, but the results will be worth it and will help your property listing positively stand out on Airbnb. The Airbnb service can help you find a professional photographer in your area to work with—visit www.airbnb.com/info/photography—or you can easily find a talented photographer on your own.

NOTE

Research from Airbnb shows that hosts that utilize professional-looking photos within their property listing and profile receive up to 20 percent more bookings and a 20 percent increase in earnings. Most hosts can recoup the money they spend hiring a professional photographer after hosting their first few guests.

TIP

Your property description is a great place to promote what's truly special or unique about your property and emphasize that you're offering a clean, comfortable, and safe place to stay. If you're targeting solo travelers, couples, business travelers, people traveling with pets, or families, for example, explain exactly why your property will appeal to a specific type of traveler.

Based on your responses to Airbnb's questions about your property, the Airbnb website will display a text-based, paragraph-long description of your property. You can leave this description as is, but to get the most attention from potential guests, take a few minutes to edit the text to be more customized to what specifically you're offering and who you're offering it to.

The Name Your Place field is where you'll compose your listing's title. It can be up to 50 characters long. Write something that is descriptive and attention-getting, and that will appeal to your target guests.

At this point, you can preview your listing and see exactly how it will appear on the Airbnb platform. Remember, do not actually publish your Airbnb property listing without adding your photos.

Step 3: Set Your Rate and Availability Dates

Before you set your rate and availability dates, there are a few preliminary items to tend to. First, you'll be prompted to answer the following questions:

- *Have you rented out your place before?*
- *How often do you want to have guests?* Your options include As Often as Possible, Part-time, or Not Sure Yet.

The Settings screen lists three separate options: Calendar, Trip Length, and Availability.

- Calendar provides month-to-month calendars and the option to manually block out specific dates that your property will *not* be available to guests.
- The Trip Length option sets the minimum and maximum number of consecutive nights a guest can book your property for. Some hosts set a two-night minimum, for example, while others allow guests to book for as little as one night. For the maximum nights, you can set this to any number that's higher than your minimum night stay. As a new host, you might want to keep the maximum stay short (a week or less), so you don't wind up with someone staying at your property for a long period, if you happen to decide against remaining a host.
- The Availability screen offers three options you can customize, including: Advance Notice, Preparation Time, and Booking Window. These options allow you to fine-tune when your property will be available for bookings, based on a series of personal preferences and the time needed for cleaning, for example.
- Use Advance Notice to set the number of days in advance guests must book and prepay for their reservation prior to their arrival. The default option

is Same Day, meaning that they can book a reservation and begin staying with you that same day. As a new host, you might require one day advance notice to give you ample time to prepare your property and communicate with the potential guests.

- Use Preparation Time to choose how much time in between reservations you need to clean your property and prepare it for the next guest. Your options include: No Prep Time, One Day, or Two Days. Airbnb will automatically adjust your property's availability based on booked reservations and the time you say is needed between them.

- Use Booking to determine how far in advance someone can book a reservation. Your options include: Any Time, Three Months, Six Months, or One Year.

Now you can set a nightly price, but be sure to do some research before you do this. First, explore the Airbnb website (or mobile app), and figure out what other hosts with comparable properties in your area are charging. Next, go online or call nearby hotels, motels, B&Bs, and/or resorts. Determine what their nightly pricing is. There are also online services that will help you set short-term rental pricing in a way that maximizes your profit potential while remaining competitive. Using one of these dynamic pricing services takes the guesswork out of price setting, especially for new hosts.

Some of the online-based, independent pricing tools you can use include:

- **AirDNA**—www.airdna.co/airbnb-pricing-tool
- **Beyond Pricing**—www.beyondpricing.com/airbnb-pricing-tool
- **Mashvisor**—www.mashvisor.com
- **PlushyHost**—www.plushyhost.com
- **PriceLabs**—https://hello.pricelabs.co/dynamic-pricing

 **WARNING**

Remember, once you accept a booking/reservation as a host, you are penalized and will receive negative ratings/reviews if you later cancel on a guest. Don't accept any reservation that you don't plan to honor.

When setting your own nightly rate, you have two options. You can choose the Price Adapts to Demand option or the Price Is Fixed option. If you select the first, adaptive option, you will be asked to set a fixed price and a price range. Then, the Airbnb service will automatically adjust your price. When local demand is high, your nighty rate will automatically be promoted as being higher.

If you select the Price Is Fixed option, this means that you set a nightly rate, and that rate will always be in effect, unless you manually change it. Regardless of which option you choose, the Airbnb service will offer tips to help you choose the best nightly fixed price or price range, based on what you're offering, your geographic location, and seasonal demand (if applicable).

 TIP

As a new host, you'll likely wind up wanting or needing to tweak your nightly pricing as you receive feedback from your initial guests and read their reviews related to the value of what you're offering. Likewise, if you improve your property or add new amenities, you'll probably want to update your pricing to reflect this.

Using Airbnb's own Smart Pricing tool, the Airbnb platform will automatically maximize how much you earn each night and, in some cases, increase the nightly rate on certain high-demand nights, just as traditional hotels do. For example, Airbnb may promote a lower rate for your property midweek but may charge a premium on weekend and holiday nights. Smart Pricing focuses on demand in your geographic area and automatically adjusts prices accordingly. Keep in mind, when you turn on the Smart Pricing feature, Airbnb will never offer your property for less than what you determine is your minimum nightly rate.

After you set your nightly rate and choose between Fixed or Smart Pricing, you'll also be given the opportunity to offer a discount to guests who book and prepay for a full week or a full month. Offering a discount encourages longer stays. By default, Airbnb recommends offering a 21 percent discount for stays between 7 and 27 nights, and a 49 percent discount for stays longer than 28 nights. However, you are free to set your own discounted rate for long-term stays.

 NOTE

> Initially, you might want to avoid accepting bookings several months in advance, because between now and then, you may wind up raising your rate or altering your amenities/offerings. Once you accept an advance reservation, the nightly rate that was quoted at the time of the booking is how much that guest will pay. You cannot change the rate after a reservation has been confirmed.

Step 4: Request Additional Guest Information

The Review Airbnb's Guest Requirements page gives you the opportunity to obtain additional information from prospective guests, including a confirmed email address and phone number, profile photo, and payment information. The guest will also agree to adhere to your published House Rules and share details about the purpose of their trip when requesting and booking a reservation.

If you want to gather additional information from prospective guests, click on the Add More Guest Requirements option, and then choose: Government-Issued ID Submitted to Airbnb, and/or Recommended by Other Hosts, and/or Have No Negative Reviews.

If you live alone and are renting out a guestroom or area of your home where you'll also be staying, consider activating these additional options to help ensure your personal safety and well-being before inviting strangers to stay in your home.

 TIP

If you turn off the Instant Book feature, be prepared to respond to reservation requests as quickly as possible (within an hour or two, if possible), or you could wind up losing the booking to someone else. Furthermore, your listing will be displayed less prominently on the Airbnb website and mobile app, and according to Airbnb, "You may only get half as many reservations." You will, however, be able to block people who you're not comfortable with from staying with you, based on information within their profile and initial text message–based communications.

From a host's standpoint, House Rules are an important aspect of a property listing. Here, you get to explain exactly what is and isn't permissible during a guest's stay. The Set House Rules for Your Guests screen offers the following options. Answer Yes or No for each:

- Suitable for Children (2–12 years)
- Suitable for Infants (Under 2 years)
- Suitable for Pets
- Smoking Allowed
- Events or Parties Allowed

There is also an Add More Rules option where you can manually add any additional rules you want to enforce when guests stay at your property (see the "Put Some Thought into Your House Rules" section for more information). Keep in mind, one of the most in-demand options guests are looking for as of early 2023 is the ability to bring their pet with them during their stay, so offering pet-friendly accommodations will be to your advantage.

 TIP

> At any time, to edit, change, or delete your property listing, sign into the Airbnb service, click on your name/photo (displayed in the top-right corner of the browser window), and then click on the Your Listing or Dashboard option that's displayed. Prior to publishing your listing, the message "In Progress" will appear in conjunction with your listing. When the "In Progress" message is displayed, only you can view your property listing. It is not yet public, and you cannot yet accept bookings/reservations.

If you're a new Airbnb host, consider turning off the Instant Book option on the How Guests Book screen. Simply click the Require All Guests to Send Reservation Requests option. If you select the Instant Book option, you automatically accept all reservation requests immediately. By turning off this feature, you will receive a request from each prospective guest, be able to read their profile, ratings, and reviews, and then approve or deny the reservation within 24 hours of receiving the request.

Based on the available dates you've listed, the Airbnb platform will ask that you confirm that what you've provided is accurate. To do this, click on the I Understand button, or click on the Go Back to Availability Settings button to tweak your property's dates of availability.

Prior to publishing your listing, select your desired cancellation policy. This is the policy that your guests will need to adhere to if they book a prepaid reservation and then want or need to cancel or change that reservation. Airbnb allows you to choose between a Flexible, Moderate, Strict, Super Strict 30 Days, Super Strict 60 Days, or Long-Term policy. Read the description for each option carefully before selecting one, because the option you choose directly determines how you'll handle guests who want to cancel or change their reservation.

Once you fine-tune each section of the property listing, be sure to click on the Preview button one final time to make sure all the information is accurate, and that what you've written contains no spelling or punctuation mistakes. When you're ready, click on the Finish the Listing button to publish your listing.

Create a Compelling Host Guidebook

A Host Guidebook is a section of your property listing that includes your personal suggestions when it comes to what people should see and do in the area when they visit. Your Guidebook can include a listing and description of local restaurants, food delivery options, shops, points of interest, landmarks, parks, tourist attractions, bars, beaches, airports, access to public transportation, or anything else nearby that you think potential guests will want to know about.

The locations for listings you add to your Host Guidebook will appear on the map that accompanies your property listing that shows the location of your property. To create or customize an optional Host Guidebook, sign into your Airbnb account, click on the Manage Listings option, and then click on the Manage Listing and Calendar option. Next, click on the Guidebook option. Follow the on-screen prompts to create or edit your Host Guidebook.

Based on all the Host Guidebooks created within your geographic area, a more general City Guidebook is also published online within the Airbnb site. This allows guests looking to stay in or near a particular area to learn more about that area prior to making their reservation.

Put Some Thought into Your House Rules

The House Rules you create are presented as part of your property listing, and potential guests must agree to these published rules before they can make and confirm their reservation. As a host, you'll also want to review your House Rules verbally when guests arrive at your property and present them with a printed copy of these rules upon their arrival. You'll read more on this in Chapter 6, "Responding to Broken Rules."

The goal of the House Rules is to help maintain your peace of mind as a host and to ensure your guests treat your property and belongings appropriately. It encourages your guests to act in a manner that will not bother you, other guests, or your neighbors.

If guests violate your House Rules, you have the option of canceling their reservation without penalty and asking that guest to leave your premises. The Airbnb Customer Service team can help you deal with this type of situation when and if it arises.

Above and beyond the House Rules that Airbnb recommends, you can add additional rules that cater to your own wants, needs, and property. The following are a few additional House Rules you might want to implement:

- No drinking or drug use (including legalized marijuana).

- No excessive noise, loud music, or socializing between 11 p.m. and 8 a.m.

- If you allow pets, no dog walking on the front lawn. (You might state that guests must clean up after their dog and choose to provide complimentary poop bags for their use and a place to dispose of the used bags.)

- No trespassing in the basement/attic.

- No entering the host's own bedroom/bathroom.

- No eating in the bedroom.

- No moving or touching the artwork or antiques displayed within the property.

In addition to House Rules, consider creating a printed house manual for your property. This will be a short document that you present to your guests that offers easy-to-understand, step-by-step instructions for:

- Using the appliances in the kitchen
- Using the laundry facilities
- Where to park their car
- Where to find the iron and ironing board
- How to use the coffee machine
- How to log in to the Wi-Fi
- How to turn on and use the hot tub
- How to use the TV and cable box
- Where to find extra sheets and blankets
- How to lock/unlock the front door

After compiling a list of the most asked questions from your guests, you'll want to revise this house manual as needed to answer these questions.

Attracting Specific Types of Guests

Based on how you present your listing, you will be able to weed out certain types of people from requesting a reservation, and if you have the Instant Book feature turned off, you always have the option of reading a potential guest's profile, ratings, and reviews before accepting their reservation.

For example, if you do not want infants or kids staying at your property, do not promote your property as being family-friendly. However, if you want short-term business professionals to stay with you, make sure you list the property as being suitable for business travelers and offer amenities that will appeal to these people.

Within your personal profile, if you enjoy quiet and solitude within your living space, mention this, but also make sure that you stipulate no groups or parties are allowed, and within your House Rules, you explain that loud noises or rowdiness is not acceptable.

Without discriminating against specific groups of people, you can describe yourself within your profile and property listing and stress that you're looking to host like-minded guests with similar interests.

Offer the Best Collection of Amenities to Your Guests

Regardless of what type of property you're offering on Airbnb, it's expected to be clean, safe, and comfortable. You're also expected to provide essentials, such as clean towels, bedsheets, soap, and toilet paper, plus have one or more smoke detectors, carbon monoxide detectors, fire extinguishers, and a basic first-aid kit on hand.

 TIP

Potential guests can search the Airbnb service for property listings based on specific amenities that are offered. By providing a broad selection of the most sought-after amenities, your listing is more apt to be noticed when it shows up based on a potential guest's personalized search parameters. Be sure to create and promote the most comprehensive list of amenities possible. For example, don't just say the property has a full kitchen. Describe the major appliances in that kitchen, including the microwave, coffee maker, and dishwasher, for example.

There are many potential amenities you can offer that will make your property that much more appealing to potential guests. Some of the most in-demand amenities that potential guests will appreciate include:

- A selection of free snacks and/or drinks, including bottled water
- Access to a full kitchen, with a coffee maker

- Bedroom windows that open (with a view) but that have curtains or shades for privacy
- Closets with hangers and/or drawer space within a dresser
- Desk and/or workspace
- Easily accessible and available on-site or nearby parking
- Fireplace
- Fully equipped dining room (you provide dishes, silverware, glasses, etc.)
- Heat and/or air-conditioning
- Hot tub / swimming pool
- In-home gym (workout equipment)
- Iron and ironing board
- Multiple power outlets and/or an available power strip within each bedroom
- Nightstand with reading lamp
- Premium bedding, blankets, and pillows (If you offer Egyptian cotton sheets with a high thread count, for example, this should be promoted within your property listing.)
- Secure lock on the bedroom door
- Shampoo, conditioner, hair dryer, and other extra toiletries in the bathroom
- Television with cable/satellite TV programming available
- Travel-size toiletries (complimentary), ranging from shampoo and conditioner, to soap, mouthwash, toothpaste, etc. (These can be purchased for about $1 each from a dollar store, supermarket, or pharmacy.)
- Wi-Fi

Making your property pet-friendly and allowing guests to bring their pet(s) may be a sought-after amenity by some potential guests, but if there's no place for guests to walk their dog, or if you're concerned about the pets soiling your carpets, ruining your furniture, or making too much noise, think twice about allowing pets. If you do allow pets, consider providing food and water bowls, dog toys, poop bags, complimentary dog treats, a dog bed, and other amenities the pet owner can use. For an additional fee, you could also offer a pet-sitting or dog-walking service through a professionally licensed third party.

 TIP

If you opt to include a dog bed and dog bowls, don't forget that these, too, will need to be cleaned and sanitized in between guests.

Meanwhile, by offering two or more bedrooms with different bed configurations and promoting your property as "family-friendly," you're more apt to attract parents traveling with their kids. If you're looking to provide family-friendly accommodations, you may want to include a video game system, board games, and/or toys within your list of offered amenities.

 TIP

Based on the types of guests you're looking to attract, offer bed configuration(s) that will appeal to these people. A couple will likely want a queen- or king-size bed, while a solo business traveler will appreciate a queen-size bed for extra space and comfort. Friends traveling together typically prefer separate twin- or queen-size beds, or two separate bedrooms. Parents traveling with kids will want one queen- or king-size bed, along with a twin-size bed for each of their kids. A traditional mattress and box spring are typically preferred over a sofa bed or air mattresses.

Don't Forget to Protect Yourself and Your Property

If you're not familiar with smart home equipment, it's time to get up to speed, as having some of this gear within your short-term rental property will make your job as the host easier. For example, consider installing a smart lock and video doorbell at the front and back doors.

While you may choose to install security cameras on the outside of your property, many guests will be leery about finding security cameras inside the property. A smart thermostat will help you keep utility bills lower and allow you to control the heat and/or air conditioner remotely, if necessary.

With a smart door lock, you can create access codes for each individual guest that activates on the time/day they're set to arrive and then automatically expires at the conclusion of their reservation. This can be done from your own smartphone. It eliminates the need to distribute traditional metal keys that could get lost or stolen.

Using smart lighting with motion sensors, you can turn on/off lights outside or inside the home remotely for added safety and security. Visit any consumer electronics store or hardware store to learn about the smart home equipment you can easily and inexpensively add to your short-term rental property. You can also use any search engine and enter the search phrase "Best smart home equipment for Airbnb" to discover what's available and the best ways to use the latest technology as a host.

As an Airbnb host, you'll ultimately be inviting strangers to stay at your property. Thus, it's in your best interest to make sure all your belongings and furniture, for example, are properly protected. Plus, it's important that you have ample liability coverage, in case someone is injured on your property. Before you begin hosting guests, be sure to speak with a licensed insurance agent in your state to determine what type of insurance and how much coverage you need.

If you plan to host families with kids or allow pets in your home, additional insurance may be required. Likewise, if you have valuable belongings, antiques, or artwork within your property, you may also need additional insurance. Determine your insurance needs, and make sure the appropriate policies are active, *before* paying guests start staying at your property.

WARNING

Think twice before offering a crib or specialized gear for infants/toddlers within your property, or you could be held accountable if, for whatever reason, the infant or young child is injured using that crib or child-specific furniture. Instead, promote that the bedroom has ample space for parents to bring and set up their own pack-and-play crib, for example.

Meet Airbnb Superhost Mary Shimshea

Based in Allentown, Pennsylvania, Mary Shimshea is an experienced Airbnb Superhost. She owns a five-bedroom home, which she is paying off using revenue she earns by hosting guests through Airbnb.

How did you get started with Airbnb as a host?

Mary Shimshea: "I live in the home and invite guests to stay with me in my home's various bedrooms. I live near a college and a hospital, so prior to getting started with Airbnb, I was renting two of the rooms on a long-term basis to college professors. One of the professors told me about Airbnb. I visited the Airbnb website and decided it was worth a try.

"I started by doing some research in my immediate area to see how much local hotels, motels, and bed-and-breakfasts were charging. I also checked what other Airbnb hosts were charging and evaluated what they were offering for that price. I have always seen myself as a natural host. I like to entertain."

As a host, what are some of the extra things you do for your guests?

Mary Shimshea: "Some of the extra things I do for my guests include providing menus for local restaurants in each of the guestrooms and displaying the clean and folded towels within nice baskets. First and foremost, I treat my guests just as I would want to be treated if I were traveling."

What has it been like for you offering your home as a short-term rental through Airbnb?

Mary Shimshea: "I have welcomed guests from around the world. I have had so many truly nice people stay with me. I try to cater to college professors, business professionals, and doctors who are traveling for work. Most of my guests want a clean and comfortable place to sleep at night, so they don't fully utilize the dining room or patio that I have set up for my guests."

Since your goal is to attract medical professionals, professors, and businesspeople as guests, what are some strategies you've adopted to make this happen?

Mary Shimshea: "Within my property listing, I use phrases like 'cozy room with balcony,' 'serene and clean,' and 'spacious room with privacy' to describe the guestrooms. I've discovered that people like to learn about the area, so I stress that the house is located across the street from a wonderful breakfast restaurant and is a short walk from a beautiful park. Even though I live next to a college, I have a strict policy against accepting college kids as guests. Before accepting a reservation, I always review the potential guest's profile and make sure that I'd be comfortable having that person or couple stay in my home. You can get a pretty good idea about what to expect from a guest, based on the reason they provide for their trip."

What are some of the things you do to earn five-star ratings from guests?

Mary Shimshea: "My guests appreciate the clear effort I put into making the house as comfortable as possible for them. As a result, I have received almost all five-star ratings and very positive reviews. The single most sought-after amenity I offer is Wi-Fi. This is something that almost everyone requests. I also offer televisions with cable TV programming, a yard with a barbecue set up, and use of a full kitchen. I have made the house's main dining room into a comfortable tearoom where people can relax. I have my own pets, so I decided to accept pets and have wound up getting bookings, specifically because my home is pet-friendly."

What are some of the other things you do to encourage more bookings?

Mary Shimshea: "I am willing to welcome people with a late arrival time. I have had travelers show up after 10 p.m. because of travel delays, and they were very pleased that I was happy to welcome them in person when they arrived. I have found that travelers coming from a long distance appreciate the ability to check in late and be welcomed upon their arrival. Most of my guests stay for one or two nights, although occasionally I welcome a guest for a full week. I had one guest stay for four months. He had a local, short-term job in the area and needed a place to stay without having to sign a one-year lease."

How much interaction do you typically have with your guests?

Mary Shimshea: "I leave that entirely up to each guest. Some people want to go right up to their bedroom and be left alone. Others enjoy sitting with me on the porch and chatting for hours at a time. No matter what, I am always at home to welcome each guest when they first arrive. I like to be at the front door to greet each guest and to offer them a bottle of water. My guests seem to appreciate this."

What do you think are the qualities that make you a good host?

Mary Shimshea: "I consider myself to be a spiritual person who enjoys interacting with and hosting other people. Being an Airbnb host is not for everyone. If you're uncomfortable with the idea of a stranger sleeping in your home and you don't have another property to offer as a short-term rental, this is not something you should pursue. If you do decide to become a host, make sure you're open and honest with your prospective guests in terms of the information you provide in your profile and listing. One thing I require is that people who are interested in staying with me have a picture of themselves within their Airbnb profile."

Do you have smart locks with a digital code on your front door?

Mary Shimshea: "Yes. Not having to distribute and then collect keys makes things a lot easier. Also, in terms of House Rules, one of the things I state is that people stay quiet after 10 p.m., so that everyone can get sleep and live in harmony. As a host, being able and willing to provide guests with information about where to go, where to eat, and what they can do during their free time is important. I have found that being attentive to guests leads to positive ratings and reviews. For me, the biggest challenge is always being available to my guests, while also being able to enjoy my life in retirement. The biggest perks of being a host for me are that I am continuously meeting new and interesting people and, at the same time, earning extra money while doing something that I really enjoy."

Creating an attention-getting personal profile and property listing on Airbnb is your first big step toward becoming a successful and money-earning travel host. However, setting your rates is also an extremely important task that'll impact how much money you can ultimately earn. The next chapter focuses on calculating your expenses, setting your base nightly rate, and maximizing your profit as an Airbnb host.

CHAPTER 3

Planning for Profit and Setting Your Rates

A lot of factors should go into setting your nightly rate as an Airbnb host. Unfortunately, there's no preset formula that guarantees success or that you'll generate a profit. While this chapter will help you identify many of the key considerations and options available when it comes to setting your prices, you first need to fully understand and calculate all your expenses.

 NOTE

According to Mashvisor (www.mashvisor.com/blog/category /investor-blogs/airbnb-rentals), "Airbnb short-term rentals are becoming the choice of many property investors in recent years, replacing traditional rentals as the optimal rental strategy in many U.S. real estate markets." It's no doubt that short-term rentals are revolutionizing real estate investing for investors. Many investors are now considering short-term rentals due to the higher profit potential they offer. In addition, they give you the flexibility to decide your nightly rate, as well as choose the number of nights to make the property available for booking.

Chapter 9, "Managing Finances for an Airbnb Hosting Business," offers work-sheets and strategies for calculating all your business-related expenses—from cleaning fees and the cost of amenities to repairs, ongoing maintenance, increased utility costs, property management fees, upgrades to your property (such as the addition of smart locks and other smart home gear), insurance, the cost of fur-niture, and marketing costs. It doesn't take a financial genius to know that your earnings as an Airbnb host must exceed the total of your expenses, plus compen-sate you for your time, and allow you to generate a profit (not just break even).

When it comes to setting your prices, once you understand your costs, there are still a lot of factors to consider, which is the focus of this chapter. Remember, for each booking through Airbnb, as the host you'll typically be charged a flat ser-vice fee of 3 percent of each guest's total booking, so be sure to calculate this fee into your cost of doing business, your nightly pricing, and your overall budget.

What the Airbnb Service Fee for Hosts Covers

Listing your property on Airbnb is free. However, for each booking, you'll pay a 3 percent service fee to Airbnb. This is a flat fee based on the booking subtotal. It's calculated based on your nightly price, plus any optional fees you decide to charge guests (such as a cleaning fee). It does not include additional fees and taxes that Airbnb charges its guests for each booking.

In general, guests making a booking through Airbnb will pay around a 14 percent Airbnb Service fee on the booking subtotal (as of early 2023). The Airbnb fee for guests is added to their total booking at checkout. In addition to a guest's nightly rate, all additional fees, such as the cleaning fee, extra guest fee, pet fee, and refundable security deposit (if applicable), are displayed along with the local taxes and the total price for their entire booking. Everything but the 3 percent fee charged to hosts is now clearly itemized for guests.

The 3 percent booking fee paid by hosts is used by Airbnb to provide 24/7 customer support, marketing to guests, AirCover protection for hosts and their property, and the educational resources available to hosts. To learn more about Airbnb's AirCover protection for hosts, point your web browser to www.airbnb.com/aircover-for-hosts.

What Type of Accommodations Do You Plan to Offer?

Pretty much before anything else, it's important to determine what type of accommodations you plan to offer and figure out who your target guest will be. For example, you could offer a single bedroom with a shared bathroom and the most basic of accommodations, with a flexible cancellation policy at a very competitive price. Doing this will typically attract younger, budget-conscious travelers looking for a good deal on their accommodations.

If your property permits, you also have the option of renting out multiple bedrooms within your home simultaneously (to the same or different guests), again with basic accommodations, but this could generate more revenue. Yet another option is to rent out your entire property. If you go this route, you could provide basic amenities with a flexible cancellation policy and charge a highly competitive rate to help ensure more frequent bookings, or you could upgrade the amenities, go with a more rigid cancellation policy, and charge a higher rate to travelers looking for alternative accommodations to a hotel or motel (but who are willing to pay an equivalent nightly fee).

For hosts willing to make a more substantial investment in their property to provide higher-end, more luxurious accommodations (and offer more personalized attention to their guests), this will attract more affluent travelers looking for comfort as opposed to bargain accommodations. You might not book your property as frequently, but you'll potentially earn a higher nightly rate.

More and more travelers who use Airbnb are looking for higher-end and extremely unique accommodations, or higher-end accommodations with an experience tied into their stay. For this, they're willing to pay a significant premium. The type of property you're able to offer, and the quality and selection of amenities that go along with each booking, will play a significant role in how much you can charge for accommodations as a host. But, as you're about to discover, there are other considerations that go into pricing, too.

Determine Your Property's Short-Term Rental Value

Before you can set your nightly pricing, you need to understand what you're offering and what potential guests are willing to pay for that type of accommodation. The more space, privacy, luxury, and uniqueness you're able to provide to guests, the more you'll be able to charge. That said, your income potential for renting out one room of your residence that will accommodate one or two people will be much lower than renting out an entire multi-bedroom house or apartment that can accommodate an entire family, for example.

Most Profitable U.S. Cities to Operate a Short-Term Rental Property

According to projections published by DPGO Software, Inc. (www.dpgo.com /go/best-places-to-own-an-airbnb-in-2023), in December 2022, the most profitable cities in the USA to operate a short-term rental property in 2023 include:

- Austin, TX
- Denver, CO
- Kauai, HI
- Miami, FL
- Palm Springs, CA
- Phoenix, AZ
- San Francisco, CA
- The Poconos, PA

Beyond just the space or property type you're offering for accommodations, some of the other factors that go into price setting include:

- Your property's geographic location and popularity (being located close to a tourist attraction, theme park, lake, ocean, ski resort, or special event will allow you to charge a premium). Short-term rental properties in regions that attract a lot of tourists tend to have a higher occupancy rate and have a higher nightly rate based on demand. If your property is not in a major tourist area, you'll do better if it's close to public transportation, restaurants, activities, recreation centers, and shopping, for example. Hosts with properties close to hospitals or colleges tend to attract longer-term guests.

- The collection of amenities being offered. Amenities go beyond offering an iron and shampoo. Some amenities that are desirable include a swimming pool, fireplace, hot tub, fully equipped chef's kitchen, or a spectacular view.

- How many people your space can comfortably accommodate. This determines if you'll attract solo travelers, business travelers, couples, or families.

- The type of guests you're looking to attract. By catering to upscale guests, families with kids, people traveling with pets, honeymooners, or business travelers, for example, and offering accommodations and amenities that'll appeal to your intended guests, you can often charge premium rates.

- Seasonality. Ideally, you want your short-term rental property to be in demand throughout the year. However, many places attract seasonal tourists, whether it's for water-based activities in the summer or skiing in the winter. If your property will only attract bookings during certain times of the year, make sure you'll be able to maximize revenue during that period, and consider offering significant discounts to increase your occupancy rate during the off-season(s).

- Your ratings and reviews as a host.

- Whether or not the property is pet-friendly, family-friendly, or suitable for a special occasion (such as a honeymoon).

- If the property is equipped for remote workers or business travelers.

- If the property is handicap accessible or suitable for guests with special needs; this, too, can increase your occupancy rate, but not necessarily allow you to charge a premium rate.

- Whether what you opt to charge is in line with your business goals and profit objectives.

TIP

As you're first starting out, consider charging a lower nightly rate, even if it means taking a slight financial loss. This will allow you to potentially generate positive ratings and reviews, learn more about hosting from real-world experience, identify any mistakes you've already made, and figure out exactly what guests expect from you and the accommodations you're offering. After hosting a handful of guests successfully and ironing out the kinks, that's when you should raise your prices.

Analyze Your Local Competition

Start by exploring the Airbnb website (or mobile app) and figure out what other hosts with comparable properties in your area are charging. Be sure to check pricing for weekdays, weekends, holiday periods, and weekly rates for each property. Pay attention to the amenities and type of property being offered. As a potential guest looking for accommodations, you can use Airbnb's filters to match the type of accommodations you're planning to offer in your geographic area.

As you evaluate your local competition, pay attention to whether Instant Booking or Self Check-In options are offered, whether the competition is offering standard Airbnb accommodations, accommodations operated by a Superhost, operating an Airbnb Plus property, and what additional fees the individual hosts are charging.

The Difference between a Superhost and an Airbnb Plus Property

An Airbnb Plus property is one that has been verified for offering both quality and design, while a property operated by a Superhost is one that has earned the title by meeting or exceeding Airbnb's Superhost criteria.

There are a few differences between a property offered by a Superhost and an Airbnb Plus property. A host will automatically become a Superhost if they meet specific standards (which are outlined here: www.airbnb.com/help/article/829). For a property to receive the Airbnb Plus ranking, the host must be invited into the program after developing a reputation for offering what Airbnb refers to as "outstanding service and demonstrating they genuinely care." Airbnb Plus properties and their hosts must meet specific style, comfort, and hospitality standards. The program standards are outlined here: www.airbnb.com/help/article/2675. As of early 2023, the Airbnb Plus and Airbnb Luxe programs were not being promoted as heavily as the Superhost accreditation as a standard for quality.

Once you've become acquainted with your local competition from other Airbnb hosts, go online or call nearby hotels, motels, B&Bs, and/or resorts. Determine their nightly pricing and what amenities these properties offer. Ultimately, you need to be able to justify your pricing, in part, based on what others are charging for similar accommodations.

How to Set or Adjust Your Pricing

When you're ready to set your default nightly pricing, log into your Airbnb account and access your property listing. Click on the Pricing and Availability option and then choose Pricing. Next, select the Edit option associated with Nightly Price. Enter your new or updated price, and then be sure to click on the Save option. Keep in mind, anytime you update your pricing moving forward, the new price will only apply to new reservations and bookings, not reservations that are already pending or confirmed.

Beyond just setting a standard nightly rate, you have the option of listing a higher or lower rate during specific time periods. For example, you can charge a premium during the last week in December and the first week in January. To set pricing for specific dates or date ranges, once you're viewing your property listing, select the Calendar option, select one or more dates, choose the Nightly Price option, and enter your custom price. Be sure to click on Save when you are done. The new rate during the date(s) you selected will now automatically override your default nightly rate, as well as the Smart Pricing rate, weekend pricing, or long-term pricing you may have already set.

What to Consider When Setting Your Rates

Beyond setting a default nightly rate for your property, you may choose to charge added fees for specific services and require a refundable deposit. Then, based on demand and other factors, you may opt to increase that nightly rate on weekends (Friday and Saturday nights), during holiday periods, and/or during peak travel times (such as school vacation periods).

Or, depending on your goals, you might opt to attract more guests by offering various types of discounts or promotions. As you're about to discover, Airbnb gives hosts a lot of flexibility when it comes to setting their pricing. Let's look at some of your options.

Pros and Cons of Short-Term, Weekly, and Long-Term Rentals

In addition to taking advantage of Airbnb's own Smart Pricing tool, which automatically adjusts your nightly rate based on demand (which will be explained shortly), beyond setting a default nightly rate, you have the option of setting special weekend pricing, as well as discounted rates for weekly, monthly, or even longer-term bookings. For weekly bookings, for example, Airbnb recommends offering at least a 25 percent discount off your default nightly rate. For a monthly booking (28 consecutive days or longer), Airbnb recommends offering at least a 50 percent discount off your default nightly rate.

 NOTE

In November 2022, NerdWallet (www.nerdwallet.com/article/travel /airbnb-pricing-statistics) published data indicating that, on average, hosts offered a 32 percent discount for weekly stays and a 46 percent discount for a 28-consecutive-night or longer stay. The research showed that hosts generally prefer having fewer bookings to manage, while ensuring occupancy and having to deal with fewer cleanings between guests.

These discount recommendations are just general guidelines, not requirements. Some hosts opt to offer just a 10 percent discount for weeklong bookings and a 20 to 30 percent discount for monthlong bookings, for example. But most travelers using Airbnb to find accommodations expect to receive some type of discount if they book an entire week (seven or more nights), a month (28 or more nights), or for an even longer term. For example, if your property is located close to a college, you might attract visiting professors or students looking to stay with you for an entire semester (or longer).

When you're offering your property for short stays, with a bit of luck and hard work, you'll hopefully achieve an above-average occupancy rate for your region. You'll be able to charge your full nightly rate (or even a premium during peak times) to your short-term guests. However, you'll have a lot of guest turnover. This means having to clean your property more often, manage more bookings, and have more interaction with a greater number of people.

 TIP

One of the easiest ways to encourage longer bookings is to offer a generous weekly-, monthly-, and long-term-stay discount, and then provide amenities and furnishings that'll make long-term guests feel more like being at home. If you know you typically have a low occupancy rate during certain times of the year, instead of going with no income during non-booked nights, offering a discount for longer stays will help you find guests looking to stay longer. This could increase your occupancy rate and potentially allow you to earn more money (compared to having more non-booked, zero-revenue-generating nights in any given month).

Consider Separate Weekend Pricing

As an Airbnb host, you have the option of requiring guests looking to book weekend accommodations to reserve Friday, Saturday, *and* Sunday night (or just Friday and Saturday night), as opposed to just one weekend night. You can typically charge a higher rate than your default rate for weekend accommodations, but this is at your discretion.

Seasonal Pricing

If your property is a cottage located by a lake or beach and its location is subject to seasonal weather, during peak months it makes sense to offer a higher seasonal rate when the weather is warm. But, to generate revenue during the off-peak season, seriously consider lowering your nightly rate significantly as the appeal of the property during cold-weather months will likely diminish. Before you start setting seasonal pricing, determine how demand for your property and its perceived value to guests will fluctuate throughout the year.

Airbnb Smart Pricing: Automatically Adjusting Prices Based on Local Demand

The Smart Pricing tool offered by Airbnb automatically studies the local demand for accommodations in your area, and then considers more than 70 other factors to calculate the best pricing for your accommodations. Once you turn on this feature, your rates are updated automatically by Airbnb, based on things like lead time, local popularity, seasonality, listing popularity, and your review history.

After turning on the Smart Pricing tool, be sure to set a minimum nightly price within this tool to ensure you never lose money (based on your expenses) and that you're able to generate a profit.

Consider Additional Discounts

Airbnb offers hosts a handful of other discount options that can be extended to potential guests, at the host's discretion. There are several reasons why you might want to offer a discount. For example, you might want to increase your number of bookings during a certain period, encourage guests to provide referrals to their contacts, or entice past guests to become repeat guests.

 TIP

Yes, it's possible for a host to offer multiple discounts within their property listing using what Airbnb refers to as "Rule Sets." Before using this feature, a host should understand how multiple discounts are applied by Airbnb and the impact offering multiple discounts will have on their income. For an up-to-date description of how Airbnb applies multiple discounts to a single booking, point your web browser to www.airbnb.com/help/article/2061.

New Listing Promotion

For all new listings on Airbnb, a host can offer a "New Listing Promotion," which Airbnb boasts will allow new hosts to obtain their first three bookings up to 30 percent faster. For a new listing with zero bookings, when a host activates the New Listing Promotion option, Airbnb will offer an automatic 20 percent discount to guests for the first three bookings the new listing receives. This is a way to quickly attract guests and help them overlook the fact that, as a host, you don't yet have any ratings or reviews.

> ✏ **NOTE**
>
> When you opt into the New Listing Promotion option as a host, it will automatically apply to eligible guest bookings within the next 90 days. The discount automatically expires after the property's third booking or 30 days after the promotion opt-in date (whichever happens first).

Early-Bird Promotions

This is a discount a host can offer for bookings made well in advance. The host determines the amount of discount and how far in advance the booking must be made for it to apply.

Last-Minute Discounts

This is a discount a host can offer for a booking made last-minute. The host can choose what constitutes a "last-minute" booking, although this is typically one week or less, or less than 24 hours. The host also determines the size of the discount offered.

Custom Promotions

Offering a custom promotion is yet another way a host can attract more interest in their property listing(s) and ultimately generate more bookings. Keep in mind, not all property listings are eligible to offer custom promotions. For example, Airbnb Plus, Airbnb Luxe, and hotel listings are not eligible for this type of promotion. To set up a custom promotion, access your property listing, select the listing's calendar, and click on the Promotions option. Next, choose the dates you want the promotion to be active and the discount you want to offer (which must be at least 10 percent).

Send Special Offers to Specific People

Providing top-notch accommodations combined with superior customer service as a host will help you earn positive ratings and reviews, which will ultimately allow you to attract more bookings. At the same time, it gives you the opportunity to acquire positive word-of-mouth advertising from your guests and potentially have them back as a return guest in the future. All this positively impacts your earning potential as an Airbnb host.

One way you're able to reward guests who come to you through a referral or who are repeat guests is to send them an invite with a special offer through Airbnb's messaging system. When someone contacts you through the messaging system, as a host, you can send them an invitation to book that includes a custom, discounted price that you have set. The recipient of the offer then has 24 hours to accept it and complete their booking at the discounted rate.

 NOTE

> The difference between a promotion and a special offer is that a promotion becomes part of your listing and applies to everyone, while you determine exactly who will receive a special offer and how much of a discount each specific potential guest will receive.

The special offer you send will provide a discount to your nightly rate, cleaning fee (if applicable), and extra guest fees (if applicable), but it does not discount the Airbnb service fee a guest would normally pay, the security deposit you require as a host (if applicable), or the taxes the guest is charged. A special offer provides a way for you to reward guests or potential guests who have been loyal or that you wish to extend a special rate to.

For up-to-date information about how invitations and special offers work, point your web browser to www.airbnb.com/help/article/35.

TIP

For up-to-date directions and guidelines for changing or withdrawing a special offer that's already been sent, point your web browser to www.airbnb.com/help/article/844.

Consider Adding Extra Fees to Your Nightly Rate

Above and beyond what you choose to be your nightly, weekly, monthly, or long-term rate to offer your property as a short-term rental, Airbnb allows you to tack on additional charges to be paid by the guest, including a cleaning fee, extra guest fee, resort fee, linen fee, management fee, or community fee.

One benefit to listing certain fees separately is that you can display an initially lower nightly rate to attract a prospective guest's attention. However, once they look at your property listing, Airbnb will calculate and display the total cost of their stay (including the extra fees). What you'll find is that most guests are willing to pay an extra cleaning fee, for example, if they're offered accommodations that have been professionally cleaned and sanitized in between guest bookings, and that they have access to professionally cleaned bedding, linens, and towels.

If you choose to add special fees, proceed with caution as the added expense will often deter budget-conscious guests from booking your property. But you may be able to attract more affluent guests looking for more luxury or unique accommodations that are as clean and comfortable as a hotel, but that offer a homier atmosphere and vibe.

Independent Tools to Help You Generate the Highest Revenue Possible

There are many independent online services that will help you set short-term rental pricing in a way that maximizes your profit potential while remaining competitive. Using any of these services allows you to use analytics and real-time data to take the guesswork out of price setting, especially for new hosts.

Many of these services will also help you predict your average occupancy rate during any given period, based on the type of property you're offering and your location. At the same time, you'll be given data that shows when you should increase or decrease your nightly rate, and by how much. Armed with the right data, you can determine how much income potential your property will likely generate each month of the year, so you can easily compare your costs with potential earnings to predict your profits rather accurately.

Some of the online-based, independent pricing tools you can use include:

- **AirDNA**—www.airdna.co/airbnb-pricing-tool
- **AllTheRooms**—www.alltherooms.com
- **Beyond Pricing**—www.beyondpricing.com/airbnb-pricing-tool
- **Mashvisor**—www.mashvisor.com
- **PlushyHost**—www.plushyhost.com
- **PriceLabs**—https://hello.pricelabs.co/dynamic-pricing
- **Transparent**—https://seetransparent.com

Especially if you're a new Airbnb host, consider using at least one of these independently operated tools to help you set your pricing. While some of these services have fees associated with them, the additional profit you ultimately earn will easily help you offset the cost.

Set Your Cancellation Policy

Airbnb offers hosts the choice of adopting one of several booking cancellation policies. The goal is to choose a policy that protects your own financial interests, but that also offers potential flexibility for your guests. The Standard Cancellation policies apply to stays shorter than 28 consecutive nights. While they're subject to change, as of early 2023, your cancellation policy options include:

- **Flexible Cancellation**—This allows guests to cancel their reservation up to 24 hours before check-in and receive a full refund. If the guest cancels before the 24-hour deadline, you as the host will not be paid. However, if the guest cancels within the 24-hour window prior to check-in, they'll be charged for one night. Meanwhile, if they check in, but opt to check out early, they'll be charged for the nights they've stayed, plus one additional night.

- **Moderate Cancellation**—If a guest wants to receive a full refund for their booking, they must cancel at least 30 days before their scheduled check-in. In addition, they can receive a full refund within 48 hours of making their initial booking (if they cancel at least 14 days prior to check-in). If the guest chooses to cancel between 7 and 30 days prior to their check-in date, as the host, you get paid 50 percent for all nights booked, and if they cancel less than 7 days prior to their check-in date, you receive 100 percent of all nightly fees.

- **Firm Cancellation**—For a guest to receive a 100 percent refund, they must cancel at least 30 days prior to their scheduled check-in date. However, if they cancel between 7 and 30 days before check-in, as the host, you still get paid 50 percent of the fees paid. If they cancel less than 7 days before check-in, you're entitled to be paid 100 percent for all nights booked. When you choose this policy, guests have the right to cancel the reservation and receive a 100 percent refund if they cancel within 48 hours of initially making the booking.

- **Strict Cancellation**—For a guest to receive a full refund, they must cancel their booking within 48 hours of making the initial reservation and cancellation must be at least 14 days before the guest's check-in date. However, if the guest chooses to cancel their booking between 7 and 14 days before their check-in date, as the host, you'll be paid 50 percent of the nightly fees. And if they choose to cancel less than 7 days prior to check-in, they'll forfeit 100 percent of their accommodation fees.

- **Nonrefundable**—As a guest finalizes their booking, they can receive an immediate 10 percent discount if they lock in their booking and choose the nonrefundable option. This feature must be activated by the host as part of their listing. Once the booking is paid for and confirmed, it's not refundable or cancellable.

 TIP

For up-to-date information about your available short-term cancellation policy options, as well as your long-term rental cancellation policy options, point your web browser to www.airbnb .com/resources/hosting-homes/a/choose-the-right-cancellation -policy-for-you-19.

Regardless of which cancellation policy you adopt for your guests, you may want to be somewhat flexible if legitimate extenuating circumstances with your guests arise. Keep in mind, because of the COVID-19 pandemic, guests often seek out accommodations that offer a more flexible cancellation policy, but as the host, this typically does not work out to your advantage financially, aside from the fact that you're more apt to attract the booking in the first place and will likely generate more bookings over time.

NOTE

According to Mashvisor's research published in early 2023 (www
.mashvisor.com/blog/virginia-beach-short-term-rental/#more-301008),
"One major challenge the industry's been facing in recent years is
the COVID-19 pandemic. With the travel industry on its knees, there
weren't enough guests to book short term rentals two years ago.
Fortunately, the industry is now slowly inching its way to full recovery."

Once your guests arrive and check in, regardless of the cancellation policy you've adopted, they have the right to request a full refund if the property is deemed inaccessible, unclean, or unsafe, or if the guest can't reach you (the host) to check in. In addition, if the guest contacts Airbnb directly within 24 hours of check-in and reports a serious issue that the host is unwilling or unable to address, the guest may be granted a full refund. The guest can also request a full refund from Airbnb if an extenuating circumstance exists. Airbnb's acceptable extenuating circumstances are outlined here: www.airbnb.com/help/article/1320.

The Financial Benefits of Becoming a Superhost

You already know that becoming a Superhost requires you to meet the spe-cial requirements outlined by Airbnb. With this designation, your property listing(s) and profile will automatically display a Superhost banner for as long as you retain this accreditation. Achieving Superhost status will take extra time and effort on your part—not just when it comes to providing superior accommodations that are clean and comfortable, but also in the customer service you offer both to prospective guests before they book and to paid guests once they check in through the time they check out.

You may be asking, what's in it for you? The simple answer is that savvy Airbnb travelers know to look for the Superhost banner and often will go out of their way to book a property operated by a Superhost. Over time, this generates more bookings for you and likely sets you apart from your local competition. In addition, the Superhost designation typically allows you to charge a premium. How much of a premium you can charge will vary based on your location, time of year, regional demand, and related factors.

For example, if you were an Airbnb traveler and chose to seek out accommodations for four nights in downtown Boston, Massachusetts, July15 through July 19, 2023, and then use the filters option to select Entire Place (which could be an apartment, condo, or home), one bedroom, one bed, and one bathroom for two people, more than 450 properties would be listed. If you select the Superhost option, however, the number of available options for a traveler drops to around 140 and the average nightly price is often slightly higher. Experienced Airbnb travelers know they're virtually guaranteed to have an exceptional experience staying with a Superhost, so it's in your best interest to work toward earning this designation.

Meet Airbnb Superhost Alyson Chadwick

Several years ago, Alyson Chadwick inherited a family house in Long Island, New York, and decided to use it to host short-term rental guests through Airbnb to pay off the second mortgage on the property.

What made you get involved with Airbnb as a host?

Alyson Chadwick: "The home I inherited has a second mortgage, but it also had a fully finished and separate apartment in the basement. After redecorating the basement apartment, in April 2020, I listed it on Airbnb to help cover the mortgage payments."

How has the experience as a host been for you?

Alyson Chadwick: "Overall, it's been favorable. I had never done anything like this before, but there was a learning curve in the beginning. Over time, I discovered that providing coffee, snacks, and oatmeal, for example, is something the guests really appreciate. Obviously, I try to keep the property as clean as possible, but there are some people that will never be happy. They'll complain about absolutely everything. When I've had to deal with difficult guests, Airbnb's support team has been there to support me."

Before becoming an Airbnb host, did you do any research about local laws or regulations pertaining to short-term rentals?

Alyson Chadwick: "I knew New York State has some strict rules, so I did some research to discover that I must collect a hotel tax that I must pay once per quarter. I found speaking with a few tax professionals helped me ensure I was adhering to all the rules and keep[ing] everything aboveboard."

In your opinion, what is the most compelling reason why someone should become an Airbnb host?

Alyson Chadwick: "If you have extra space in your home or have an extra property you can use for short-term rentals, it can be a very good source for a secondary income. Being a host can also be fun. My grandmother built our family home in 1961. Now that she's passed, I know she'd appreciate that people are still enjoying her home, because she loved to entertain here. It's been fun to get to know people from all over the world. I've also had people come back to stay with me up to four times in a single year."

What are some of the strategies you discovered for creating an attention-grabbing property listing on Airbnb?

Alyson Chadwick: "I think the main attraction for my place is the location. The house is right on the water, about a mile from Stony Brook University and the historic town of Stony Brook. I have not had to do a whole lot to promote the property, because since I started with Airbnb, I have had an 85 to 90 percent occupancy rate."

Do you have any tips for creating eye-catching photos for a property listing?

Alyson Chadwick: "I took the photos myself initially, but I wound up getting some help from professional photographers. I think the most important lesson I learned was to show the property in photos as it is. This sets realistic expectations from guests. You don't want them to show up expecting one thing, only to find something else entirely. This leads to bad reviews and, as a host, you're setting yourself up for failure."

How do you set your nightly pricing?

Alyson Chadwick: "I use Airbnb's Smart Pricing tool. Initially, I set my prices very low, because I started listing the property in April 2020, which was during the COVID-19 pandemic. I was lucky because I wound up hosting some visiting nurses who were working at the local hospital, so they wound up staying with me for several months. I offer a discount for extended stays, but for everything else, I rely on Airbnb's pricing tool to set my rate automatically."

In addition to coffee and snacks, what are some of the other amenities you've discovered guests really appreciate?

Alyson Chadwick: "Because the house is right on the water, I offer inner tubes, kayaks, life vests, and beach towels so people can easily take advantage of the water. The house has an outdoor barbecue, and guests seem to really like that."

What were some of the mistakes you made early on as an Airbnb host, and what did you do to fix them?

Alyson Chadwick: "I don't think I was as detail oriented as I should have been early on. While I have a professional cleaning service come in between guests, early on, I did not take the time to check their work to ensure the property was spotless and ready to welcome new guests. I have since become much more detail oriented and conscious of how spotless the property needs to be. I also found out that I need to be available in some capacity 24/7 to deal with emergencies. I come and go as I need to, but I have someone else who lives at my house full-time, so one of us is always on the property when we have guests.

"We are literally upstairs from the basement apartment, so if someone has a problem, they can call, text, or come knock on my door to reach me. I encourage people to reach out, because if they have a problem, I can't fix it if I don't know about it."

For a typical guest, how much interaction do you have with them?

Alyson Chadwick: "This really varies based on the guest. There are some people who have a lot of questions about the area and will spend a lot of time with me getting to know more about it. There are plenty of other guests that just want to know the code for the door, and then want to be left alone during their stay. I try to give people as much privacy as possible. I had one guest stay with me for five months, so we wound up going to dinner several times. I perform stand-up comedy locally, so if I am performing, I will sometimes invite guests to a show and get them free tickets. Typically, I perform on Long Island and in New York City."

Has a guest ever done anything to make you uncomfortable?

Alyson Chadwick: "I have had a few people want to extend their stay but want to pay me directly instead of going through Airbnb. I never want to do that because of the insurance issue. Plus, if they stayed with me without going through Airbnb, based on New York laws, if they refused to leave, it would be more difficult to evict them."

When you were creating your House Rules, were there any rules you needed to add because it became necessary based on a guest's behavior?

Alyson Chadwick: "No. People have been very respectful of me and my property. While I state no parties or large gatherings are permitted, I had one guest ask me if they could invite a few friends over for dinner, and I was cool with that. Originally, I had a no pets policy, but more recently, I have begun allowing pets, and that's worked out very well. In terms of House Rules, first determine what you will and will not tolerate in your home and then write up clear rules based on that."

What do you do to help ensure your guests will wind up giving you the best reviews possible?

Alyson Chadwick: "I go out of my way to make sure the property is as clean and comfortable as possible. I also respond as quickly as possible to questions, concerns, or problems that potential or booked guests have. I always have people on call, like a plumber, who can fix a clogged toilet anytime it's needed, for example. I deal with any problems that arise immediately. My goal is to be very responsive to people. Because my property is a bit older, I spend a lot of time keeping up with maintenance issues to make sure everything is working and comfortable for guests. I think guests really appreciate that I make myself available to answer their questions about the area."

Do you have any other advice for up-and-coming Airbnb hosts, based on your experiences?

Alyson Chadwick: "I think whatever you can do to make your space welcoming will go a long way toward keeping your guests happy. For example, providing complimentary bottles of water to guests when they check in is a small touch that people appreciate. Because my property is so close to a historic village, which is a tourist destination, I try to incorporate some of that local charm into the property. For example, the complimentary coffee I provide to guests is from a local coffee shop, and I provide a lot of printed information about the historic area.

"Once piece of advice I can offer is that when you encounter a guest that you know will never be happy, do what you can to make the experience as pleasant for everyone as possible and continue to act professionally. Understand you can't please everyone, and you can't take it personally if you go out of your way to provide a pleasant experience for your guests but they do not appreciate any of your efforts."

Reasons to Reinvest in Your Airbnb Hosting Business

Some hosts get involved with Airbnb for the experience of meeting new people, while others are strictly in it for the money. If your goal is to earn the highest revenue possible, without making a huge initial investment, you can start by offering basic accommodations, but over time, reinvest your earnings into your business so you can upgrade your amenities, enhance the furnishings and décor, and provide a more luxurious experience for your guests. And for this, you can charge more money.

Initially, you might furnish your home with affordable IKEA furniture, for example, and acquire the most affordable bed linens, bath towels, mattresses, and no-name amenities (like shampoo, soap, etc.). However, if you upgrade to high-end linens, expensive towels, more comfortable mattresses, and more luxurious brand-name amenities, and can describe them within your listing, this will attract more affluent guests willing to spend more money for their accommodations.

And then once you're earning top dollar from one property and have a steady income from that, you can use those profits to make a down payment on additional properties to grow your business (again without having to initially invest a fortune). If you're interested in investing in multiple properties to operate as short-term rentals through Airbnb, be sure to read Chapter 11, "Ways to Make Being an Airbnb Host Your Full-Time Career."

CHAPTER 4

How to Use the Airbnb Website and Mobile App

Airbnb is an online community and service. It's available 24 hours per day, seven days per week—from any computer or mobile device that connects to the internet. To access Airbnb from your internet-connected computer, use your favorite web browser—such as Microsoft Edge (Windows PC), Safari (Mac), Google Chrome (PC/Mac), Foxfire (PC/Mac), Opera (PC/Mac), or DuckDuckGo (PC/Mac)—and visit www.airbnb.com.

What makes using Airbnb incredibly convenient for you as a host is that virtually all the same tools that are available from your computer are also available using the Airbnb mobile app from your internet-connected smartphone or tablet. These tools include the ability to manage your account, create or edit your personal profile, create and manage your property listing(s), manage bookings, and interact with (potential) guests.

Because you can access Airbnb via any desktop computer, laptop computer, or mobile device, you don't always need to sit in front of a computer at your desk to manage online tasks associated with being an Airbnb host. These tasks can be handled from virtually anywhere, which gives you a tremendous amount of freedom and flexibility. Thus, to be a truly efficient Airbnb host, you'll probably want to invest in a reliable smartphone or tablet (with cellular data connectivity).

A smartphone can use a cellular data connection (which you pay for through your cellular service provider) or Wi-Fi to connect to the internet and allow the smartphone to access Airbnb's service via its mobile app. However, if you opt to use a tablet, such as an Apple iPad or Samsung Galaxy Tab, based on your lifestyle and where you'll be using it, you can choose between a Wi-Fi-only tablet, or a slightly more expensive tablet with Wi-Fi plus cellular (LTE) internet connectivity.

A Wi-Fi-only tablet allows you to connect to the internet (and use the Airbnb mobile app) anytime the device is connected to a Wi-Fi hot spot, which could be from your home, at work, at school, at a public library, at an internet café or coffee shop, at a hotel, or at any airport, for example. However, if you're driving around in your car, or not within the signal radius of a Wi-Fi hot spot, the Wi-Fi-only tablet will not be able to connect to the internet. Thus, the Airbnb mobile app won't function. In this situation, a tablet with cellular plus Wi-Fi connectivity is required.

 TIP

When relying on your mobile device to manage your Airbnb account, you don't need to keep the Airbnb mobile app continuously running on your smartphone or tablet. Instead, simply set up the Notifications and Alerts options (which on an iPhone/iPad is done from the Notifications menu within Settings, not from the Airbnb app itself). Your smartphone/tablet will automatically receive a text message, or your smartphone or tablet will automatically receive a Push Notification, anytime a (potential) guest sends you a message, you receive a new booking, or something related to your Airbnb account needs your attention.

Remember, whether you're using a computer or mobile device to manage your Airbnb account to handle all the administrative hosting tasks related to the service (including managing reservations and communicating with guests via Airbnb's messaging service), you'll need to have a continuous and reliable internet connection. The good news is that you do not need the latest model computer, smartphone, or tablet to access the Airbnb service. The equipment simply needs to be capable of connecting to the internet and running a web browser (for computer users) or running the Airbnb mobile app (for smartphone and tablet users).

 NOTE

> If your web browser is set up to remember your website-specific usernames and passwords, and sign you into each website upon a return visit, each time you revisit Airbnb.com, your name will be displayed in the top-right corner of the browser window, instead of you having to go through the Sign In option manually.

Get Acquainted with the Airbnb Website

Virtually everything you'll be doing online related to your responsibilities as an Airbnb host is handled directly from the Airbnb platform (www.airbnb.com). Once you have bookings and you're in contact with your guests, some of this communication can also be done via email, by phone, or through social media (Facebook, Twitter, Instagram, LinkedIn, or Snapchat, for example). However, for your own security, it's best to communicate with your potential guests and booked guests as much as possible through the Airbnb messaging service, because a detailed transcript of all that transpires is maintained by Airbnb.

As you learned from Chapter 2, "Get Started as an Airbnb Host," one of the first things you'll need to do once you opt to become an Airbnb host (or use the Airbnb service as a guest) is create a personal Airbnb account. This can be done from the Airbnb website or mobile app.

Then, to proceed with becoming an Airbnb host, create one or more property listings, which can be done from the Airbnb website or mobile app, although it's much more convenient to do this from a computer with a larger screen. How to set yourself up as an Airbnb host was covered within Chapter 2.

Once your personal account and property listing(s) are created, everything having to do with managing your account and listings, as well as virtually all administrative and financial tasks associated with being a host, is handled from the Airbnb website. So, it's important that you become familiar with what's possible and develop a basic understanding of how to navigate around the site.

Depending on whether you have your computer's web browser set up to remember your website-specific usernames and passwords, it may or may not be necessary to sign into the Airbnb website each time you access it. If after you've set up your Airbnb account you're required to sign in during subsequent visits, click on the Log In option that's displayed in the top-right corner of the browser window once the Airbnb homepage has loaded.

 **WARNING**

> As an Airbnb host, if you have a desktop computer set up in your property that your guests will have access to, do not allow the computer to remember your usernames or passwords. You do not want one of your guests being able to hack into your Airbnb account and take control of it. For your own security, make sure you always keep your Airbnb account password private.
>
> Obviously, this security precaution applies to all your usernames and passwords for your online banking, investment, online shopping, and credit card management accounts. To make things easier, use a secure password manager application, such as Dashlane, NordPass, Keeper, 1Password, RoboForm, or LastPass to securely keep track of all your usernames and passwords. These applications work with both Windows and Mac computers, as well as iOS and Android-based mobile devices. Do a search for any of these applications using your favorite internet search engine, such as Google or Yahoo.

Handling Hosting-Related Administrative Tasks from the Airbnb Website

Keep in mind, the Airbnb website (like the service itself and its community of users) is continuously evolving. New features and functions are always being added, and the design and user interface of the website is periodically tweaked. As a result, your navigation experience when you access some of the features and functions outlined in this chapter will likely be different.

At any time, if you have a question about using a specific website feature or function, simply access the service's Help option. On a computer, click on your profile icon in the top-right corner of the web browser window and then click on the Help option displayed within the pull-down menu that appears. Within the Search field that appears on the top of the screen, type a keyword, question, or search phrase that relates to what you need help with. Alternatively, click on the Host or Experience Host tab that's displayed below the Search field to view a list of popular help-related topics. You'll discover the overall design and user interface associated with Airbnb.com is well designed, intuitive, and easy to navigate.

Figure 4.1 offers a rundown of some common administrative tasks for hosts available from the Airbnb website's Account menu screen.

Figure 4.1   Airbnb.com Commonly Used Account-Related Features

Account Menu Option	What It's Used For	How to Access It
Personal Info	Enter or update your personal contact information and basic details about yourself. From here, you can also upload your government-issued ID.	Click on the Personal Info option, which is part of the Account menu, or visit www.airbnb.com/account -settings/personal-info.
Login & Security	Update your Airbnb account password and activate additional security-related features. It's also possible to link your social media accounts to your Airbnb account from here or deactivate your Airbnb account altogether.	Click on the Login & Security option, which is part of the Account menu, or visit www .airbnb.com/account-settings /login-and-security.

Account Menu Option	What It's Used For	How to Access It
Payments & Payouts	Review payments, payouts, coupons, gift cards, and tax payments related to your Airbnb account.	Click on the Payments & Payouts option, which is part of the Account menu, or visit www.airbnb.com/account-settings/payments/payment-methods.
Notifications	Determine what types of notifications you want to receive from Airbnb. Be sure to adjust all the settings displayed below Offers and Updates, as well as the Account tabs.	Click on the Notifications option, which is part of the Account menu, or visit www.airbnb.com/account-settings/notifications.
Privacy & Sharing	Access and control privacy settings related to your Airbnb account. Be sure to adjust all the settings listed below the Data, Sharing, and Services tabs.	Click on the Privacy & Sharing option, which is part of the Account menu, or visit www.airbnb.com/account-settings/privacy-and-sharing.
Global Preferences	From here, you're able to adjust your language, currency, and time zone.	Click on the Global Preferences option, which is part of the Account menu, or visit www.airbnb.com/account-settings/preferences.
Travel for Work	Used more by Airbnb travelers, this option allows you to link your work email with your Airbnb account. This makes it easier to track work-related travel expenses.	Click on the Travel for Work option, which is part of the Account menu, or visit www.airbnb.com/account-settings/airbnb-for-work.
Professional Hosting Tools	From here you can access a variety of tools useful to Airbnb hosts who manage several property listings at once. For example, you can link a company name to your Airbnb account.	Click on the Professional Hosting Tools option, which is part of the Account menu, or visit www.airbnb.com/account-settings/professional-hosting.
Referral Credit & Coupon	Access information related to guest referrals and account sign-ups that you get rewarded for soliciting.	Click on the Referral Credit & Coupon option, which is part of the Account menu, or visit www.airbnb.com/invite.

TIP

Quick access to most Airbnb hosting tools offered by the Airbnb.com website can be found by visiting the Dashboard (www.airbnb.com /home/dashboard). You'll need to sign into your Airbnb account to access details pertaining to your account.

Once you create your first property listing by clicking on the Airbnb Setup button and then going through the step-by-step process presented to you once you've initially set up your Airbnb host account, you'll have access to a main host menu with the Today, Inbox, Calendar, Insights, and Menu tabs listed at the top of the browser window.

Click on the Today tab, and below the Your Next Step heading will be several buttons, including Turn Instant Book On or Off, Set Up Your Calendar, Pick Your Policy for Cancellations, Add Your House Rules, and Offer Special Promotions. Click on each button, one at a time, to adjust the various settings within each submenu before you publish your property listing.

Click on the Inbox tab to read and respond to messages from prospective guests. This is Airbnb's own messaging/email system that allows you to securely communicate with people without disclosing too much information about yourself, your phone number, your personal email address, or your property address. Once someone confirms and pays for a booking at your property, Airbnb will provide them with additional details about you and your property.

Click on the Calendar option to set up the dates when your property is available for booking, and what the default nightly rate is for each date (or date range). Be sure to click on the Pricing and Availability option (located in the top-right corner of the default monthly calendar view) to adjust a wide range of options pertaining to pricing, discounts, additional charges, taxes, trip length, calendar availability, calendar syncing, and sharing settings. For example, from this menu, you can add a cleaning fee, pet fee, extra guest fee, and alter your nightly rate for weekdays versus weekends.

Click on the Insights tab to reveal a submenu consisting of more tabs displayed across the top of the browser window that offer options related to Opportunities, Reviews, Earnings, Views, Superhost, and Cleaning.

Click on the Menu icon to reveal a pull-down submenu that gives you control over host-related features related to your Property Listing, Reservations, the Create a New Listing option, Guidebooks, Transaction History, Explore Hosting Resources, and Connect with Hosts Near You. Before publishing your property listing, go through every submenu option and customize each setting, plus utilize the free resources that Airbnb makes available to hosts.

Keep in mind, as you navigate around the Airbnb website, there are often multiple ways to access commonly used features and functions. For example, hyperlinks or buttons that will help you navigate are often located near the top-center of the browser window or are embedded in the contents of specific Airbnb web pages.

How to Set Your Payout Preferences with Airbnb

As an Airbnb host, you want to be paid in a timely, accurate, and convenient manner. Well, all money that exchanges between Airbnb hosts and guests happens via the Airbnb platform. This provides one centralized place where all Airbnb-related financial transactions are handled, which makes bookkeeping that much easier for hosts like you.

 **WARNING**

As an Airbnb income-earning host, you will need to pay taxes. This is not something that Airbnb handles on your behalf. It is your responsibility, based on the location of your property and where you live. Be sure to determine what taxes you're responsible for, what tax forms need to be completed and submitted, and that your tax debt is paid on time. Failure to pay all the proper local, state, and federal taxes could result in high fines from the government and could easily lead to other legal problems. It's a good strategy to consult with an accountant who is familiar with short-term rentals and get help setting up or handling your bookkeeping and tax-related paperwork so that tax payments are paid correctly. Airbnb offers some helpful information that describes your tax obligations as an Airbnb host. This can be found at www.airbnb.com/help/article/481 and www.airbnb .com/help/article/2523.

Before welcoming your first guest as an Airbnb host, it's important that you provide Airbnb with the appropriate financial information needed for you to make and receive payments through the service. It's then your responsibility to keep this information up to date, if your bank account details ever change, for example.

To set up Airbnb's Payment Methods and Payout Preferences from your computer, follow these steps:

1. Go to www.airbnb.com and sign into your Airbnb account.

2. Click on your username or profile photo thumbnail that's displayed in the top-right corner of the web browser window.

3. From the menu that appears, click on the Account option.

4. Click on the Payments & Payouts option, and then click on the Payments tab. Next, click on the Manage Payments button. You also need to click on the Add Payment Method button. This is required if you're an Airbnb host or a guest, as the payment method(s) you add will be used to make payments to other hosts when you travel, or potentially to issue refunds to your guests.

5. When you click on the Add Payment Method button, an Add Card Details window will appear with Visa, MasterCard, American Express, and Discover card logos displayed at the top of this window.

6. Enter your Card Number, Card Expiration Date, Card Security Code, First Name, Last Name, Postal Code, and Country.

7. Click on the Done button to continue. After completing the payment method section, details about that credit or debit card will be displayed under the Payment Methods heading. You can then add an additional credit or debit card to the account, if you wish, and then choose which card you want to be your default card when making payments through Airbnb.

8. Once you've added one or more payment methods to your Airbnb account, click on the Payouts tab at the top of the Payments & Payouts menu screen. You must now set up a payout method in order to be paid by Airbnb for your hosting service—to receive payments from guests. Keep in mind, Airbnb transfers the funds that are owed to you approximately 24 hours after a guest's scheduled check-in time. It then takes time for the funds to appear in your account. How much time it takes to receive your money will be based on the payout method you select, as well as your bank or financial institution.

9. Click the Payouts tab found on the Account menu screen, and then click on the Set Up Payouts button.

10. From the Let's Add a Payout Method screen (www.airbnb.com/account-settings/payments/payout-methods/add), select your billing country/region, and then choose how you'd like to get paid. Your options include Fast Pay, Bank Account, PayPal, or Payoneer. Select one of these options.

   - *Fast Pay.* To use this payment method, you must have a debit card issued in your name that displays the MasterCard or Visa logo. When a payment is issued to you, you will receive it in 30 minutes or less, but you'll need to pay a 1.5 percent transaction fee (up to $15) to receive your funds.

   - *Bank Deposit.* This takes between three and five business days for funds to appear within your account; however, there are no money transfer fees. This method works only on business days, so no transactions take place on weekends or bank holidays. If you choose this method, you will be prompted to enter the name associated with the bank account, select the type of account it is (checking or savings), and then provide the bank's routing number and your unique account number. This is information displayed in the lower-left corner of your printed checks, or it can be obtained from your bank. Click the Finish button after entering this information.

- *PayPal.* This option takes one day (or less) to process and receive your funds, but you first need to set up a separate PayPal account (www .paypal.com). If you opt to transfer funds out of your PayPal account once they're received, however, you will have to pay PayPal withdrawal fees.

- *Payoneer Prepaid Debit MasterCard.* If you choose this option, you will be mailed a physical prepaid debit card. Money you earn from Airbnb will be transferred to this prepaid account and can be spent using the prepaid MasterCard you receive. However, if you use this card at an ATM to withdraw cash, ATM withdrawal fees will apply. It takes one day or less for Airbnb to transfer funds to you using this method. To set up a Payoneer Prepaid Debit MasterCard account, the Airbnb website will transfer you to a separate website, which will request your name, address, and other relevant information. For more information about the fees associated with this option, visit: www.payoneer.com/fees.

All financial information you provide to Airbnb will be kept confidential. You, however, must not allow unauthorized people to gain access to your Airbnb account. Be sure to keep your login information private. Once you've set up your Airbnb Payout Preferences and begin earning money, access your Transaction History at any time by pointing your web browser to www.airbnb.com/users /transaction_history once you've set up your hosting account. This is information you'll need to keep track of your personal finances and income, as well as when it comes to tax return preparation and filing.

Discover How to Use the Airbnb Mobile App

The Airbnb mobile app for the Apple iPhone or iPad can be used to handle almost all the same tasks as you'd otherwise handle from the Airbnb website. You can find, download, and install the app for free from the App Store (https://apps.apple .com/us/app/airbnb/id401626263). From your mobile app, follow these steps:

1. Launch the App Store app from the Home screen on your iPhone or iPad.

2. On an iPhone, tap on the Search icon at the bottom of the screen, or on the iPad, tap on the Featured icon, and then tap on the Search field that's displayed in the top-right corner of the tablet's screen.

3. Within the Search field, type "Airbnb," and when the search results are displayed, tap on the Get button that's associated with the Airbnb app listing (from Airbnb, Inc.). Follow the same process as you normally would to download and install a new app onto your mobile device.

4. Once the app is installed, the Airbnb app icon will be displayed on your iPhone or iPad's Home screen. Tap on the app icon to launch the app.

5. From the opening screen, tap on the Log In option to sign into your Airbnb account.

6. When prompted, enter your Airbnb account username and password, and then tap on the Yes, Notify Me button when the Turn On Notifications? option is displayed. The Airbnb mobile app will go online, access the Airbnb platform, and allow you to manage all aspects of your account if your iPhone or iPad maintains its internet connection. From left to right, the following five command icons are displayed along the bottom of the screen:

   - **Explore**—As an Airbnb traveler, explore property listings and book reservations.

   - **Wishlists**—Access property listings you've favorited as an Airbnb traveler.

   - **Trips**—Manage your bookings as a traveler.

   - **Inbox**—Access Airbnb's messaging service.

   - **Log In**—Log into your Airbnb account.

   - **Profile**—This icon will replace the Log In icon once you've logged into your account. From below the Account Setting heading, scroll down to the

Hosting heading and select the Switch to Hosting option to access host-related tools. Once you do this, the hosting tools and related menus offered by the Airbnb.com website become accessible to you via the mobile app.

 NOTE

If you use an Android-based mobile device, the Airbnb mobile app for Android works very much the same way as the iOS (iPhone/iPad) version. You can find, download, and install the Android app by visiting the Google Play Store and searching for it using the Search tool, or by visiting https://play.google.com/store/apps /details?id=com.airbnb.android.

Get Social with Airbnb

Airbnb's official Facebook page allows employees to interact with its community members and allows hosts to communicate informally among themselves. To "Like" this page and become active on it, you must have an established Facebook account, which you can set up for free by visiting www .facebook.com or by using the official Facebook app on your mobile device.

Once you're active on Facebook, visit www.facebook.com/airbnb to access Airbnb's official Facebook page, and click on the "Like" button that's associated with the page to join it. From this Facebook page, you can participate on the message board, view photos and videos, plus learn about upcoming events. Airbnb is also active on YouTube (www.youtube.com/user/Airbnb), Twitter (@airbnb or @airbnbhelp), Instagram (www.instagram.com/airbnb), and LinkedIn (www.linkedin.com/company/airbnb). There are also a variety of Facebook groups specifically for hosts to interact with one another and share information. Before you publish your property listing on Airbnb, consider asking one or more of these hosts to review your listing and offer their recommendations.

For more personalized guidance as a host, you can be matched up with a Superhost for free. This person can act as a mentor as you're getting started. To contact a Superhost, visit www.airbnb.com/hosting, sign into your account, and then scroll down to the We're Here to Help heading and click on the Superhost referral button. As a new host, you also get free access to Airbnb's Specialized Support team. From the Hosting menu page, again scroll down to the We're Here to Help heading and click on the Contact Specialized Support button. Yet another option is to access the online-based Airbnb Host Community Center, where you can interact with other Airbnb hosts (https://community.withairbnb.com/t5/Community-Center/ct-p/community-center).

If you have an urgent question, one way to reach Airbnb directly is via Twitter, using the @airbnbhelp username when posting a tweet that contains your question. This is a public forum, so be careful about posting any personal information within the message.

Yet another way to interact with fellow Airbnb hosts in your city is to participate in an in-person Airbnb Meet Up. These are informal gatherings that are scheduled throughout the world by Airbnb hosts. For more information about how to participate, visit www.airbnb.com/meetups.

Once you've created your property listing, you'll need to set up your short-term rental property so it's ready to welcome guests. The focus of the next chapter is on how to prepare your property so it meets Airbnb's guidelines and will appeal to your future guests.

CHAPTER 5

Preparing Your Property

Before accepting your first booking as an Airbnb host, it's necessary to prepare every aspect of your property for guests. To provide a clean, comfortable, efficient, visually pleasing, and safe environment, some of the things you'll probably need to do include:

- Rearrange some of your existing furniture to make the living space more accessible and comfortable for guests.
- Remove clutter and personal items from where your guests will be staying.
- Remove political and/or religious décor or paraphernalia from where your guests will be staying.
- Fine-tune the overall décor.
- Ensure that the living space is safe for guests.
- Install proper indoor and outdoor lighting and safety equipment as needed.
- Invest in the purchase of furniture, beds, mattresses, bedding, towels, and amenities to be used by your guests.
- Thoroughly clean the property, and hire an optional professional cleaning/maid service you'll use on an ongoing basis.

- Make sure all your appliances, home electronics, Wi-Fi, and other equipment are fully functional.

- Have copies of front door keys made, or install smart door locks with a programmable keypad so guests can easily come and go as they please using a numeric code that you provide.

- Write a house manual for your guests that outlines how everything in your home operates and recaps your House Rules.

- Collect menus from nearby restaurants (and determine which restaurants deliver, as well as their delivery hours), as well as brochures from nearby attractions and points of interest to have on hand for your guests.

To accomplish some of these tasks, chances are you'll need to make an up-front financial investment, which hopefully you'll quickly recoup once you start having paid guests stay at your property. Another approach is to handle the most important tasks first, initially charge a lower nightly rate, and then use your profits from paying guests to improve the property over time. Then, as the living space becomes more comfortable and luxurious, begin charging a higher nightly rate.

 TIP

> Visit the local department of tourism for your town, city, or region and collect brochures for local activities, attractions, historical sites, museums, and other points of interest your guests might be interested in visiting. For a listing of travel and tourism offices listed by state, point your web browser to www.usa.gov/state-travel-and -tourism. Once your short-term rental property is ready to accept guests, consider creating a brochure about your property and providing copies to your local tourism office so your information can be distributed to interested travelers.

Think Safety First

In addition to acquiring all the necessary insurance, make sure your property provides the safest living space possible. Be sure to install and test the smoke detectors, carbon monoxide detectors, fire extinguishers, flashlights, and have a first-aid kit on hand, for example. Also, check every piece of furniture to make sure it's working properly, sturdy, and safe (for adults and kids alike).

Some of the additional safety-oriented measures you should take care of include:

- If you have a large bookcase or display cabinet, make sure it's securely bolted to the wall and can't accidentally fall on and injure someone.

- If you're allowing guests to use your kitchen appliances and/or laundry facilities, make sure the equipment is functioning properly, up to date with maintenance, and clean.

- Check all the electrical wiring in your home, and make sure it's up to date with building codes and that you don't have any unsafe extension cords or wires on the floors or walls that guests can trip over or get themselves caught on. This is particularly important if you'll be allowing families with young kids or pets to stay at your property.

- Make sure your flat-screen television is securely bolted to the wall or mounted on a stand that can't accidentally get knocked over.

- Install nonslip mats on the floor of each shower and/or bathtub.

- Install or make sure all lighting in the exterior of your home is functional, and consider adding an automatic timer so the parking area/driveway and main entrance to your property is well lit from sundown to sunrise. This can easily be achieved using smart lighting.

- Ensure that all the interior lighting fixtures and lamps are functioning properly, are sturdy, provide ample lighting, and are easily accessible. Also keep a supply of extra light bulbs on hand.

- Install separate door locks (which lock from the inside) on each guestroom door, so guests will feel safer at night while they're sleeping. In addition, for less than $20 per door, you can easily install a hotel-style door latch (also referred to as a door reinforcement lock).

TIP

Be sure to leave open space within each guestroom, especially if it's a small space. Remember, people will have luggage with them and will need to place their suitcases where they're easily accessible. Consider adding a luggage rack in each guestroom for the added convenience of your guests and so they don't accidentally ruin or scratch the furniture, for example, by piling their suitcase on top of it.

Decorating and Furnishing Your Property

When it comes to decorating and furnishing your short-term rental property, think in terms of efficiency, functionality, durability, comfort, and appearance. There are several directions you can go. Either offer low-end furniture that's durable and charge a lower nightly rate or go all out and offer high-quality furnishings and décor that will allow you to charge a premium nightly rate.

If you go with the economical and affordable approach, furnish your guestroom(s) the same way you'd furnish a college dormitory—with basic, low-cost, but highly durable furnishings that include a bed, nightstand, dresser, mirror, trash can, lamp(s), nightstand light, and possibly a desk and desk chair. Functionality takes precedence over appearance and luxury, but you should still offer clean and comfortable accommodations.

Keep in mind that most people travel with a notebook computer, tablet, smartphone, e-reader, digital camera, and/or other consumer electronics that need to be plugged in to charge. Whenever possible, offer multiple, easily accessible electrical outlets in each bedroom, or include an extension cord and a multi-outlet power strip (with a surge protector) within each guestroom.

By taking the economical approach, you can do your furniture shopping at IKEA (www.ikea.com) or another low-cost furniture store, decorate the guestroom walls with one or two posters or pieces of generic (non-offensive) artwork, and offer decent, but inexpensive bedding (sheets, blankets, pillows, etc.) that you purchase from IKEA, Target, Walmart, or Costco.

As for the kitchen and dining room area, if you take an economical approach, consider offering plastic dishes, silverware, and cups that won't break and that are easily washable or disposable. Provide paper towels and paper napkins that can be thrown away after use (as opposed to dish towels or cloth napkins that need to be laundered). In the bathroom, offer clean towels and bathroom mats (that can be laundered and bleached), plus always put extra emphasis on the cleanliness of the bathroom itself. Your guests should never see mold, mildew, soap scum, or dirt anywhere in the bathroom (including on the floor, as well as in and around the sink, toilet, shower/bathtub, or on the shower curtain).

 NOTE

> Within the guestrooms, remove all your own personal items from the closets, dresser drawers, nightstand drawers, and under the bed. Each bedroom that you offer to guests should be void of your own belongings, and like any traditional hotel room, include nothing that promotes or conveys your own political or religious beliefs.

The Furnishing, Décor, and Amenities You Provide Can Impact Your Nightly Rate

If you opt for a higher-end approach to your furnishings and décor to provide a more comfortable and luxurious living space for your guests, you should promote this approach within your Airbnb property listing, and it should be reflected in your nightly rate. People will pay more for luxury and added comfort.

When you opt to take this approach, the expectations of your guests will be much higher. The up-front cost to decorate and furnish each guestroom or your entire property will also be higher, but you should easily be able to recuperate the additional costs by charging a higher nightly rate.

By targeting a higher-paying clientele, understand that they'll expect nicer furniture, more luxurious bed linens, pillows, and blankets, and more elegant artwork and décor, plus fancier and brand-name amenities. These people will be harder to please and potentially less apt to write unsolicited reviews (unless they're very disappointed with their experience staying at your property).

On the plus side, if you have a flare for interior decorating and hospitality, you can do more, be more creative, and showcase some of your personal taste with your selection of furniture, décor, and artwork. You can also include extra amenities, like fresh flowers in the bedrooms.

 TIP

If you target a high-end clientele by offering a property in the middle of an upscale community or neighborhood and you'll be charging a premium, consider hiring a professional interior decorator to decorate the property, especially the bedrooms. Again, focus on comfort, efficiency, safety, and cleanliness, in addition to appearance. For example, in addition to providing a basic iron and ironing board, offer a clothing steamer as well.

Invest in Basic Amenities for the Added Comfort of Your Guests

By increasing your nightly rate by just a few dollars, you can easily afford to offer a selection of complimentary but low-cost amenities that your guests will appreciate.

 WARNING

Charging a higher nightly rate means inviting higher expectations from your guests. You can't get away with offering cheap, uncomfortable bed linens or old and saggy mattresses. Failure to offer accommodations that meet the guest's expectations will result in bad ratings and reviews, which will have a long-term detrimental impact on your success as an Airbnb host.

Figure 5.1 features a checklist that describes a range of common amenities you should consider offering your guests. Each time you're about to welcome new guests, refer back to this checklist and add a checkmark to indicate you've purchased and provided the items. Whenever possible, buy amenities in bulk to save money. You can shop at places like Costco, BJ's Wholesale Club, Amazon, a local supermarket, pharmacy, or a local dollar store for many of these items. However, if you're trying to cater to an upscale clientele, only provide name-brand and higher-quality amenities whenever possible.

Figure 5.1 Common Amenities to Offer Your Guests

Amenity Description	Amenity You Plan to Offer Guests	Purchased and Ready for Guests	Product Brand & Quantity Needed for Each Guest
Bottled Water	☐	☐	
Plastic/Paper Cups	☐	☐	
Travel-Size Toiletries (Shampoo, Conditioner, Hand Soap, Mouthwash, Skin Cream, Toothpaste, Dental Floss, Cotton Swabs, Makeup Remover, etc.). Each guest should be provided with a new, unopened selection of these amenities.	☐	☐	
Toilet Paper (In addition to providing a new roll next to every toilet, be sure every bathroom contains several extra rolls.)	☐	☐	
Tissues (next to every bed and in every bathroom)	☐	☐	
Hair Dryer	☐	☐	
Iron and Ironing Board (Clothing steamer is optional.)	☐	☐	
Can of Lysol or an Air Freshener (in each bathroom)	☐	☐	
Hand Sanitizer	☐	☐	

Continued on next page

Amenity Description	Amenity You Plan to Offer Guests	Purchased and Ready for Guests	Product Brand & Quantity Needed for Each Guest
Sanitizing Wipes	☐	☐	
Bedsheets, Pillowcases, Duvet, and Blankets (made from hypoallergenic materials)	☐	☐	
Bath Towels, Hand Towels, and Washcloths (Offer multiple sets, including extras, for each guest, based on the duration of their stay.)	☐	☐	
KN95 Masks (several for each guest)	☐	☐	
Welcome Basket Containing a Selection of Prepackaged Snacks	☐	☐	
Wi-Fi Throughout the Property	☐	☐	

If you're offering higher-end accommodations at a premium nightly rate, consider including the additional amenities listed within Figure 5.2.

Figure 5.2 Premium Amenities

Amenity Description	Amenity You Plan to Offer Guests	Purchased and Ready for Guests	Product Brand & Quantity Needed for Each Guest
Selection of Current Magazines	☐	☐	
Fresh Muffins and Juice Every Morning	☐	☐	
Access to a Coffee Machine with a Premium Selection of Coffees, Teas, and Hot Cocoa	☐	☐	
Down Comforter on Each Bed (with a Luxury Duvet Cover)	☐	☐	
Smart TV (at least 50 inches) with Cable TV or Streaming (Netflix, Hulu, Disney+, etc.). Access within the Bedrooms and Living Room	☐	☐	
Bottle of Wine Upon a Guest's Arrival	☐	☐	

Amenity Description	Amenity You Plan to Offer Guests	Purchased and Ready for Guests	Product Brand & Quantity Needed for Each Guest
Vase with Fresh-Cut Flowers in Each Guestroom	☐	☐	
Real Wood Furniture and/or Antique Furnishings (that add elegance and character to each guestroom)	☐	☐	
Guestrooms Decorated and Furnished around a Theme, like Victorian, Contemporary, Tuscan style, Traditional, Coastal/Beach, Western/Rustic, Tropical, or Nautical	☐	☐	
In-Home Gym/Workout Equipment, an In-Home Sauna, a Hot Tub, and/or Other Fitness Equipment	☐	☐	
A Fan, Air Conditioner, and/or Portable Heater in Each Guestroom (so guests can control the temperature)	☐	☐	
Plush Cottom Robes and Disposable Slippers for Your Guests	☐	☐	

As you choose furniture, décor, appliances, and consumer electronics to install within the property and plan how you'll arrange the property and guestrooms, consider ongoing maintenance issues—what will be involved with keeping everything functional. Figure out who will handle the maintenance, and the cost of that ongoing maintenance.

If you opt to welcome families with kids to your short-term rental property, consider offering kid-friendly amenities, like a video game system, board games, toys, and age-appropriate books. Also, make sure you remove any foods or snacks that contain nuts that kids might be allergic to. Meanwhile, for a property that will be pet-friendly, consider equipping the house with dog bowls and a dog bed, for example. Remember, everything extra you choose to add will need to be cleaned and sanitized in between each guest visit, so this will provide more work for your cleaner.

Think about the last time you stayed at a hotel or motel and what complimentary amenities were offered within the guestroom. Try to offer as many of these as possible. Whenever applicable, provide single-use, prepackaged amenities.

Especially if you're catering to guests paying a premium nightly rate, everything within the property will be expected to be fully operational, so when something breaks, you'll need a plan in place to have it repaired quickly and affordably.

Do a cost/benefit analysis when choosing new furniture and amenities for your property. For each thing you will need to spend money on, determine how it will impact the comfort and happiness of your guests, and whether the added investment can be recuperated over time with a small increase in your nightly rate.

Buy Enough for Everyone

When stocking up on items that will be used consistently by your guests, make sure you acquire enough of everything for each guest, and have enough of everything on hand if you wind up having guests back-to-back (and won't have time to go shopping or do laundry before your next guest arrives).

For example, for each bed, you'll need multiple sets of sheets, pillowcases, blankets, comforter covers, and pillows. For guests that stay a week, you might opt to launder the bedding one or two times during that period. However, if you'll be having one-night guests check in every day, you'll need to strip the bedding between each guest and obviously provide clean and fresh bedding for each guest.

By utilizing a comforter cover, you can easy wash the cover between each guest and launder the actual comforter only once every few weeks, especially if you're offering a flat top sheet as well.

For bedding, figure out how many sets of sheets, pillows, and blankets you'll need on hand for each bed, based on how frequently guests will be staying at your property and how often you plan to do laundry.

As for pillows, keep in mind that some people prefer more than one, and some people prefer down filling, while others require synthetic, memory foam, latex, or cotton filling due to allergies, so for each bed, you'll want to have at least two or three pillows on hand, made from a selection of different materials.

 TIP

> For sanitary reasons, seriously consider enclosing each of your mattresses in a plastic mattress cover that will keep bedbugs and bodily fluids from reaching the mattress itself. Also, refrain from utilizing decorative throw pillows on the bed or offering extra blankets that are made from materials that can't easily be laundered.

Consider offering one bath towel, one hand towel, and one washcloth per guest, per day. Again, based on the number of guests you plan to have staying with you simultaneously, and how often you plan to do laundry, always have enough clean towels on hand, keeping in mind that, periodically, a guest will have the need for extra towels. If your property is near the beach, a lake or the ocean, or has access to a pool or hot tub, be sure to provide your guests with separate beach towels as well.

Have enough dishes, coffee mugs, glasses, and silverware on hand in your kitchen so two or three meals can be served without having to do dishes. Then, stock up on disposable items, like garbage bags, selections of travel-size toiletries, toilet paper, tissues, dish soap, laundry detergent, hand sanitizer, and other necessities that you will continuously need on hand. (Go with unscented laundry detergent.) Again, consider shopping at a wholesale club, like Costco or BJ's

Wholesale Club, to save money, assuming you have the storage space available for the items you buy in bulk. Also, make sure you do not use perfumed or heavily scented air fresheners or cleaning products in your rental property, as some people are allergic to these chemical-based odors.

 TIP

> Be sure to offer a laundry basket for guests to leave their used (dirty and wet) towels once they're done using them. If they'll be expected to reuse towels, be sure ample towel rack space is provided in the bathroom or guestroom, so the towels can dry off between uses and not get moldy.

Provide a Detailed House Manual

In Chapter 3, the concept of creating a house manual (in addition to a list of House Rules) was introduced. While House Rules provide guidelines for how guests are expected to act while staying at your property, a house manual is a document that outlines all the most important information your guests will need to know while they're staying with you. This printed document should be provided to your guests upon their arrival or can be placed within the guestrooms where each guest will be staying.

Upon a new guest's arrival, you'll want to verbally go over the House Rules, provide a property tour, and offer brief demonstrations on how various things work. However, you can assume that only a small fraction of what you say will be remembered. Therefore, a printed house manual is important. If you plan to greet your guests remotely, consider offering a video-based house tour that they can watch at their convenience via their internet-connected mobile device or computer.

NOTE

Create a master shopping list for yourself with items you'll require on an ongoing basis and the quantity you need of each item. Then, in between shopping trips, update the list as needed. You can create the list on paper or use a mobile app on your smartphone or tablet.

The house manual should include a printed copy of the House Rules, as well as separate instructions for operating equipment that could be confusing. This can include easy-to-understand, step-by-step directions for:

- Unlocking and locking the front door.
- Turning on and using the television / home theater system and operating the cable box or streaming device connected to the television. (Also include a list of TV channels/networks you receive, and their corresponding channel numbers.)
- Using the washer and dryer.
- Using the coffee machine.
- Connecting to the Wi-Fi.
- Where it's okay to park and parking rules or local laws that guests need to adhere to.

Have Restaurant Recommendations On Hand for Your Guests

Chances are, many of your guests will want to know your personal recommendations for nearby restaurants or bars or may want referrals about which restaurants deliver. Consider providing a detailed restaurant list, along with walking or driving directions to the most popular restaurants. You should also have a selection of menus on hand. This information should be included within your house manual.

In addition to the restaurants that offer their own delivery service, determine if your geographic area is serviced by mobile apps and websites like Grubhub (www.grubhub.com) or Uber Eats (www.ubereats.com). These services determine the user's location, locate all of the participating restaurants in the nearby area, display menus for those participating restaurants, and then accept orders to be delivered, whether or not the restaurant itself offers a delivery service.

Grubhub, Uber Eats, and other food delivery apps like them can be acquired for free from the App Store (iPhone/iPad) or the Google Play Store (Android smartphones and tablets). Once you determine that one or more of these apps/services work in your geographic area, consider recommending them to your guests who are looking to have food or meals delivered.

Also, within your house manual, be sure to include answers to the most asked questions you receive from guests, including:

- Directions to the closest grocery store, pharmacy, convenience store, and gas station

- A sampling of menus and walking/driving directions to a selection of popular restaurants that are nearby

- Information about popular attractions, landmarks, points of interest, and things to do in the area, including movie theaters

So that you can easily keep your house manual up to date, consider using a three-ring binder and covering each topic on a separate page within the binder so you can easily update and replace specific sections or pages without having to reprint the entire manual.

Include a copy of your house manual within each guestroom and point it out during your initial tour. To serve its purpose, your house manual should be clearly written, comprehensive, well organized, and easy to understand. It should also display your cell phone number prominently, so guests can call or text you with questions if you're not available in person.

TIP

In addition to offering a detailed house manual, make it clear to your guests that you, as their host, are always available to answer their questions or address their concerns in person. Make sure you provide guests with your cell phone number so they can text you with questions during their stay or call you if their need is urgent. Once you start receiving the same question(s) repeatedly from guests, consider updating your house manual to include the appropriate answer(s). If you work with a property manager, their contact information should be prominently displayed within your house manual.

 TIP

To easily differentiate between incoming personal and guest-related calls, it's easy to add a second phone number (with a unique ring) to your smartphone or landline. From your smartphone, for example, access the app store and within the Search field, enter "second phone number" or "virtual phone number" to find apps that offer this functionality for a low monthly fee.

Manage Your Time and Responsibilities

As a host, you'll have to do a series of tasks and chores daily, as well as complete a separate selection of important tasks after each guest leaves and before your next guest(s) arrives. You may also assign separate responsibilities to your professional cleaning service.

To ensure that you don't forget an important task or chore, write out detailed checklists and schedules that include everything that needs to be done, and when.

Include everything from laundry, washing dishes, sweeping the floors, and vacuuming the carpets to cleaning and sanitizing the bathroom, paying monthly bills (cable TV, utilities, landscaping, cleaning crew, etc.), replacing the bedding and making the beds between guests, and doing the necessary shopping.

Especially as a new host, it's essential that everything within your property always be clean, on hand, and ready for your guests. Remembering to do everything will require planning and organization on your part.

Cleaning and Preparing for Your Guests

To some extent, your guests should be expected to clean up after themselves from day to day and leave your property exactly how it was found when they first arrived. You'll discover, however, that your guests are not always so considerate or responsible.

 **WARNING**

A guest should never have to look for a new roll of toilet paper in the bathroom or come to you to report that you've run out of toilet paper. This, and situations like it, will virtually guarantee you receive a bad rating and review and cause serious inconvenience for your guests.

It's your job as the host to do a daily inventory of all items on hand that could run out and ensure there's always an ample supply of everything, including clean towels, toilet paper, coffee, bottled water, tea, and paper towels.

Especially if you're renting one or more guestrooms in the home where you also live, as the host, you'll need to get into the habit of doing some basic cleaning daily, whenever you have guests staying with you. Basic chores, like wiping down the bathroom, sweeping the floors, emptying trash cans, dusting, and making sure the dishes are clean, all become your responsibility.

If you're renting out an entire home or apartment for multiple nights, many of these basic housekeeping tasks can be left to your guests, provided you give them whatever is needed to handle them. Then, when each guest checks out, you will need to go into the property to clean up, sweep, vacuum, dust, change the bedding, sanitize everything, organize the bathroom, and prepare the property for the next guest(s).

 **WARNING**

There was a short-lived trend amongst Airbnb hosts where guests were required to launder their own bedding and towels at the conclusion of their stay. This turned out to be a mistake and a requirement that most guests found unacceptable. Generally, if a hotel or motel would not require a guest to do something, you should not either.

Depending on how much you're charging and how busy your schedule is, it may make financial sense to hire a professional house cleaner to come in one or more times per week, and in between guests, to give the property a proper and thorough cleaning. Choosing this option obviously costs money, but it also means you'll need to find and develop a business relationship with a trustworthy and reliable housecleaning service or cleaner. If you hire a service, be sure to hire one that has done background checks on its employees and that has adequate insurance.

 NOTE

If you're offering services or amenities that truly add value to someone's stay, consider building the cost of these extras into your published nightly rate, instead of listing extra fees for them within your property listing. However, you don't want your nightly rate to appear much higher than nearby properties when potential guests are evaluating their options.

Manage Your Cleaning Services

In addition to online services and mobile apps, like Angi and Thumbtack, there are services, like TurnOverBnb (https://turnoverbnb.com), that specialize in helping hosts find a cleaning service or independent house cleaner. There are also Facebook groups for Airbnb hosts and an interactive community of hosts on the Airbnb website where you can exchange referrals. After all, one of the biggest challenges hosts have is finding and keeping a reliable cleaning service. Most experienced hosts agree that an important qualification to look for in a cleaning service or house cleaner is having previous experience cleaning short-term rental properties.

Then, even once you find a cleanings service or independent house cleaner, try to develop a long-term and trusting relationship. You'll always want to check their work before a new guest checks in. If you can't do this in person, insist that the cleaning service send you photos of every area of the property that they clean, so you can do a visual inspection to ensure everything was done correctly and that your property is ready to welcome a new guest.

Just as an airplane pilot uses a printed preflight checklist before every single flight, no matter how many flights they've piloted and how much experience they have, so, too, must an Airbnb host develop a detailed checklist of all cleaning-related activities that must be done to their property in between guests if they want to maintain a consistent level of cleanliness. Create a second checklist of all cleaning-related activities that need to be done once per month or once per season, such as shampooing the carpets, doing a deep clean on the oven, cleaning the dryer's air duct, washing the windows, etc. By using checklists, you're able to set clear expectations for your cleaning service so they know exactly what needs to be done during each visit and they have no excuse for forgetting an important step. This also helps you maintain a consistent quality standard for your guests.

Every cleaning and property preparation detail or step, such as laundering and then inspecting the linens, blankets, pillows, and towels for stains, discoloration, or rips, should be included within the checklist, as should a list of everything that goes into making each bed properly. For example, the cleaner should ensure the mattress cover is on the mattress and that it's covered with a clean, fitted sheet. Each bed should also include a top sheet and a predetermined number of pillows and blankets. The made bed and related furnishings should look exactly how it looks in the property listing's photos.

Something as simple as not emptying the trash cans could impact a review, so even minor cleaning-related details should be included within your checklist. Likewise, all dishes, glasses, and utensils should be counted, cleaned, and put in their proper place, all surfaces should be dusted and sanitized, and all carpets should be vacuumed using a commercial-quality vacuum with air filtration.

Sample cleaning checklists that you can use as a template, but will want to customize for your unique property, can be found at:

- https://hosttools.com/blog/short-term-rental-tools/airbnb-cleaning-checklist
- https://turno.com/airbnb-cleaning-checklist
- https://blog.hostgpo.com/good-cleaning-checklist-for-airbnb
- www.lodgify.com/guides/airbnb-cleaning-checklist
- https://www.quilldecor.com/blog/the-ultimate-cleaning-checklist-for-you-airbnb

In conjunction with the personalized printed checklist that you and your cleaners can rely on, take photos of what the property should look like before each guest arrives so you and your cleaners have a visual reference—from how the beds are made, to the organization of the bathroom and kitchen. To consistently earn five-star reviews, as a host, you must be consistent with all your cleaning practices.

Cleaning Supplies and Equipment to Have On Hand

If you choose to clean your property yourself in between guests, you'll need to have a comprehensive selection of cleaning tools and products on hand to do the job right. Figure 5.3 offers a checklist of recommended cleaning products you should always keep on hand.

| Figure 5.3 | Cleaning Tools and Products Checklist |

On Hand	Cleaning Product	Brand Used
☐	Bleach	
☐	Broom and dustpan	
☐	Bucket	
☐	Carpet Cleaner	
☐	Dishwashing Detergent	
☐	Disposable Gloves	
☐	Duster	
☐	Face Shields & KN95 Face Masks	
☐	Floor Cleaner	
☐	Furniture / Wood Polish	
☐	Garbage Bags	
☐	Glass Cleaner	
☐	Laundry Detergent	
☐	Laundry Stain Remover	
☐	Microfiber Cleaning Cloths	
☐	Mold Cleaner	
☐	Mop	
☐	Multi-Surface Cleaner	
☐	Multi-Surface Disinfectant	
☐	Oven Cleaner (if applicable)	
☐	Oven Degreaser (if applicable)	
☐	Paper Towels	
☐	Scrub Brushes	
☐	Scrub Pads (for kitchen dishes, glasses, pots, pans, and flatware)	
☐	Shower Cleaning Detergent (disinfect, remove soap scum, remove mold)	
☐	Toilet Cleaning Brush and/or Toilet Cleaner	
☐	Vacuum Cleaner (preferably bagless)	

TIP

Even if you have your property professionally cleaned in between guest stays, be sure to provide cleaning and sanitizing supplies for use by your guests. This should include an ample supply of paper towels, multi-surface cleaner, disinfectant wipes, antibacterial hand sanitizer (in each bedroom, bathroom, and common area), and disinfecting hand soap near every sink. When stocking up on these supplies, make sure you provide sanitizing products that are approved by the U.S. Environmental Protection Agency (EPA) or the European Chemicals Agency.

Should You Charge a Cleaning Fee?

Airbnb allows hosts to add an optional cleaning fee to their nightly rate. If you opt to charge this, your guests expect you to hire a professional cleaner to ensure the property is clean, sanitized, and ready for them upon their arrival. Make sure you allow enough time in between bookings to properly clean your property. When each guest arrives, the property should be ready for them.

For your long-term guests (staying one week or longer), devise a cleaning schedule so they know what day(s) the bedding and towels, for example, will be laundered, and/or when the maid service will be visiting and need access to their guestroom or the property where they're staying.

If you're charging a premium rate for a guest to rent your entire property, adding a cleaning fee will likely be expected. However, if you're renting a single guestroom in a competitive marketplace, guests will likely balk at an added cleaning fee, especially if you're one of the only hosts in the geographic area charging one.

TIP

To find a professional cleaning service in your area, seek out a referral from someone you trust, do a Google search, or see if a national housecleaning chain, such as Merry Maids (www.merrymaids.com), Molly Maid (www.mollymaid.com), or MaidPro (www.maidpro.com), operates in your area. You can also find local housecleaning services or independent cleaners through an online-based referral service, such as Angi (www.angi.com) or Thumbtack (www.thumbtack.com).

Pay Attention to Airbnb's Five-Step Cleaning Process

As a result of the COVID-19 pandemic, Airbnb now requires all hosts to follow a five-step cleaning and sanitizing process for their property. The five steps include:

- Step #1—Prepare for the Cleanup In Between Guests
- Step #2—Do the Cleaning
- Step #3—Sanitize
- Step #4—Do a Walk-Through and Check Everything
- Step #5—Reset

For more information about this policy, point your web browser to www.airbnb .com/help/article/2809.

WARNING

As an Airbnb host, you must abide by Airbnb's published COVID-19 Safety Practices, in addition to the five-step cleaning process. Failure to comply will result in Airbnb revoking your host status and deleting your property listing(s). Since the COVID-19 Safety Practices continue to change, based on guidance from the World Health Organization and U.S. Centers for Disease Control, be sure to read up on the latest guidelines published on Airbnb's website (www.airbnb.com/help /article/2839), and then check this website frequently to learn about any policy changes.

Attract Business Travelers with an Airbnb Business Travel Ready Listing

In addition to vacation or leisure travelers, Airbnb caters to business travelers by offering accommodations that meet a specific set of requirements that are designed to appeal specifically to businesspeople traveling for work, as well as remote workers. Property listings that qualify to accept business travelers are specifically set up to handle their unique needs.

As an Airbnb host, you can apply to become a Business Travel Ready property, if you're offering an appropriate type of accommodation, the required selection of amenities, and you meet the other requirements outlined by Airbnb.

To see the most up-to-date list of requirements for becoming an Airbnb for Business host, visit www.airbnb.com/business-travel-ready and www.airbnb.com /resources/hosting-homes/a/how-to-make-your-space-comfortable-for-remote -workers-236.

Assuming your property qualifies, some of the additional services and amenities you'll need to provide as a host include:

- 24-hour check-in

- Maintaining a strict no-smoking/no-pets policy

- Offering business-friendly amenities, including fast and reliable Wi-Fi, a laptop-friendly workspace, iron, hangers, hair dryer, and shampoo

The benefits as a host providing work-friendly accommodations are that your property listing will be showcased to business travelers, you'll wind up with more bookings, and you can typically charge a higher nightly rate. You'll also potentially

receive more midweek or longer-term bookings, especially during nonpeak vacation periods.

Decide Whether or Not to Deal with Keys

Every time new guests arrives at your property, you'll need to provide them with an
easy way to come and go as they please, 24 hours per day, during the length of their
stay. One option is to provide them with a copy of the traditional metal house key(s)
needed for entry, which you'll then need to collect upon each guest's checkout.

One problem with using a traditional key distribution method is that it becomes
the guests' responsibility to lock the door after them each time they leave and not
lose or forget the key, which will be needed to let themselves back in.

Available from any hardware store, you can replace the traditional key-entry
locks on your front door with a digital smart lock that requires a numeric code
for entry and that automatically locks itself each time the door is shut. No actual
keys are required. These smart locks can also be added to bedrooms for the added
security and privacy of your guests.

Some of the more advanced keyless-entry smart locks can be programmed and
remotely controlled using a smartphone app or computer software. As the host,
this means you can quickly change the entry code as often as you like (in between
guests, for example), from anywhere you have internet access.

Smart locks are available from many manufacturers, starting as low as $50 each
(although plan on spending between $150 and $300 for a quality smart lock with
plenty of features). Most smart locks can be installed within 30 to 60 minutes on
your own, using basic tools. However, any local locksmith can also install them.
Once installed, some of these smart locks allow the host to use their smartphone
or computer to track when guests come and go and ensure the door otherwise
always remains locked. If someone forgets their code, the host can also remotely
unlock the door using their internet-connected smartphone or computer from
virtually anywhere.

In addition to the keyless-entry smart locks that are available from your local
hardware store, Airbnb has teamed up with a company called RemoteLock to

offer a selection of keyless-entry smart door lock options specifically to Airbnb hosts. To learn more, visit http://remotelock.com/airbnb. As you'll discover, the cost of RemoteLock's offerings range from $199 to $469 per lock. (Keep in mind, less expensive options may be available from hardware stores and other online-based vendors.)

 TIP

To shop online for the selection of smart locks available from Home Depot, visit www.homedepot.com/s/smartlocks. To shop for these locks online from Lowe's, visit www.lowes.com/search?searchTerm= smart+locks. You'll also discover Amazon.com offers a vast selection of smart locks that can replace your existing door locks. To find them, visit www.amazon.com, and within the search field, enter the phase "smart locks."

New Hosts Should Hold a Dress Rehearsal

As a new travel host who has just made your property ready to invite guests, one of the optional things you can do to ensure everything will go smoothly with your paying guests is to hold a dress rehearsal. Just before you publish your Airbnb property listing, invite one or more of your close friends to stay with you and pretend to be an Airbnb guest. Have them stay in your guestroom(s), use your property, and experience everything that a paying guest would experience. Then, get their honest feedback, and make whatever adjustments are necessary.

You can also take this a step further and have your friends book a paid stay at your property through Airbnb. This allows them to provide you, as the host, with your first review once their visit is complete. You can always reimburse your friends for the money they paid and consider the fee you paid to Airbnb for the booking as a cost of doing business.

Either approach will allow you to practice being an Airbnb host, without the risk of making mistakes that could result in a bad review from a paying guest.

Meet Airbnb Superhost Lauren Aumond

Within just a few years of becoming an Airbnb host, Lauren Aumond and her husband now own and manage nine short-term rental properties along with three long-term rental properties. As Superhosts, they have welcomed more than 300 guests in the last two years. You can preview some of Lauren Aumond's Airbnb property listings by visiting her website (https://adultingiseasy.gumroad.com).

How did you first get started with Airbnb?

Lauren Aumond: "I originally started with a long-term rental duplex in St. Petersburg, Florida. My next goal was to purchase a second long-term rental property rather quickly. As I was looking for the perfect property, I discovered an actual working bed-and-breakfast that was for sale. It was built in 1901 and contained three bedrooms and two full baths. Immediately outside of this bed-and-breakfast were two additional stand-alone cottages.

"The area in Florida where this property is located is very tourist based, so my husband and I quickly pivoted from doing only long-term rentals to using the bed-and-breakfast property to host short-term rentals through Airbnb. This all happened in 2019, right as COVID-19 started to happen. After purchasing the property, we put an additional $150,000 worth of work into the property. We later took about $100,000 out of that property and purchased an additional duplex about 30 miles north of the bed-and-breakfast property.

"By December 2021, I pulled additional money out of the existing properties via a 1031 exchange to purchase another six-unit apartment building, half of which are now used for short-term rentals. Ultimately, I wound up with nine short-term rental listings and three long-term rental units."

Do you manage all the properties yourself?

Lauren Aumond: "Yes. However, both me and my husband also have full-time, 9 a.m. to 5 p.m. jobs. We now use a property management system, called OwnerRez [www.ownerreservations.com], which integrates directly with Airbnb. As we expanded, we switched all of the locks on the properties to utilize smart locks, which we manage using an application called RemoteLock [https://remotelock .com/learn-more-about-remotelock]. And we also use PriceLabs [https://hello .pricelabs.co], which is dynamic pricing software that also integrates with Airbnb.

"Now, when someone books one of our properties through Airbnb, they get an automated message from me that thanks them for their booking. We then follow up with an email sent via Airbnb Relay, requesting them to submit their refundable deposit and that asks them to sign a rental agreement. Three days prior to their check-in, they receive their welcome information for checking in. The rest of the process, which includes their check-in details, is sent via email, and is also fully automated."

What's your secret for hiring a reliable cleaning crew to turn over and clean your properties in between bookings?

Lauren Aumond: "I found our current cleaning service through an Airbnb Facebook group, but it's taken a bit of trial and error to find the right fit. The big challenge is finding a cleaner that's consistent and reliable. For example, we had one cleaner for a short time that was a smoker, and she smoked when cleaning the linens, which caused a cigarette smell to permeate within them. This resulted in complaints, so we had to let her go. Our current cleaner gets an email notification through OwnerRez each time we get a new booking, so she knows which units need to be cleaned and when. Finding reliable cleaners and landscapers has been an ongoing challenge.

"At this point, I will only hire a cleaner if they have previous experience cleaning Airbnb properties and come highly recommended by their references. They need to be able to deal with last-minute bookings and provide a consistent level of service. One responsibility of our cleaners is to take an inventory of the property each time it's cleaned to ensure nothing has gone missing or has been damaged. They also need to make sure the property is stocked with everything that's needed, including the right number of pillows and towels, for example.

"To maintain consistent quality control, I pay careful attention to the reviews we receive, and I do personally communicate with guests. In every communication the guest receives from us, there's a message that invites them to contact me anytime with questions or concerns related to their stay. If there are any issues, I want to know about them immediately. I share the reviews with the cleaners. I also make a point to randomly visit the various units in person to get a close look at things. I have accepted that I am not always in control, but if we keep receiving those five-star reviews as Superhosts, I am willing to give up some control to people we trust."

What have you done to make your properties unique and set them apart from other Airbnb properties in your area?

Lauren Aumond: "It depends on the property, but one thing I pay attention to is landscape design. I want our guests to get that Florida feel as soon as they arrive. I believe that starts before they walk through the front door, so the landscaping features palm trees and flower beds. When someone looks at one of our property listings, I want them to look at it as an oasis."

How often do you update your Airbnb property listings?

Lauren Aumond: "Airbnb's algorithm likes active hosts. Every Monday, for example, I make a point to leave a review about all our guests who stayed with us during the previous week. I also respond to all the reviews I have gotten. I also change headings, pictures, and descriptive text for each property at least once per month. Each week, I make a point to update three or four property listings at a time.

"Within the text portion of the listings, I purposely use language that assumes the guest is already interested in staying with us. For example, I'll say something like, 'You'll just love the porch swing.' I want the prospective guests to picture themselves staying at the property. I also provide information about how close the beaches and airport are, for example. I want people to see and learn about the area where they'll be staying, so they understand what they can be seeing and doing while staying with us. One detail that I recently started adding to each listing is the Wi-Fi speed and show a screenshot from a Wi-Fi speed test. Anytime I get the same question three times about a property, I will update the listing to include a detailed answer to that question."

Do you take your own property photos or use a professional photographer?

Lauren Aumond: "I have done both, but I recommend using professional photography within your property listing. Spending money on a professional photographer is a good investment. Anytime we make a change to any of the properties, I want to immediately showcase that within the photos featured within the property's Airbnb listing. For these updates, I often take my own photos using my smartphone, but I have the professional photographer return once per year to update all the photos."

Do you have a general strategy for nightly pricing for your various Airbnb properties?

Lauren Aumond: "We offer nice, clean, suitable places to stay that have a Florida feel, without a ton of high-end bells and whistles. We price our properties in the average to lower end of the scale compared to local competition. We do, however, require a $100 to $250 refundable security deposit. We probably lose some bookings because we require a security deposit, but it's something we do to help us protect our business. Out of more than 300 guests in the last two years, we've only had to keep two security deposits, however. If someone books a reservation with three to four guests, we do charge an extra guest fee because that means they'll be using the sofa bed. Having to change the linens and clean up after the extra people upon their checkout takes the cleaner more time."

Since you host so many guests each year, how often do you replace things like the pillows, blankets, linens, and towels?

Lauren Aumond: "There is no set schedule, but everything gets replaced at some point during each year, as soon as we notice a non-removable stain, rip, or signs of wear and tear that makes something look old. All the mattresses and pillows have protectors on them. I purchase linens, towels, and other items we go through often in bulk from Costco or Amazon. We make a point to use all white towels and linens, because they can be bleached, and it makes everything look extra clean for the guests."

Not All Rules Were Made to Be Broken

One of the potential problems with welcoming strangers to stay at your property is that not everyone is as courteous as you'd like. Some people might not be respectful or try to keep your home clean, for example. No matter how clear you are when spelling out your House Rules and explaining the financial consequences to a guest who chooses to break those rules, once every so often you might encounter a difficult guest who disregards your House Rules. How to safely deal with rule breakers is what's covered in the next chapter.

CHAPTER 6

Responding to Broken Rules

Airbnb is successful because it's built a loyal and global community that's comprised of travelers and hosts. Whenever someone sets up an Airbnb account and plans to be a guest at someone's property, they agree to adhere to basic rules of conduct. Likewise, hosts agree to follow Airbnb's guidelines and requirements for providing their paid guests with a clean, safe, and comfortable space to stay.

Airbnb's business model relies heavily on each user's willingness to follow the rules and to be respectful, honest, and law abiding. For example, guests are expected to leave a host's property exactly how they found it and not steal anything or cause damage. They're also expected to follow the rules outlined by Airbnb and their host during their stay.

Most of the time, everyone follows these Airbnb-imposed guidelines, and the overall experience for the host and guests is a positive one. One incentive for following the rules is that hosts and guests both get to publish ratings and reviews about one another on the Airbnb platform, and these reviews are available for all to see.

As a host, receiving bad reviews and low ratings is tantamount to your past guests warning your future guests against staying with you. Because the Airbnb community relies so heavily on reviews, it forces hosts to provide the best experience possible for their paying guests. Hosts with bad reviews don't get bookings. It's that simple.

> **WARNING**
>
> Should Airbnb guests wind up with many bad ratings and reviews, and/or have their account suspended by Airbnb, it's all too easy for that same person to simply create a new account, using an alternate email address or someone else's information. Thus, while ratings and reviews are a good indicator for what you, as a host, can expect from your guests, unfortunately this is not a foolproof system. That said, Airbnb does try to encourage everyone to verify their identity by providing a government-issued ID upon setting up their account.

Likewise, as a guest, receiving bad reviews and low ratings will prevent someone from being able to use Airbnb in the future to book accommodations. Initially, they will be prevented from staying with hosts who have turned off the Instant Book feature, and who evaluate the ratings and reviews of their potential guests before accepting a booking. Then, after an account holder receives multiple negative reviews and ratings, Airbnb will often terminate that account altogether.

To help hosts and guests establish trust between parties, Airbnb has multiple features in place, including the review and rating system, the Verified ID system, and the Host Guarantee. As a member of the Airbnb community, once travelers establish their free account, they have the ability to report (flag) any profile, property listing, or message that they believe is offensive, discriminatory, that does not adhere to Airbnb's policies, or that they believe is suspicious.

> **TIP**
>
> Every day, many thousands of travelers stay with hosts based on bookings made through Airbnb. Most bookings happen without a hitch. Chances are, this will be your experience as well. However, as a host, have plans in place to handle situations that go wrong.

If You Live Alone, Take Extra Precautions

If you're a host who is single, lives alone, and who will be renting out one or more guestrooms within a property where you're also living, it's important to always take extra precautions before inviting strangers into your home. Sure, insurance will cover your property and belongings against theft or damage, but you also need to consider your own security and well-being.

This is where common sense and trust comes into play. As was discussed in previous chapters, as a host, you can turn *off* the Instant Book feature. This requires potential guests to contact you and request a booking. It then gives you the opportunity to review their profile, read their past ratings and reviews, and have text-based correspondence with that potential guest *before* they're able to confirm their booking and show up to stay in your home.

As you review a potential guest's profile, ratings, and reviews, if for whatever reason you're not comfortable having that person stay with you, simply reject the booking request. Accept booking requests only from people you feel comfortable inviting into your home. Yes, this will result in potential lost revenue, but it will also help ensure your safety and peace of mind as a host.

In situations where you will be alone in your home with a stranger staying with you, have plans in place to protect your safety. For example, have a friend or neighbor check in on you, have a sturdy lock installed on your own bedroom door, and determine in advance exactly how you'll handle situations that make you uncomfortable or feel unsafe. Also, keep your cell phone with you, in case you ever need to call 911 quickly.

Airbnb has a team in place that is responsible for investigating all content that is flagged by its users. While communicating with potential guests or booked guests via Airbnb's secure messaging service, either party always has the option to flag a message they receive that makes them uncomfortable or that they believe is inappropriate. Simply click on the flag icon to do this. However, if at any time you feel your safety or well-being is in jeopardy, or you're being threatened or harassed, call the police immediately.

TIP

Feeling secure goes both ways. The more ways you (as a host) get verified, the more credibility you'll have, and the safer a potential guest will feel booking a reservation to stay with you.

Develop Clear House Rules That Leave No Room for Interpretation

The importance of developing a clear set of House Rules has been discussed several times already. These rules need to be presented as part of your property listing on Airbnb and agreed to by your guests when they confirm their booking. You'll also want to verbally review the House Rules upon your guests' initial arrival and have a printed copy of the House Rules waiting for them in their guestroom (within the house manual, for example).

Assuming your guests are willing to adhere to their promise and obligation to follow your House Rules, this should eliminate a lot of potential misunderstandings and problems. Remember, your House Rules should be written in a way that protects you (the host), your property and belongings, as well as the other guests who are simultaneously staying with you (if applicable), and your neighbors.

It's important to understand that, as a host, you are not allowed to utilize House Rules to discriminate against potential guests or paying guests. Airbnb has a firm policy against publishing any content within your profile or property listing, for example, that promotes hatred, racism, discrimination of any kind, harassment, or harm against any individual or group.

In addition to this blanket policy, hosts must adhere to all their local, state, and federal laws pertaining to discrimination, which, in the United States, includes what's mandated within the Fair Housing Act and Americans with Disabilities Act. For more information, visit www.airbnb.com/help/article/483/airbnb-s-nondiscrimination -policy. This policy gets periodically updated so be sure you're familiar with the latest revisions.

NOTE

As you're creating your list of House Rules, check a handful of other property listings from Airbnb hosts who have received a lot of positive ratings and reviews and who have earned the Superhost accreditation. These hosts have updated and tweaked their House Rules over time, based on their own firsthand experiences dealing with guests. Thus, they may give you good ideas about rules you'll want to adopt that relate to your unique concerns and property.

Airbnb's AirCover Offers You Protection as a Host

To learn more about AirCover, point your web browser to www.airbnb.com/help /article/3142. If you need to file a claim related to damage protection, you can file a reimbursement request by visiting this website: www.airbnb.com/resolutions. However, if you (as a host) are found legally responsible for a guest's injury or damage to or loss of their property (such as their personal belongings), you'll need to file a liability claim by pointing your web browser to this address: www .airbnb.com/insurance/form.

What to Do When Guests Don't Follow Your Rules or Something Inappropriate Happens

Your experiences as an Airbnb host will hopefully be consistently good. However, if you wind up welcoming a guest who doesn't follow your rules, who places you in a dangerous situation, or who causes damage to your property, you'll want to take immediate action. The safety of yourself, your family, your pets, your neighbors, and your property must always come first and be your primary concern.

Depending on the severity of the situation, what House Rules have been broken, and the behavior of your guest, you typically have several options when dealing with a problem, including:

- Ignore the minor infraction, and simply deal with it. Then wait for the guest to check out on their prearranged date. If necessary, you can file a claim with Airbnb or your insurance company to recover a financial loss due to damage caused by your guest.

- Have a discussion with your guest. Provide a friendly reminder that they have violated a House Rule and give them a chance to apologize and remedy the situation.

- Report the violation to Airbnb and follow the directions you're provided. How to do this is explained shortly.

- Evict the guest from your property prior to their planned checkout date. Do this by following the guidelines provided by Airbnb.

- Call the police or dial 911 immediately. Obviously, this is the most drastic measure.

 TIP

If at any time you feel like you're in danger, call your local police or dial 911 immediately, and if possible, leave the property, and wait in a safe location for the authorities to arrive.

Which option you choose should obviously be based on the severity of the situation, whether you (or your family, pets, other guests, or neighbors) have been put in harm's way, and/or whether the guest's actions have resulted in financial loss for you and/or damage to your property.

If possible, try to approach the situation with a business mindset, as opposed to an overly emotional one. You can always write a strong negative review about that guest once they leave, plus provide them with a low rating.

Consider Acquiring Optional Short-Term Rental Insurance

For protecting your property and belongings, in addition to having appropriate liability insurance in place for your property, along with traditional homeowner's or renter's insurance, a handful of insurance companies have begun offering specialized short-term rental insurance that's designed specifically for travel hosts who have paying guests staying in their home or in a property they own or lease.

A few companies that offer short-term rental insurance include:

- **InsuraGuest**—www.insuraguest.com
- **Proper Insurance**—www.proper.insure
- **Safely**—https://safely.com
- **Steadily**—www.steadily.com/get-a-quote/short-term-rental-insurance

Again, Airbnb offers AirCover to protect you and your property. Understand, however, that while the description for the host protection may sound good, depending on the situation, it may not fully cover you from a financial loss if a problem occurs. Having your own insurance as well is a smart strategy.

 **WARNING**

If Airbnb's system determines you are declining many booking requests, this could negatively impact your property listing's search result placement on the Airbnb platform. If you have accepted a reservation request and then canceled it, you could be subject to cancellation penalties and become ineligible for Superhost status, unless the reason for cancellation is considered by Airbnb to be an "extenuating circumstance."

To avoid penalties, document your reason for canceling a guest's confirmed reservation. Acceptable reasons include maintenance issues that will impact your ability to host, death of a family member, serious illness, severe property damage, a natural disaster, or political unrest.

How to Report Violations of Your House Rules to Airbnb

Prior to or during guests' stay at your property, you have the option to decline or cancel their reservation, if a guest violates one or more of your House Rules. However, you must follow the guidelines provided by Airbnb to do this.

Through AirCover, Airbnb has published a series of detailed standards and expectations to which everyone—guests and hosts alike—is expected to adhere to. As a host, familiarize yourself with these policies that relate to safety, security, fairness, authenticity, and reliability.

From your computer, visit Airbnb's Resolution Center (www.airbnb.com /resolutions) to request money for refunds, services, or damages related to a reservation or guest. For this feature to work, there must be an eligible reservation within the Airbnb system.

If you're trying to recover money from a guest who has caused damage, for example, from the Resolution Center, click on the Request Money button, and then follow the on-screen prompts. Remember, you have up to 30 days after a guest's checkout date to pursue this option. It will be much easier to recover compensation for damages or a broken rule if your House Rules are clearly spelled out and there is a specific financial penalty associated with breaking each rule. For example, a $500 additional cleaning fee if someone smokes inside of a house where it's stated that absolutely no smoking is permitted. Be sure to list a specific financial penalty for breaking each rule.

Plus, if you charge a refundable deposit at the time a booking is made, this, too, will make it easier to recover money for damages. This is another way to protect your property, but many Airbnb travelers don't like having to pay a refundable deposit.

 TIP

You always have the option to contact Airbnb's Customer Service department by pointing your web browser to www.airbnb.com/help /contact-us.

How to Evict a Guest from Your Property

Assuming you're not in danger, but a guest will not leave your property, one option as a host is to contact Airbnb via its website (www.airbnb.com/help/contact_us) or by phone, and then follow their recommendations to get a guest to leave peacefully. If your need to evict a guest is more pressing, or you feel you're in danger, contact the police.

What If the Problem Is Your Fault?

If, as a host, you make a mistake that impacts the quality of your guest's stay, try to rectify the situation during your guest's stay to avoid a negative review. However, if someone is injured on your property, it's essential that you make sure the guest receives the medical attention required, and that you document everything that happens. If the guest refuses medical attention after an injury, have him or her put this in writing.

Once an incident happens, immediately create a detailed timeline, write everything down, take pictures, and try to find people who witnessed the events that led to the incident and the incident itself. Work with the local authorities as necessary, and consult with your lawyer, insurance company, and Airbnb as soon as possible.

What to Do If You Become a Victim of Airbnb-Related Fraud

While Airbnb-related fraud is not a common occurrence, it has been known to happen all over the world. For example, fraud occurs if a guest tries to extort money or a free stay from the host for any reason that is based on lies. In some cases, guests have been known to use the threat of a bad review to extort money or a free stay from the host.

According to Airbnb's website, "By posting a review, you agree to follow all Airbnb guidelines and policies, including the Extortion Policy, which Airbnb may enforce at our sole discretion. Failure to do so may result in the restriction, suspension, or termination of your Airbnb account." To learn more about Airbnb's Extortion Policy, visit www.airbnb.com/help/article/548/what-is-airbnb-s-extortion-policy.

Another rare issue that's been reported by Airbnb hosts is that guests invade the designated private areas of the host's property when the host is not home. One reason why a guest might invade a host's privacy is to steal or make copies of personal documents that provide the information needed for identity theft or other types of financial fraud.

As a host, consider investing in a personal safe, or keep financial documents, credit card statements, bank statements, your passport, and other legal documents locked up and away from where they can easily be viewed or taken by a guest. If someone is renting your entire property, put your incoming personal mail on hold or have your personal mail diverted to a post office box (as opposed to having it delivered to your actual address). You could also consider installing a security camera or motion sensor near the outside entrance to the designated private areas of the property that you also keep locked (such as your personal bedroom or the basement).

 NOTE

> Keeping *all* your personal, financial, tax-related, and legal paperwork and files off property, at another residence, within an in-home safe, or within a local bank's safety deposit box is a smart strategy. Also, do not keep a large amount of cash or expensive jewelry on the property when hosting guests.

If a guest gains access to your personal, legal, tax-related, and/or financial documents, this could lead to identity theft, credit card fraud, or other problems that you might not discover right away. In addition to storing these documents in a secure way, add password protection to your desktop and laptop computer(s), turn on the features that prevent guest users from installing or deleting software on that computer, or better yet, prevent guests from using any computers where you have personal, financial, or legal documents stored or from which you handle your personal finances or online banking.

If you suspect you may be a victim of identity theft, visit the Federal Trade Commission's IdentityTheft.gov website immediately (www.identitytheft.gov).

 TIP

Invest in a paper shredder and use it to destroy any paper-based documentation that you ultimately want to throw away. Don't just leave documents, bills, or bank statements, for example, that you plan to discard in a trash can that your guests have access to.

Another way to help protect yourself as a host is to initially communicate only with potential guests via Airbnb's secure messaging system. Until the potential guest books and pays for a reservation, Airbnb does not disclose your address, phone number, last name, or any other personal information about you.

If it becomes necessary to communicate with your paying guests on a more personal level, refrain from sharing too much information about yourself or providing details about your life that a potential criminal could use for identity theft or other fraudulent purposes. For example, be extremely cautious if a guest asks questions like, "Where do you do your banking?" or "How and where do you manage your retirement account or investment account?"

 WARNING

Whether or not a local or state government will strictly uphold ordinance that prevents hosts from using their property for short-term rentals can vary greatly and could change at any moment. Regardless of what advice you're given from the Airbnb website, make sure you fully understand the current local laws and ordinances that are in place related to your geographic area before offering your property as a short-term rental.

Meet Superhosts Chris and Joan Christiansen

Based in Silicon Valley, Airbnb Superhosts Chris and Joan Christiansen are a married couple who rent out rooms in their home via Airbnb—mostly to business professionals and students. They've been doing this successfully for more than seven years.

How did you get started with Airbnb?

Chris Christiansen: "What started it was that our kids grew up and moved out, so our home had several empty bedrooms. A friend of mine is a travel writer who spent more than six months staying at various Airbnb properties, so he gave us some guidance and encouragement. In our home, we currently have up to four separate bedrooms available for short-term rental."

Joan Christiansen: "We removed all reminiscences of our kids' belongings from each bedroom and replaced the décor and furnishings, so the bedrooms appeal to our guests. All our kids are grown and have their own homes, so they understand that their childhood bedroom is no longer their space anymore."

What makes your property unique?

Chris Christiansen: "Our home is located just a few blocks from one of the Google shuttles, so we've hosted Google interns for summers [when] they found us by determining where the shuttle stops are and then comparing that to where Airbnb properties are located. Outside of Airbnb, we've never done any marketing or advertising to promote the property."

Joan Christiansen: "I think the photos of our property that are featured within our Airbnb listing really do a good job at highlighting the space. We've taken all the photos ourselves. We would probably benefit from showcasing professionally taken photos, because we've had guests arrive to check in and say the house is much nicer than they thought it would be based on the photos. In addition, I think our location plays a huge role in the popularity of our property.

"Another thing we do is stay on top of all the changes constantly being made to the Airbnb platform, so when they expand the list of amenities we can highlight within the listing, we always update our listing to reflect the new options that apply.

Once Airbnb updates its master amenities list, even if a host offers those amenities, if they don't update their listing, it will look like the host does not offer them."

Before you started with Airbnb, what research did you do regarding local laws?

Chris Christiansen: "We did a lot of research on nightly pricing options and what the competition was doing, but we did not do any formal research about local laws. Airbnb, however, does have relationships with various municipalities in the San Jose area, so the service automatically collects and pays local taxes that are required, which makes our bookkeeping job a lot easier."

What would you say is the absolute best reason to become an Airbnb host?

Joan Christiansen: "We welcome a lot of international travelers. Our property is not located within or near a major tourist destination, so when we first started, we were not sure if anyone would be interested in staying with us for their vacation. The location, however, does appeal to a lot of business travelers, as well as temporary Google employees and interns who are in town for work for a three-month stretch.

"One of the most fun things is getting to know people from different parts of the world. It does vary a lot from guest to guest about how much they'll interact with us. Some guests are just looking for a place to sleep and we might say 100 words to each other over a three-month period. There are, however, plenty of guests we've become friendly with. In fact, we were recently invited to the wedding of one of our earlier guests."

Chris Christiansen: "Being able to cover our entire mortgage payment from the money earned from Airbnb is also a nice perk, especially since hosting is something we both really enjoy doing. We don't provide any meals for our guests, but they do have full access to our kitchen. Most people, however, don't eat here. Again, because of our location, we rarely have a vacationing guest stay for just a weekend, for example. Most are long-term bookings for one or two weeks, or up to three months. We've had some bookings from international guests, like a college student from Brazil, who started out with a weeklong booking as she was looking for long-term accommodations in the area, but they wound up staying with us for many months, instead of renting her own apartment. We currently don't offer one-night stays."

Do you think it's easier to accommodate long-term guests as a host, as opposed to accepting shorter bookings?

Joan Christiansen: "I think it's much easier to manage long-term guests in our home. Through Airbnb, this gives us a lot of flexibility, because we can schedule periods when we don't want guests in our home—when our own family comes to visit, for example. In between long-term guests, this gives us a chance to handle upkeep and maintenance issues and do a deep cleaning of the property without inconveniencing any guests."

Chris Christiansen: "As soon as we started hosting guests in our home, we hired a professional cleaning service to come in on a regular basis. A professional cleaner will do a much better job than we could do and it's more convenient for us."

How do you set your nightly pricing?

Joan Christiansen: "At first, I just did research on Airbnb to determine what similar properties in our geographic area were charging. I did not even know that dynamic pricing applications, like AirDNA [www.airdna.co/airbnb-pricing-tool], even existed. One thing we no longer do is accept the Airbnb recommended pricing, because I have found that it's very low and far less than people are willing to pay. We may lose a few bookings by avoiding the use of Airbnb's smart pricing tool, but over time, we've made more money. While we do not use Airbnb's smart pricing tool, we have purposely underpriced at various times, especially if someone we like has been staying with us and they want to extend their stay."

Chris Christiansen: "We also do not accept instant bookings. Because we're offering a shared space, we want to know in advance who will be staying with us and be able to refuse a booking. That said, we've never had a bad experience with a guest staying in our home. We have, however, had to tweak our House Rules for long-term guests to make it clear that they're responsible for cleaning their own dishes in the kitchen, for example. We also had a problem with people taking dishes into their bedroom to eat a meal, but not returning their dirty dishes to the kitchen when they were done. They were leaving dirty and smelly dishes in their bedroom until the cleaner removed them.

With multiple unrelated guests staying with you in your four bedrooms at any given time, do you ever have scheduling issues for them using the bathrooms or kitchen?

Joan Christiansen: "We have found that Google feeds its employees three times a day, so when we have one of their employees or interns staying with us, they rarely eat in our home, and they never cook for themselves. As for the bathrooms, two of them have their own full bath, while two bedrooms share a bathroom. I will never rent those two rooms that share a bathroom to guests who are not related or who are not traveling together. If I rent just one of those rooms to a single person or couple, I will automatically block that other room during their stay. That's my own policy. We have our own private bathroom, and there is a shared bathroom downstairs."

Since you do not accept instant bookings, are there specific types of guests you don't accept bookings from?

Joan Christiansen: "We do not allow families traveling with kids, because our home is not set up to accommodate them. We are also not pet-friendly. We have these polices clearly spelled out in our property listing on Airbnb."

What do you do on an ongoing basis to help ensure very positive reviews from guests?

Joan Christiansen: "We are very nice and accommodating people. In addition to that, I stay on top of cleaning responsibilities and replace anything, like towels, pillows, or linens, that start to look too worn."

On a day-to-day or weekly basis, how much time do you spend doing host-related duties?

Chris Christiansen: "Joan does most of the work related to being an Airbnb host. For her, it's a part-time job, especially since we have a cleaning service. Joan, however, does all the laundry in between a guest's stay, so how much work she has depends on how often people are coming and going. Even with the cleaning service, she always does extra cleaning when needed, to make sure there are never any candy wrappers or dust under the bed, for example."

Are there any other tips or pieces of advice you think new Airbnb hosts will find useful?

Joan Christiansen: "I think we're a bit unique in that we cater mostly to businesspeople. One thing we don't offer in any of the bedrooms is a TV, but nobody has ever asked for one. We found that our guests tend to stream their TV shows and movies from their laptop computer or tablet. We do have a large-screen TV in the living room, which is a common area, but people rarely use it. However, if we were catering more to vacationers, for example, I think having TVs with cable and streaming service access would be much more important. We do provide good Wi-Fi throughout the home, including within all of the bedrooms."

Communication Is Essential

As an Airbnb host, you have many opportunities to communicate with your prospective and booked guests, using text messaging, through phone conversations, and ultimately in person once the guest arrives at your property. Each time you have an interaction with a (prospective) guest, you can create a positive experience, or you can conduct yourself in a way that's off-putting and unprofessional. The choice is yours, and the result of each communication will ultimately contribute to whether someone offers you a booking, and then whether or not you receive a positive review and rating from that guest.

Thus far, you've read a handful of strategies that can help you consistently offer your guests top-notch hospitality. In the next chapter, more emphasis is put on how you should communicate and interact with people as an Airbnb travel host.

CHAPTER 7

Best Practices for Communicating with Guests

Good communication and hospitality skills are probably the most important talents you can possess if you want to be a host who consistently earns great reviews. Becoming a host is something you have chosen to do. It's a job that comes with a handful of responsibilities. Communicating and interacting with your guests in a positive, helpful, and unobtrusive way is among those responsibilities. And it's a very important one.

 TIP

The trick to communicating with guests properly is to gauge each guest's interest in how and when they want to be communicated with. You don't want to ignore them (unless this is something they request), but you don't constantly want to engage with them if they want their privacy. While you, or someone who represents you, needs to be available 24/7 if a problem arises, with a bit of experience and by using the strategies offered within this chapter, you'll discover the best and most effective ways to communicate with your guests.

By clearly and honestly conveying information in a friendly way, right from the start of each interaction you have with a prospective guest, you can easily avoid misunderstandings and help to ensure that each guest's stay goes as smoothly as possible. Doing this also benefits you, because as the host, you'll experience less hassle and have a much higher chance of earning positive reviews.

Your communication and hospitality skills are used when creating your personal profile and property listing, because what you write sets a tone and allows your potential guests to establish their initial expectations related to their upcoming stay. However, how you present yourself as a host once you start interacting through messages, email, or in person goes a long way toward making your guests feel welcome and comfortable when staying at your property.

 **WARNING**

> Unfortunately, there are some guests who, no matter how hard you try to appease them, will never be happy or content. They'll complain about the most mundane things, just because they can. In some cases, this is a ploy to get a discount. For some, complaining is just part of their personality. As a host, you'll want to identify these people early on and be prepared to deal with them as best as you can, while always maintaining a professional and friendly demeanor.
>
> The best thing you can do is listen. Try to determine why the guest is unhappy, make it clear you understand their grievance (no matter how ridiculous you think it is), and convey that you want to help. Try to apologize and appease them before they write a bad review or give you a bad rating. Some difficult and opinionated guests just want to be heard. Attempting to deal with their grievance before they check out and leave your property is your best approach.

You'll have the opportunity to communicate with your (potential) guests many times, including:

- During the inquiry process (via Airbnb's messaging system) when a potential guest can ask questions.

- During the reservation booking process (also via Airbnb's messaging system), when a potential guest requests a booking, assuming you have Airbnb's Instant Book feature turned off.

- Once a reservation has been made, when you need to coordinate with the guests when they'll arrive, plus answer any additional questions they have.

- When your guests arrive at your property and you potentially welcome them in person, provide a tour, and help them get settled in. This is best done in person by you, or someone acting as your representative, but as you'll learn shortly, it can be done other ways, too. Some hosts have devised ways to welcome their guests in an entirely automated way. This is perfectly acceptable, if your guests understand the check-in process in advance.

 TIP

You'll utilize your communication skills during all aspects of interaction you have with your prospective guests prior to their booking, upon their arrival, throughout their stay, and when they check out. This communication can happen using Airbnb's messaging system, via email, through text messaging, on the telephone, by leaving handwritten notes for your guests during their stay, and, of course, in person. Take advantage of these opportunities to make your guests feel welcome and comfortable.

- Throughout your guests' stay you can (and should) check in with them periodically to see how their stay is going, determine if they need anything, and ask if they have any questions or concerns. You can do this in person, by phone, or by text message. Depending on each guest's preferences, and the expectations you've set, you can be as involved as you'd like during a guest's stay by offering your services as a tour guide, dining companion, or informal concierge who is on hand to answer questions beyond the scope of their stay at your property.

- During the checkout process. This, too, should ideally be done in person by you or someone representing you, but it can be done in other ways as well. This is your final chance to iron out any problems before a guest writes and publishes their rating and review related to their stay.

In most cases, guests are paying less to stay at your property than they'd have to pay to stay at a hotel, motel, or bed-and-breakfast. As the host, you're not expected to offer the same level of personalized attention, service, and hospitality. After all, people who work at these places have had professional training to serve in the hospitality industry. However, if you're charging premium rates for a more luxurious property, guests will have much higher expectations that you'll need to properly manage with superior customer service.

 TIP

Your hospitality skills refer to your attitude, personality, and willingness to welcome your guests and make them feel truly welcome. It relates to how you interact with your guests throughout their stay and your actions in terms of whether you go out of your way to ensure the comfort and happiness of your guests. As a host, always acting in a professional manner is essential, no matter how your guests choose to act (even if they get angry or emotional). This continues to be essential even when you don't agree with their complaints, thoughts, or opinions.

Most of your guests will welcome communication with you and the hospitality you offer. Your guests will typically reward these extra efforts by providing you with an excellent rating and review (assuming the property itself meets or exceeds their expectations). Keep in mind, however, your guests are more apt to write a bad review or give you a bad rating for the most inconsequential thing but may not choose to provide a thoughtful and positive rating and review if they're happy with their stay and you've met or exceeded their expectations. Again, your goal as a host is to avoid those negative ratings and reviews—especially if your goal is to become a Superhost or you plan to continue offering your property as a short-term rental through Airbnb indefinitely.

 **WARNING**

> Airbnb will automatically delete words or phrases from a text-based conversation that's held using the messaging service if the content of that text reveals personal contact information. Until a host has a confirmed reservation, Airbnb requires that communication between the host and a potential guest happen exclusively through the platform's messaging system. Any attempt to share your contact information, including a phone number, email address, or social media username, will be blocked by the service.

Airbnb's Secure Messaging System

Airbnb's secure messaging system is provided for several important reasons. First, it allows (potential) guests and hosts to communicate using a real-time text messaging system, without having to reveal any personal information about themselves, such as their last name, phone number, or address. It's also convenient. One party can send a message, and the other party can respond instantly, or at their leisure, yet it's possible to have a full conversation and exchange important information.

For everyone's safety and security, the messaging system also maintains a complete record of every conversation that transpires, so you can easily look back and remember what you've been discussing. You will also have proof to show to Airbnb or the authorities if someone says something offensive, threatening, or inappropriate.

While you're engaged in a text messaging conversation, as a host, it's possible to view a guest's full profile and past reviews, view their payment details and reservation dates, see your own availability calendar, and quickly see things like reservation confirmations, preapprovals, special offers, or the rate a (prospective) guest is or will be paying. Also, while engaged in a conversation via the messaging service, a host can handle administrative tasks, like accepting or declining a reservation request.

 NOTE

> A message thread is a conversation between two parties that's displayed in the order that the messages were sent and received. A complete conversation transcript is created and viewable. Each conversation you have with a specific person is stored as a separate message thread, so you can quickly switch between conversations. This can be done via the Airbnb website and the Airbnb mobile app. Thus, you can easily communicate with people from your desktop computer, laptop computer, or mobile device, and switch between these devices as needed. You don't need to be tied to your desk to provide prompt responses.

This communication option becomes available the instant a potential guest sends an inquiry to a host or submits a reservation request. To use this service, it is necessary to be logged into your Airbnb account via the website or mobile app. In fact, anyone can freely switch between logging in to Airbnb via their internet-connected computer's web browser or the Airbnb mobile app, and all messaging content will remain synced and up to date.

To access the messaging system, click on the Messages option, and then from your Inbox, click on the message thread for the text message conversation you want to participate in. From the Messages option, you can respond to any incoming message, compose and then send a new message, or go back and review older messages (or complete message threads).

It's important to understand that this method of communication is not designed to manage lengthy conversations. Often, when people use a messaging service, like Facebook Messenger, to communicate with their friends or family members, they use emoticons, cute abbreviations, or sentence fragments within their messages. This is appropriate and acceptable. Keep in mind, when you're communicating with potential or actual guests, this is for business purposes, so your conversation should be friendly, but adopt a more professional approach that's void of emoticons and abbreviations like "LOL" (laugh out loud) or "TTYL" (talk to you later).

Try to use full sentences and phrasing that allow you to convey as much information as possible, in a way that's easy to understand and not open for interpretation or misunderstandings. Also, as a host, focus on providing the fastest response time possible, so your (potential) guests do not have to wait for multiple hours (or longer) to receive an answer to an important question. Hosts are expected to respond to incoming messages quickly and professionally. You should avoid using prewritten (canned) responses that are impersonal. In fact, refer to the person you're communicating with by name when it's appropriate and convenient.

Also, make it clear you understand what's being asked and respond accordingly. For example, if someone asks what your pet policy is, a good response might be, "Thanks for asking that, [insert name]. Our pet policy is…" Even if your property listing offers the answer to a question that's been asked, never refer someone back to the listing. Simply respond to the question by answering it in a complete, easy-to-understand, and friendly way.

 TIP

Just as with other online messaging services, the one offered by Airbnb allows you to participate in, and quickly switch between, multiple conversations (with different people). To help jog your memory about whom you're conversing with, you always have the option to click on the user's name to review their profile. It's also possible to scroll backward in each conversation to refresh your memory about what was previously discussed. Of course, you can also keep written notes about each person you're communicating with.

One of the nice features offered by the Airbnb messaging system is that it allows you to receive a push notification (alert or text message) on your smartphone each time a new incoming message or response to a previous message is received. Be sure to turn on this feature so you never miss an important message and you're able to respond to each incoming message as quickly as possible.

 TIP

A push notification or text message will be sent to your smartphone when you turn on Airbnb's Notifications feature. This means you don't have to constantly log into and check the Airbnb website or mobile app for new messages. Instead, you'll be alerted as soon as one is received. Once you receive a notification or text message, respond to the message as quickly as possible and provide a personalized and friendly response.

Remember, Airbnb does not permit hosts or guests to solicit the exchange of money directly between two parties. Any money that's exchanged (to pay for a reservation, cleaning fee, security deposit, or anything else) must go through Airbnb's platform. If a guest tries to extort money from you for any reason via the messaging system, or if a message is received that is inappropriate or threatening, immediately flag that message by clicking on the flag icon, and then do not continue communicating with that person until you have consulted with Airbnb.

Get to Know Your Guests before They Check In

Before guests arrive at your property to check in, the Airbnb messaging service offers a secure and somewhat informal way to interact with these people. As the host, it's important for you to be open and honest when responding to questions or concerns. If you're not honest or embellish the truth about something, you're apt to create false expectations. Doing this will often annoy a guest and result in a bad rating and review. However, you can also use this communication as an opportunity to get to know your guests in advance, by asking them questions and holding short, friendly conversations.

Without delving too deeply into someone's privacy, you can pose questions like:

- Have you ever been to this area before?

- What is the main reason for your visit?

- Do you want some advice about the fun things to do while you're here, so you can make advanced reservations and plan your itinerary?

- What are some of the things you plan to do while you're here?

- Would you be interested in spending some time during your stay so I can be your informal tour guide and show you around the area?

- As your host, I am happy to serve breakfast each morning or have muffins and coffee on hand. Is this something you're interested in?

- Do you have any special needs or allergies that I should know about that relates to your stay?

- What are your favorite hobbies? You can also share details about your own hobbies and offer to share that experience with guests.

You can also use this pre-arrival communication to share information with your pending guests and help you determine how much interaction they're looking to have with you (or your representative) once they arrive. For example, if they'll have a car, you can tell them where they should park when they arrive and what the local parking rules are. You can also ask questions about what time they'll be arriving, so you can be on hand to welcome them.

Immediately upon a guest's arrival, most will appreciate it if you offer them a bottle of water as you welcome them. If a guest is paying top dollar to use your entire property for a week or longer, you might also consider giving them a bottle of wine and some snacks as a welcome gift.

Welcome Guests in Person

Many hosts believe that it's important to be on hand at their property when guests first arrive. If you're not there in person, consider having your property manager or representative welcome them. This allows you to meet guests in person and handle some important tasks, including:

- Providing a tour of the property
- Reviewing the House Rules
- Helping guests settle in
- Providing front door keys (or a keyless-entry code) so guests can then come and go as they please
- Assist the guests in carrying their luggage to their guestroom

During the initial welcome, be sure to make your guests feel as comfortable as possible and make it clear that you're available to answer their questions or address any concerns they have. During the tour, explain what areas of your property are private. Then, at the conclusion of the property tour, ask if guests need anything right away, or if they anticipate needing extra blankets, pillows, or towels, for example. Also inquire if the guestroom temperature is comfortable for them, and let them know how to adjust the temperature, if possible. Finally, make it clear that you (or your representative) are available 24/7 if an emergency or serious problem arises. Explain the best ways to contact you, whether it's via your cell phone or, if you live on the property, by knocking on your door.

Other Ways to Welcome Your Guests

If, for whatever reason, you can't be on hand to welcome your guests when they first arrive, you have two options. First, have a representative (who you trust) welcome them. This can be a hired property manager, a neighbor, friend, or family member. Second, you can prearrange how and where guests will obtain a key (or keycode) to the property, and then provide them with a detailed welcome letter and house manual that provides all of the information they need to know. You can then follow up with a phone call or text message to ensure they've arrived and settled in smoothly.

This second option is the least personal but is typically used if you're renting out a vacation home or secondary property that is nowhere near your primary residence. Should you opt to utilize this method, have multiple contingency plans in place in case there's a problem upon their arrival that requires in-person attention.

 TIP

> Having someone who represents you, such as a neighbor or property manager, welcome your guests is less personal than handling this task yourself. Make sure the person who will greet your guests is friendly, knowledgeable about the property, reliable, and equipped to handle any situations that may arise, including an unexpected early or late arrival by your guest.

Interacting with Guests during Their Stay

Whether you're living at the property and sharing it with your guests, or your guests have rented your entire property for one day, several days, a week, or longer, maintaining an open line of communication with them is essential. It's important that you make your guests feel comfortable contacting you with their questions, problems, or concerns—before and during their stay.

For example, if your guests are staying in a guestroom that they find too hot or too cold at night, and this impacts their quality of sleep, they need to feel comfortable asking you how to adjust the temperature or for alternate types of bedding and blankets, to rectify the situation.

As the host, if you're nowhere to be found, and guests are not comfortable calling or texting you, and they're forced to be uncomfortable during their stay, this will ultimately be held against you when they write their review. However, this is an example of a problem that could easily be addressed and fixed if you're accessible.

 TIP

Common questions you'll need to be able to address quickly include helping guests connect to the property's Wi-Fi and explaining how to use the television set (with whatever cable, satellite, or streaming services are accessible). If you provide appliances, such as a washer and dryer or coffee maker, the guest may need instruction or a demonstration on how to use this equipment, even if you include step-by-step directions within the house manual.

If you work during the day, or are unreachable during specific hours, make this clear up front. Then, make a point to check in periodically with your guests during a break from work, to respond to their messages as quickly as possible.

In addition to waiting for your guests to reach out to you, plan to initiate contact with them periodically during their stay. For example, when they wake up, be on hand in the kitchen or living room to say "good morning" and offer them some coffee. As they're going out for dinner in the evening, ask how their stay is going, and determine if they need anything.

If you suspect your guest does need something, and you can predict this need, offer it before they ask. Understanding and anticipating the wants, needs, and concerns of your guest will help you become an excellent host.

Keep in mind, there's a big difference between being available and attentive and being intrusive. If your guests want to be left alone and have minimal interaction with you, respect their wishes, but also be attentive to providing what they need. In this situation, perhaps leave a handwritten note on their bed (or attached to the outside of their guestroom door) that says, "I hope you're enjoying your stay thus far. Please let me know if you need anything." Be sure to include your cell phone number within the note.

 TIP

> Your house manual should be included in the welcome letter presented to guests upon their arrival. To download a free sample welcome letter that you can customize to include your own property's information, visit https://hosttools.com/blog/short-term-rental-tips /airbnb-house-manual.

If you sense that a guest wants to spend time chatting or join you for a meal, consider extending a friendly invitation, making sure it will not be perceived as an unwanted sexual advance. Some hosts take on the same role as someone who runs a professional bed-and-breakfast and go out of their way to provide ongoing, professional-level hospitality, as well as personalized service and extra amenities during a guest's stay. Others focus on their core responsibilities as a host—to provide a clean, comfortable, and safe place to stay—but are less social with their guests during the length of their stay. The approach you adopt is up to you and should be based on your own personality and long-term goals as an Airbnb host.

Again, how much interaction you have, and when this interaction takes place, is a matter of what you're willing to offer, while respecting your guests' wishes and needs. Look for subtle cues from your guests in terms of what their expectations are from you as the host, and then do your best to meet or exceed those expectations.

TIP

Often saying something as simple as, "Good morning," "How is your afternoon going?" "Are you comfortable in your guestroom?" or "Do you need any additional pillows or blankets?" will go a long way toward making a guest feel good about having you as a host.

Recap of What Your House Manual Should Include

Your house manual should be a well-written and easy-to-understand document that welcomes your guests and goes on to explain your House Rules and everything they need to know about the property to get the most enjoyment during their stay. The house manual should be included within your property listing (as part of the Guest Resources section) and available in printed form upon each guest's arrival.

Each topic within the house manual should be given its own descriptive heading/title. Some hosts choose to create a separate printed page for each topic and provide the entire document in a three-ring binder with printed section tabs for easy reference.

At the very least, your house manual should include the following information:

- A welcome message.
- Your contact information, including your phone number and email address. Make it clear what the best way to reach you is during the day and at night.
- Check-in and check-out times.
- Parking instructions.
- Directions for connecting to the property's Wi-Fi (from their laptop computer and mobile devices).
- A complete list of House Rules.

- Directions for how to use all applicable equipment and appliances, including the smart door locks / alarm system, coffee maker, washer/dryer, and television set.

- How and where to find local transportation. Consider providing up-to-date schedules and route maps, or the website address or mobile app for the public transportation services in your area.

- A listing of fun and interesting things to do, including local attractions, museums, historical sights, and activities.

- A listing of local restaurants and dining options, including places that offer takeout and/or delivery.

- Emergency information. This should include the phone numbers for the local police, fire department and ambulance service, information about the local hospital or walk-in medical centers, a listing of nearby pharmacies, and any other local resources you believe a guest might need. Also, list where smoke detectors, fire extinguishers, a first aid kit, and other emergency equipment are located within your property.

Recap of Common House Rules

The House Rules you choose to enforce at your property will have a lot to do with the type of guests you welcome, your personal preferences, and what you believe will keep you, your neighbors, and your guests happy. Some of the most common House Rules hosts choose to list and enforce include:

- No parties or events allowed.

- No smoking or vaping allowed (including the use of marijuana in places where it's legal).

- No illegal substances on the property.

- Your pet policy.

- No unregistered guests allowed to spend the night, and no more than [insert number] of visitors at once during the day.

- Where guests can eat and drink. For example, you could say, no food or drinks in the bedroom.

- Hours in which you enforce quiet hours. Define this by playing loud music, speaking too loudly, or turning up the volume of the TV. (This will depend on the type of property you're offering.) For example, if the guest will be sharing the property with you (as the host) or other guests, quiet hours might be from 11 p.m. until 8 a.m.

- Whether or not a guest can adjust the heat or air-conditioning.

- A request that the posted check-in and check-out times be respected unless previous arrangements are made and approved by the host.

- Your lost key policy (if you have traditional door locks as opposed to smart locks).

- How you expect furnishings to be cared for (i.e., no jumping on the beds, no moving the furniture around, etc.).

- A request that guests clean their own dirty dishes and clean up the kitchen after themselves.

- How and where to dispose of trash.

- Where and how to find or request extra towels, sheets, blankets, pillows, and other necessities, if needed.

How to Offer Additional Customer Service and Amenities

Depending on how much your guests are paying per night, what information you included within your property listing, and what expectations your guests have developed, in addition to whatever amenities you've promised within the property listing, you always have the option of offering additional amenities on a complimentary basis.

For example, if you happen to be cooking breakfast or preparing a pot of coffee in the morning, invite your guest to join you, and don't charge them for the food or coffee.

However, if you list additional services or amenities you have to offer within your property listing, and state an extra fee applies, you then can charge those applicable extra fees. For example, you might charge a per-hour rate to spend time with a guest driving them around your city (in your own car) and acting as their tour guide, allow them to rent a bicycle from you, or charge them extra for preparing them a home-cooked dinner every evening.

Based on Airbnb's guidelines, if you opt to charge a guest for value-added extras, above and beyond the nightly rate to stay at your property, these fees must be described in advance and then collected via the Airbnb platform. As the host, you're not supposed to accept payments directly from your guests for any extra services or amenities you provide. This is also the case with virtual Airbnb Experiences you offer to guests.

 TIP

> Based on your situation and what you're offering, you may discover that simply increasing your nightly rate and then providing extra services or amenities will be more acceptable to your guests, as opposed to charging them a nightly rate and then requesting additional fees for extra services/amenities that you choose not to include for that nightly rate.

The Difference between an On-Location, Local, and Remote Host

For the purposes of this book, an Airbnb host can manage their property in one of three ways:

1. They can live on the property and rent out a room or area of their home.

2. They can live and work nearby, be readily available to guests, but not live/ stay on the short-term rental property.

3. They can be a remote host (located far away from the rental property). In this situation, you'll need a representative or property manager to be near your short-term rental property.

Airbnb hosts have found all three hosting methods can be successful if handled correctly. Whichever method you opt to use, make sure your guests know how to reach someone if a question or problem arises and that there's someone you trust nearby to inspect and manage the property in between guests, make repairs (or hire repair people), and clean the property (or manage the cleaners you hire).

Hiring a Property Manager or Airbnb Local Partner Is an Option

To take some of the responsibilities off yourself, you can hire a professional property manager or Airbnb Local Partner. In addition to managing your short-term rental property, a property manager or Airbnb Local Partner can handle communication with your guests. The best way to find a reliable and experienced property manager is through a personal referral or from another Airbnb host. You can also find listings within Airbnb host-related Facebook groups or by doing a search online.

The Hostaway.com website offers free information and strategies for hiring an Airbnb property manager, which you can find at www.hostaway.com /how-to-hire-an-airbnb-property-manager.

 NOTE

According to OnlineDegree.com, "An Airbnb property manager manages one or more condos or homes that are rented out to guests as vacation properties. They're responsible for marketing their properties, managing reservations, and booking stays, as well as many of the day-to-day cleaning, stocking, and key exchange responsibilities." While compensation for property managers varies greatly, the hourly wage is between $18 and $45 per hour, with $28 per hour being the national average. By 2024, it's projected there will be more than 52,100 Airbnb property managers operating within the United States. Most are self-employed, although some work for management companies. Some property managers earn a percentage of your rental income. This percentage will range between 20 and 50 percent.

While working with a property manager costs money, it makes it easier to own and operate a short-term rental property when you don't live on that property or you're unable to dedicate the time needed to offer proper hosting services.

Another option is to team up with nearby Airbnb hosts and create a hosting team where you help each other out by serving as a host for each other's properties when needed. Information about how to create an Airbnb hosting team can be found at www.airbnb.com/help/article/970 or www.airbnb.com/help/article/2514.

Meanwhile, Airbnb also offers its "Local Partner" program, which is designed to help Airbnb hosts partner with people certified to assist with hosting duties. To learn more about this program, visit www.airbnb.com/d/hosting-services. To find an Airbnb Local Partner, visit www.airbnb.com/hosting-services/location.

Meet Airbnb Superhost Nathan Waldon

Airbnb Superhost Nathan Waldon owns and operates two gift shops in Oakland, California. Running these shops continues to be his full-time job, but he personally wanted to invest in a weekend getaway cabin in Sonoma County. Since he only utilizes this home one or two weekends per month, he discovered that offering it as a short-term rental property on Airbnb was a great way to generate enough money to cover the mortgage on the home.

He's now been operating the cabin as a short-term rental through Airbnb for more than six years and maintains his Superhost status. In early 2023, Waldon was recruited by Airbnb to be a community host leader for the Sonoma/Napa region. He now runs a Facebook page for Airbnb hosts in the region and plans networking events for fellow hosts.

What inspired you to purchase a property in Sonoma County and then offer it as a short-term rental?

Nathan Waldon: "I really wanted a vacation home for myself located in the country, since I live in a city. The Airbnb platform made it easier for me to buy the property and justify the expense, because I knew the revenue it would generate as a short-term rental would offset the cost of its purchase and maintenance. At the time, however, I did not anticipate that operating the property as a short-term rental would be equivalent to operating a small, part-time business."

How did you choose the Sonoma County location and the property itself?

Nathan Waldon: "I did a lot of research and found the perfect cabin that is right in the middle of a redwood forest, so the surroundings are spectacularly beautiful. First and foremost, we were looking for the perfect weekend getaway home for us.

"We wanted it to be located less than two hours away from the city, so commuting back and forth would not be too time consuming or difficult. We also wanted natural beauty so we could feel like we're surrounded by nature and not want to leave. As an Airbnb property, I think its popularity is mainly because of its location. It's located in a charming river town that has a very tourist-friendly and eclectic vibe. It's also less than 10 miles from the ocean and there are many local wineries nearby.

"We typically use the cabin for one weekend per month. The rest of the time, it's pretty much fully booked up by Airbnb guests. If there is a last-minute cancellation, we might drop everything and go for a second weekend during a month. Financially, Airbnb allows the cabin to pay for itself, but this took a few years to achieve. I only use the Airbnb platform to rent the cabin. I handle all the bookings myself using the Airbnb website and app. The cabin, however, is cleaned and maintained between guests by a professional service. Airbnb is a company and brand that really resonates with me. We share a lot of the same core values. Now that I am a community host leader, I have met a lot of other Airbnb hosts and have discovered it takes a certain type of person to become successful doing this. A lot of us have similar values and personalities.

"At least in my region, there is plenty of business to go around, so I have found that Airbnb hosts really support each other. It's amazing how sharing we are. The only time we tend to get tight lipped is when we find a reliable cleaning service. There is a shortage of good cleaners."

How much research did you do before purchasing your cabin?

Nathan Waldon: "I did extensive research related to individual communities, local short-term rental ordinances, and how popular specific areas are with tourists. Each county and town in California [has] its own set of regulations, which have become a lot stricter in recent years. For example, in the area where we purchased our cabin, there is a rule that each owner can only own one property that is used for short-term vacation rentals, and an LLC cannot own a short-term rental property. When I was looking at properties, I purposely chose a real estate agent who was well versed in the vacation rental business. He knew what was going on with local legislation, such as the fact that the property needed to have its own parking area, since no street parking is permitted."

Now that you've been an Airbnb host for more than six years, what would you say is the absolute best reason for someone to become a host?

Nathan Waldon: "I don't think hosting is for everyone. You don't necessarily need previous experience in the hospitality industry to be successful, but you do need to have a hospitality spirit. If you have the type of personality who likes to make people happy, those are the people who are the happiest and best hosts. If you're only in it for the money, buy a hotel. Being an Airbnb host means that you're sharing your home, whether you live in it full-time or not."

Because you live about two hours from your cabin, do you have a property manager who meets guests and handles their needs locally?

Nathan Waldon: "For me, the whole reservation and check-in process is totally automated. However, part of the local law is that I need to have someone locally who is on call 24/7 to deal with problems or emergencies. I use another local Airbnb host who lives five minutes from the cabin to be my property manager. She runs her own Airbnb short-term rental, but I keep her on a monthly retainer to manage my property as well. Over the years, we have become very close friends. Through the Facebook group I operate for fellow Airbnb hosts, we offer referral to regional professional property managers who we found to be reliable.

"Some of the things I do to weed out undesirable guests who might want to throw a party in the cabin, for example, is that I require a three-night minimum stay, particularly on weekends. Most guests who cause problems only want to stay at a property for just one night. During the week, I have a two-night minimum, but never allow just a one-night stay."

What do you do to maximize your income as an Airbnb host?

Nathan Waldon: "I keep the property in pristine condition and offer a lot of high-end and luxurious amenities that allow me to charge a premium nightly rate. The cabin is furnished with extremely luxurious bedding, pillows, and towels. The entire place is designed and decorated beautifully, both inside and outside. And I do a good job marketing this within the property listing, so it appeals to a more upscale guest. I charge premium pricing all year, and never discount my rate, even during the off-season. I also charge a higher rate on weekends and during holidays.

"Through research, I looked at comparable homes and the level of amenities they offered. When I started off, I kept my pricing in line with the competition. However, as soon as I started to earn a lot of very positive reviews, I gradually raised my rates. At this point, in my region, my nightly rate is typically the second highest on Airbnb. I think there is a mindset among upscale travelers that when they see the higher rate, they're more apt to book it because they believe they'll be staying at a more luxurious property and they're willing to pay for that experience. Over the years, I have found a sweet spot in my pricing that people are willing to pay for the accommodations I am offering them."

What are some of the premium amenities you offer to meet the higher expectations of your high-paying guests?

Nathan Waldon: "I offer nice French bath products at the ready for them. I also provide a gift for guests upon check-in, which might be a custom candle or a local bottle of wine. All the linens and towels are luxurious. The Serta mattresses, duvet covers, blankets, and towels are also all premium quality. The plush towels, for example, are imported from Belgium. Plus, the kitchen is stocked with high-end cookware and dishes. The kitchen is also stocked with high-end olive oils and spices, for example, along with every kitchen gadget you can imagine. Within the kitchen is also a library of cookbooks.

"As a rule, I replace all the white towels and linens every four months, whether they show signs of wear or not. I also provide separate beach towels, so guests are not bringing the expensive towels to the beach.

"Outside, the property offers a beautiful flower garden and separate herb garden. I encourage guests to pick fresh herbs to use when they're cooking. I try to offer an experience that a premium hotel could not, but still be within the price range of a premium hotel.

"A successful host needs to make sure all areas of their property are always clean, and that the cleaning is done consistently. One of my pet peeves is dirty windows. I don't believe this is acceptable, but I see plenty of Airbnb listings where the windows are so dirty, you can barely see out of them. Cleaning the windows, inside and outside, takes time. This is something that makes a difference, however.

"My cabin is also pet-friendly. I do not charge extra when someone brings their pet. I try to avoid having parents bring their toddlers to the cabin, because after they leave, I will find sticky fingerprints everywhere. The cleaning person literally needs to crawl around on the ground to spot all the fingerprints and smudges that are low down on the walls. My cleaner charges me based on how long she's there, so having to do extra chores to make sure the cabin is perfectly prepared for the next guests costs me more money."

What are tricks you discovered for maintaining an Airbnb profile that gets attention?

Nathan Waldon: "I think showcasing professionally taken photography is the most important thing. You need to invest in a great photographer. I make a point to completely update my photography at least every two years to reflect all the changes and upgrades made to the cabin. My listing contains at least 30 images at any given time. The photos showcase the cabin's insides, its entrance, and its outdoor surroundings. In the bedrooms, I would never include a photo that shows an extension cord running across a bedroom floor, for example. If not done correctly, photography can accentuate the negatives in a property and will draw someone's eye to those negatives. This is something you need to be mindful of when choosing your photos. Also, make sure the beds are made, the pillows are fluffed, and everything is put away and clean when photos are being taken of your property. I can't tell you how many listings I have seen of properties where the hosts didn't even bother to make the bed or clean the floors before taking their photos.

"I also think it's essential to keep the house looking fresh. I stage the house with little decorative touches that will appeal to the guests. I never forget that, as an Airbnb host, I am working in hospitality and competing with hotels that really understand how to offer hospitality.

"When composing the text for an Airbnb property listing, if you're not a good writer yourself, hire a professional copywriter who will know what words to use to make your property seem more appealing."

How important is it to be a Superhost?

Nathan Waldon: "For normal, average-priced properties it certainly does not hurt since it can be one more positive thing that sets your property apart from the competition. I also think there is a large percentage of Airbnb travelers who specifically seek out this accreditation when choosing their accommodations. If you're offering a luxury property, I feel being a Superhost is expected and an unofficial requirement."

Never Accept Money Directly from Guests

If you need to charge a guest more money to cover damages, for example, always use the Airbnb platform to handle these financial transactions. If you run into a problem, take advantage of the Airbnb Resolution Center (www.airbnb.com/resolutions).

Likewise, if guests want to extend their stay with you, this should be handled through the Airbnb platform as well. As the host, never agree to extend a guest's stay (perhaps at a discounted rate), and then be paid directly in cash for the additional nights. Among other reasons for not accepting direct payments is that most home or renter's insurance policies do not cover short-term rentals, and if you've collected money for services outside of the Airbnb platform, you will not qualify for the AirCover protection (www.airbnb.com/aircover-for-hosts) from Airbnb.

As an Airbnb host, your long-term success will depend on you following Airbnb's rules and procedures, while simultaneously catering to the needs of your guests. After all, your ability to obtain future bookings (and possibly become an Airbnb Superhost) will depend heavily on the ratings and reviews you earn. The power of positive reviews and ratings is the focus of the next chapter.

CHAPTER 8

The Power of Positive Reviews

Reviews and rating are opinions that other people rely on to make educated decisions about things like what movies to watch, what music to listen to, what products to purchase, and where they should stay when they travel. As a community, Airbnb relies heavily on a review- and rating-based system to help hosts and guest alike make intelligent choices.

Travelers can use ratings and reviews to figure out which Airbnb properties past guests have really liked and which hosts are the most hospitable, while hosts can evaluate a guest's past reviews to determine whether to accept a booking request (assuming the host has the Instant Book feature turned off).

Most Airbnb travelers base their accommodations-related decision on several factors, including location, price, property description, property photos, property reviews/ratings, and host reviews/ratings. For example, if a traveler is planning to stay for a few nights in the Washington, D.C., area and is looking for a private room, they'll have hundreds of options to choose from. Assuming they narrow down their selection to a handful of properties in the same price range, that are in the same general area, and that offer the same basic amenities, the decision about where to stay will likely come down to which property and host has the best ratings and reviews.

TIP

Keep in mind, a review on Airbnb is text-based, and is written by either a guest (to describe their experience staying at an Airbnb property) or a host (to describe a guest). Once a review is published on Airbnb, it can seldom be edited or deleted after 48 hours of being published—unless extenuating circumstances apply. However, if one party does not agree with the other party's review, a text-based comment or reply can be added that offers the other party's point of view or response.

In fact, many savvy Airbnb travelers (your potential guests) won't even consider staying at a property that doesn't have an average four- to five-star rating, based on at least a dozen reviews. Most won't stay with a host with below a five-star rating, or who has not earned the Superhost accreditation.

Each written review is accompanied by a star-based rating. The person writing a review is asked to provide between one (worst) and five (best) stars related to a series of categories, which will be discussed shortly. These individual star-based ratings are combined into an average star-based rating, which considers how many reviews the average is based on. So, if a host, for example, has an overall average five-star rating based on 50 reviews, that's a lot more impressive than a host with an average three-star rating that's based on only 10 reviews.

How the Airbnb Community Utilizes Reviews

Airbnb reviews are based on a specific person's opinions—which may or may not be accurate and that are highly subjective. For example, you might stay at a property and write a review that states the bathroom was spotless. However, someone else might visit that same property and write a less favorable review because they noticed the trash can in the bathroom had not been emptied recently and was bothered by that. An Airbnb guest might penalize a host for minor inconveniences, like finding dust under the bed or a small amount of soap scum in the shower stall. Therefore, hosts must be diligent about maintaining a spotless property, especially since many travelers are more germ conscious than ever due to the COVID-19 pandemic.

Thus, while every review and rating you receive as a host is important, and should be highly favorable, your average ratings are equally important. These consider the opinions, reviews, and ratings of multiple people. Thus, if 10 different guests rate a bathroom as being less than spotless, chances are the critique has some validity. Keep in mind, a repeated negative comment will be held against you, impact your booking frequency, and limit your ability to charge a nightly rate that's equal or higher than a host with better ratings and reviews.

Some travelers will invest the time to read every review a host and their property has received. Others will invest just a few seconds to look at the average star ratings the host and property have earned when making their decision about where to stay.

Ultimately, as a host, if you have many more negative or neutral reviews than positive ones, this is going to cost you a lot of future business. Far fewer potential guests are going to risk staying with you, especially if there are numerous other Airbnb properties in the area that have earned higher reviews and better ratings. Most Airbnb travelers are willing to spend a bit more for the assurance that where they choose to stay is clean, comfortable, and safe. Far fewer Airbnb travelers than ever before are simply looking for bargain accommodations, and those that are may not be the most desirable people for you to host.

How Reviews Work on Airbnb

When a guest looks at an initial listing for a property, each listing displays photos of the property, a headline, the nightly rate, the type of accommodation being offered (private room, shared room, entire house, etc.), and how many guests the property can accommodate. Along with other information presented in a snapshot format, a thumbnail photo of the host, the average star rating the property has received (between one and five stars), and an indication of how many reviews that average rating is based upon are also showcased.

As the host, you get to customize the listing for your property. You can write an attention-getting headline, offer a competitive nightly rate (that you set), and showcase awesome-looking property photos, for example. At the same time, you can forgo including a profile photo of yourself, or just write something very basic for your headline. Your listing, however, automatically showcases your average star-based rating and the number of reviews you've received. There's no way to hide this rating and review information.

Once you capture someone's attention with your property's listing, and that person clicks on that listing to view more information, a vast amount of additional information is displayed about your property. Plus, a potential guest can click or tap on your name and/or thumbnail profile photo to view your personal profile.

As potential guests view your full property listing, they can see all the images you've published with your listing. To keep the property listing current, which is looked upon as favorable by Airbnb's search algorithm, many hosts opt to update their property listing and photos on a regular basis. Whether you do this every two weeks, every month, or every quarter, for example, is up to you, but hosts that are diligent about keeping their profile and photos fresh tend to receive more views from potential guests. No matter how often you update your property listing and photos, however, it's impossible to hide or take attention away from your ratings and reviews.

 TIP

If your property has received no ratings or reviews to date, this is the only situation where no star-based rating is displayed, and no mention of reviews will be showcased in conjunction with your property listing. This, too, however, will often prevent cautious travelers from booking your property, unless they're given a significant discount. Therefore, it's a good strategy to have a few of your friends pay to stay at your property (at a discount) when you first open it up to Airbnb guests, so these people can provide and publish your initial reviews.

In addition to your property's average star-based rating, there's also a Ratings Summary chart, which offers average star ratings based on a handful of categories. Here's a quick alphabetical synopsis of what each of these highly subjective rating categories relates to:

- *Accuracy.* This allows someone to determine how accurate, forthcoming, and honest the host is related to their property listing, as well as the information the host shared with their guest(s) during their messaging conversations, for example. If you embellish facts, outright lie to your guests, or create false expectations, it will come back to haunt you in the form of a low Accuracy rating.

- *Check-In.* This rating relates to how welcome the guest felt when they first arrived at the property, and how smoothly the initial introductions and property tour went. If someone arrives at your property at the mutually-agreed-upon time to check in, but you are nowhere to be found, this could result in a poor check-in rating. If you're a host who relies on automated smart door locks, and you fail to provide a guest with the right code, this, too, will typically be held against you as the host. Likewise, if you welcome the guest, but forgo a tour and simply hand the guest a key, and then walk away, this demonstrates a lack of hospitality, which will typically result in a lower check-in rating, unless you've set up expectations so the guest knows they will not be greeted in person but will have easy access to the property upon their arrival.

- *Cleanliness.* This relates to the overall cleanliness of the property, including the bedroom(s), bathroom(s), and common areas. As a result of COVID-19, this is a rating that most Airbnb travelers now give extra attention and importance to.

- *Communication.* This is a rating based on a host's response time when communicating with a guest and whether the responses provided were accurate, helpful, and easily understandable. If a guest asked five questions as they booked their reservation, for example, but the host responded by answering only one of the questions after a 15-hour wait, this would result in a poor communication rating.

- *Location.* This rating relates to how convenient the property's location is to local landmarks, attractions, points of interest, public transportation, nearby shopping, restaurants, bars, or whatever the guest is personally interested in. Again, this is highly subjective, based on each guest's unique interpretation of what they deem as being convenient in accordance with the area they wanted or needed to stay in.

- *Value.* Based on your nightly rate and what your property offers in terms of comfort, cleanliness, safety, amenities, and your hospitality, each guest is asked to rate whether staying with you and paying your nightly rate is a good value. For example, if you're charging a competitive nightly rate but offering a bunch of complimentary amenities that go above and beyond what most Airbnb hosts offer, you'll typically receive a high value rating (five stars) from a guest for this category.

List All Positive Changes and Upgrades to Your Property within Your Property Listing(s)

The month and year a review was published is displayed in conjunction with each review. So, if a review is more than six months old, chances are the host has made changes to the property and its offerings, so that older review may no longer be representative of what a future guest will experience. If this is the case for your property, be sure you promote this clearly in the description.

For example, if you have added a brand-new bed with a new mattress into the guestroom, promote this in your property listing's description, and state when the new bed and mattress were added. This also applies to new appliances, new furnishings, or a redesign of a property's interior or exterior. Accompany the text describing the improvements or additions with updated photos.

Remember, if a potential guest sends you a message (via Airbnb's messaging service) prior to requesting a booking, you can use this opportunity to mention what new amenities you're now offering.

The ratings chart that's displayed with each property listing gives a prospective guest a good idea about what other people have experienced staying at the selected property, particularly if the average ratings are based on dozens or hundreds of reviews from past guests. This, too, is clearly displayed. The number next to a property listing's average star-based rating indicates how many reviews that property has received. As a host, keep in mind that not all guests will publish a rating or review after their stay, although this is strongly encouraged by Airbnb.

By scrolling down further when viewing a property listing, prospective guests can read each individual text-based review that was written by past guests. For someone to be able to write a review, however, they must have already stayed with that host as a paying guest booked through Airbnb.

 **WARNING**

Anyone who views your property description while visiting the Airbnb platform can click or tap on the Report This Listing option if they believe any information that you've provided is false, offensive, discriminatory, or misleading. Any time a listing is flagged, it will be reviewed by someone at Airbnb.

As you'll discover, some past guests will write long and detailed reviews about their experience staying at an Airbnb property (utilizing the maximum number of words that's allowed). Others will write one short sentence or phrase, like "Great place" or "We had a wonderful stay," and quickly provide their star ratings. Many guests, especially if they've had a positive experience staying with you, will forego writing a review altogether (which saves them time, but doesn't help you to build up your credibility as a host). Thus, one of your challenges will be getting your guests to write and publish a review and submit their ratings after their checkout.

It's important to understand that, as a host, the Airbnb platform automatically tracks your performance when it comes to your response rate and response times. This information is displayed as part of your property listing. This is another reason why responding to all incoming inquiries from potential guests in a very timely manner is so important.

 TIP

> When searching for a place to stay, potential guests can use Airbnb's Search tool to add a filter for properties that accept instant bookings. Some Airbnb travelers rely heavily on this feature because it saves them time when making a confirmed reservation once they choose where they want to stay. Airbnb also gives search result placement preference to properties that have the Instant Book feature turned on. As a host, the drawback to doing this is that you have no say whatsoever about who can stay with you. Once an instant booking is made by a guest, as a host, you're expected to honor it, or you will be penalized.

Some Ratings Say a Lot, While Others Don't

Many frequent Airbnb travelers take their responsibility to write a review of their accommodations and hosts very seriously. Others just publish a very short text-based review along with their rating. There are also plenty of guests who, upon checkout, never leave a review at all.

A brief review, such as, "Beautiful sunrises!!! Fit a family of five just right!!! Can't beat the waterfront access!!!" says a lot in just a few words. Another short review for the same property stated, "Property exactly as advertised. Perfect place in a perfect location. Amazing sunrise." These two, albeit short reviews, make it clear the property met expectations and that the sunrises at the location were stunning.

However, the following, more detailed review, again of the same property, is even more helpful to a potential future guest. It stated, "We decided to have a family getaway over the New Year's weekend. I am so glad I came across this Airbnb home. Entering was easy, and the house was very clean, and the location was great, at this time of the year it was so peaceful…. Just sitting in the Airbnb enjoying family was wonderful, we have plenty of food and beverage with all the necessities in the kitchen, TVs in the living room and two bedrooms, one bedroom without a TV. Exiting was easy, as we followed the directions. Thank you host."

Another longer review stated, "This stay was a weekend getaway for college friends for over 40 years. The place met our needs: clean, on the water, room for each of us to have our own beds, provided most of the amenities wanted, and peaceful. The host was always responsive to our questions before and while there. We totally enjoyed our fall beach stay. We lucked out with 70 degrees one afternoon and went to [location] after the rain blew over."

In the minute or two it just took to read these reviews; you got a pretty good understanding about the quality and cleanliness of the property and how helpful the host is. These are the types of reviews you should strive for as a host. As you probably guessed, this property has an overall 4.89 (out of 5-star) rating, based on more than 50 reviews, along with these category-specific ratings: Cleanliness: 4.8, Accuracy: 4.9, Communication: 4.9, Location: 5.0, Check-In: 4.9, and Value: 4.7.

A Property's Location Is Extremely Important, Too

Another element of each property listing is a detailed map that shows your property's location, as well as other points of interest listed within your optional house guidebook. Upon reading your property listing, a potential guest can click on the Similar Listings link that is included at the bottom of their screen or click on the Request to Book button to make a reservation if you have the Instant Book feature turned off. When the Instant Book feature is turned on, anyone viewing your listing can instantly make a confirmed reservation by clicking or tapping on the Reserve button and making their payment.

Keep in mind, when anyone using the Airbnb service views your personal profile, they can see the number of reviews you have received and whether you've been verified. Also displayed on your profile page are the reviews from guests you've received as a host, as well as reviews from hosts you've received when you've traveled and stayed at other Airbnb properties as a guest.

Many savvy Airbnb travelers will look at a potential host's profile page to read all the host's past reviews to learn more about them. These same people will look for the Verified badge and the Superhost badge when evaluating you as a potential host.

Hosts Can Be Fined for Canceling a Reservation

As a host, if you cancel a guest's confirmed reservation for a reason that Airbnb does not consider to be an extenuating circumstance, a negative review will automatically be added to your profile that Airbnb refers to as one of the "host cancellation penalties." These reviews remain visible within your profile permanently. To learn more about host cancellation penalties, visit www.airbnb .com/help/article/990/i-m-a-host--what-penalties-apply-if-i-need-to-cancel -a-reservation.

In addition to receiving a negative review, Airbnb can and will often impose a financial penalty on hosts who cancel a reservation for a reason that's not considered an extenuating circumstance. According to Airbnb's website, "Under certain circumstances, if the Host cancels a confirmed stay reservation, or if the Host is found to be responsible for a cancellation under this Policy, Airbnb may impose fees and other consequences. The fees and other consequences set out in this Policy are intended to reflect the costs and other impacts of these cancellations on guests, the broader Host community and Airbnb.... When calculating cancellation fees, the reservation amount includes the base rate, cleaning fee, and any pet fees, but excludes taxes and guest fees. If the calculated cancellation fee is less than $50 USD, it will be adjusted up to $50 USD, and if the calculated fee is more than $1,000 USD, it will be adjusted down to $1,000 USD." In other words, if a host cancels a confirmed reservation, it could wind up costing them up to $1,000.

How Ratings Affect Becoming an Airbnb Superhost

Another feature that can be used to attract potential guests to your property listing is your ability as a host to display the Superhost emblem in conjunction with your name and profile photo. To learn more about this program, visit www .airbnb.com/superhost.

As you learned from Chapter 2, "Get Started as an Airbnb Host," the Superhost designation is something you must earn from Airbnb after becoming an experienced host, by providing "extraordinary experiences for your guests." Once a host earns this designation, Airbnb reevaluates it four times per year to ensure that each Superhost has maintained the level of standards required to be called a Superhost.

In a nutshell, to become a Superhost, you must have maintained a good-standing account on the Airbnb service for the previous 12-month period, plus have hosted at least 10 stays, maintained a 90 percent response rate or better, an average star rating of 4.8 or better (provided at least half of the guests who have stayed with you publish a review), and you must complete each confirmed reservation without cancellations. Only a 1 percent cancellation rate will be tolerated. So, you must have at least 100 successful guest bookings and stays to be able to cancel just one as a host without your Superhost ranking being put in jeopardy.

 TIP

Especially when you get along well with your guests, exchange email addresses and/or social media details, and then follow up with a thank-you note one day after their checkout. Ask if they made it home safely, thank them for staying with you, and politely remind them to write a review about their experience. Of course, you should also invite them to stay with you again in the future and mention that they should feel free to tell their friends about their positive experience staying with you. At this point, you can also offer them or their friends an exclusive discount on future stays.

You can learn more about these requirements for becoming a Superhost by visiting https://www.airbnb.com/help/article/829. As a host, you do not need to apply for the Superhost designation. Airbnb automatically keeps track of your performance. If you meet the appropriate criteria, you will automatically be awarded Superhost status. Until you achieve this status, you can determine how far along you are toward earning it by viewing the Superhost section of the Dashboard any time after you become an active host.

Once you become a Superhost, you're automatically given extra benefits by Airbnb. For example, you receive extra promotional recognition from Airbnb and access to exclusive rewards. Plus, as a Superhost, you'll be invited to attend special events and preview new Airbnb features before other hosts. In addition, your property listing is more apt to be seen by potential guests, because the Airbnb platform offers a search filter option that allows travelers to view Superhost properties exclusively, once they select a destination.

Word-of-Mouth Referrals Are Equally Important

Within the Airbnb community, as a host, striving to earn the best reviews and five-star ratings is a worthwhile endeavor that will significantly enhance your credibility and reputation. Just as important, however, is meeting or exceeding your guests' expectations so that they're inclined to tell their friends, family, and others about their experience. Ideally, you want all your past guests to recommend your property to people they know and provide a specific referral to your Airbnb property listing.

Just as hotels, B&Bs, and all other businesses rely on word-of-mouth referrals to increase their business, as an Airbnb host, you can also use them to work in your favor. After all, wouldn't you prefer a potential guest who is looking to stay in your geographic area to sign into the Airbnb service and specifically seek out your property listing, as opposed to browsing through dozens or hundreds of other listings before stumbling upon yours? Plus, if a potential guest contacts you directly via a referral, you can send them a discounted booking invitation via the Airbnb platform.

While a guest is staying with you, if they tell you how much they're enjoying their stay, thank them for the kind words, and simply respond by asking them to tell their friends about their experience staying at your property. If a guest chooses to share details about their stay with you on social media, ask them to include a direct link to your Airbnb property listing within their post. This allows people to click on that link and be forwarded directly to your property listing.

Your unique property listing web page address (URL) can be found by signing into the Airbnb service and viewing your listing as a traveler. When viewing the listing, copy the URL from the address field of your web browser. It will look something like this: www.airbnb.com/rooms/########. The "#"s represent your unique listing number within the Airbnb system. You can remove any additional information within the URL that's displayed after this unique number.

10 Tips for Generating the Best Possible Reviews from Guests

The following are 10 tips that will help to ensure you earn the best possible reviews from your guests. These tips recap some of the core and most important concepts that have been discussed elsewhere in this book.

1. Respond to booking requests, questions, and concerns from potential guests as quickly as possible—ideally within one hour (or less).

2. Be honest when creating your property listing and personal profile. Develop positive but realistic expectations about what potential guests can expect from your property.

3. Offer something unique that other nearby Airbnb properties don't offer or make a point to offer a great value based on your nightly rate.

4. Set up House Rules that get everyone on the same page in terms of what guests can and can't do while staying at your property.

5. Provide a clean, safe, and comfortable environment for your guests.

6. Welcome your guests personally when they arrive, and then be on hand for their checkout (unless you set up an automated check-in and check-out system, which is perfectly acceptable, if you maintain communication with your guests).

7. Provide extra amenities, on a complimentary basis, that will make a guest more comfortable. For example, provide them with several bottles of water and snacks upon their arrival.

8. Create a clearly written and easy-to-understand home manual.

9. Check in with your guests periodically during their stay.

10. Always be polite and professional when interacting with potential and actual guests. Try to avoid allowing small disagreements or misunderstandings to escalate into formal complaints that get submitted to Airbnb.

 WARNING

If you make a genuine mistake as a host that could lead to a negative review, first apologize. Next, try to rectify the situation with your guest as quickly as possible (before they check out). Be sure to learn from your mistake, and do not repeat it. Someone looking at your profile or property listing in the future might overlook one negative review, especially if you have plenty of good reviews. But if someone sees multiple negative reviews for the same reason, it shows you're aware of a situation, but have done little or nothing to fix it. This will quickly tarnish or ruin your reputation and credibility as a host.

 TIP

One of the biggest nightmares hosts have is that a guest will use their property to throw a party. In addition to stating that this is forbidden within your House Rules, one way to help prevent this is to have a two- or three-night minimum stay and charge a refundable deposit. If someone is planning to host a three- or four-hour party, they probably won't want to pay for several nights' worth of accommodations and risk not getting their deposit back. You can also turn off Instant Bookings and, while communicating with your prospective guests, casually ask them the reason for their stay.

Responding to Negative Reviews

If, as a host, you receive a bad review from a guest, it's important to consider the following:

- You might have done something wrong as a host that resulted in you and your property not meeting or exceeding the expectations of your guest. For example, perhaps your property listing or information within your profile was misleading, badly worded, or created expectations within the guest's mind that their experience staying with you didn't live up to.

- As a host, perhaps you said or did something to anger or offend your guest.

- One or more things within your property didn't work or caused your guest discomfort.

- You did not achieve your objective of providing a clean, comfortable, and safe place to stay at a reasonable price.

To avoid receiving similar negative reviews in the future, based on what the negative review says, seriously consider what you could have done to rectify the situation while the guest was still staying with you. Next, fix whatever is wrong before your next guest checks in.

Remember, you have 48 hours after a review is published to contact the guest and try to rectify the situation, apologize, or reach an understanding or arrangement that will result in the guest modifying their review before it becomes permanently linked with your profile or property listing. Under no circumstances, however, should you ever threaten a guest, try to extort a good review, or do anything that goes against any of Airbnb's policies and guidelines.

Assuming a negative review does wind up being posted, you have 14 days to add a public response to that review. Unfortunately, this public response has no impact on the star ratings the former guest included with their review. It simply allows you to share your point of view, or your side of the story, in hopes of reducing the impact the negative review has on your reputation as a host.

Airbnb's Policies and Guidelines Are Constantly Evolving

It's important to understand that Airbnb continuously strives to provide the best possible community experience for all its travelers and hosts. Part of this commitment involves the need to occasionally adapt its policies and guidelines to meet current demands and trends in our global society. For example, when the COVID-19 pandemic first started, Airbnb initiated a series of cleaning and sanitizing protocols that hosts were required to follow.

Earlier in this chapter, web page links were provided that allow you to review Airbnb's up-to-date Content Policy and Review Guidelines. Links to Airbnb's Extortion Policy, Standards & Expectations, and Nondiscrimination Policies were listed in previous chapters. To find links for all of these documents, visit https://www.airbnb.com/help/feature/2.

As a host, it's important that you periodically review these documents, so you stay up to date on new or revised policies that govern how you host your guests, and what behaviors and actions are acceptable. For example, part of Airbnb's Community Commitment policy states, "We believe that no matter who you are, where you are from, or where you travel, you should be able to belong in the Airbnb community. By joining this community, you commit to treat all fellow members of this community, regardless of race, religion, national origin, disability, sex, gender identity, sexual orientation, or age, with respect, and without judgment or bias." If you are unwilling or unable to follow these polices as an Airbnb host, don't bother becoming one, because this revenue-generating opportunity and the Airbnb community is not for you.

NOTE

Just as it's optional for guests to write a review about their host and the Airbnb property they stayed at, it's possible (and encouraged) for hosts to write a review about each of their guests. Especially if you had a problem with a guest, writing a review will help other Airbnb hosts potentially avoid that same problem by declining that guest's booking request in the future. The time you invest writing reviews about your guests helps the Airbnb community. However, if you have something nice to say about a guest, and you publish a review on Airbnb, this might further encourage that guest to write a review about their experience staying with you, so you benefit as well.

How to Write Reviews about Your Guests

According to Airbnb's Review Guidelines, as a host reviewing a recent guest, you're asked to "stick to the facts" and provide useful information to the people who will be reading the review. Each review should simply describe your personal experience related to a guest or reservation. It can't be used to endorse or promote any harmful or illegal activity or include any type of general social commentary.

You're also not allowed to use a review to violate another person's rights, or include content that is being used for extortion, that relates to an Airbnb investigation, or that is in any way harmful, threatening, obscene, profane, vulgar, discriminatory, or defamatory. All content within your review must adhere to Airbnb's Content Policy, which you can learn more about here: www.airbnb.com /help/article/546/what-is-airbnb-s-content-policy.

The following are some host guidelines to keep in mind when writing a review about a recent guest:

- You have up to 14 days after a guest checks out to write and publish your review. Once published, the review remains online and visible indefinitely.

- A review can contain up to 500 words, and must follow Airbnb's Review Guidelines, which are listed at https://www.airbnb.com/help/article/13.

- A review of a guest can be edited for up to 48 hours after it's published online, or until that guest completes and publishes their own review of you and your property. After that time, only reviews that violate Airbnb's Review Guidelines will be removed from the service by Airbnb.

- Once a review has been published, it remains online indefinitely. It can't be deleted. It's possible for either party to write a public response that will be displayed along with the review. However, a response must be posted within 14 days after the initial review has been published.

Here are a few actual reviews of guests published by their hosts on the Airbnb platform:

- "[Name] was delightful to correspond with over the Airbnb messaging platform. He and his guests upheld all House Rules and left our beach house in sound condition upon departure. We were glad to host [Name] and his guests here at [location]. We are looking forward to having him and family back as guests in the future."

- "Perfect guest! Left the house spotless. Great communication throughout the process and just a genuinely nice person. Would gladly welcome [Name] back."

- "[Name] was a fantastic guest. Great communication and very easy to deal with. My place was left in pristine condition! I would have [Name] back again without question!"

- "It was an absolute pleasure hosting [Name]. He took excellent care of our home, and I would love to welcome him back anytime!"

- "[Name] and his family were great guests. They left my home exactly as I would have hoped, if not better. I appreciate that they were so respectful of my home. I would welcome them back to [location] and my condo any time they want to come!"

- "[Name] and [Name] were great guests. Communication with [Name] was good—proactive and friendly. They left the house in nice condition, and we'd welcome them back anytime. Thanks, [Name] and [Name]!"

As a host writing guest reviews, you may be inclined to do this in a hurry and inadvertently make grammatical or spelling mistakes. Take the time to proofread your guest reviews before publishing them.

Meet Megan Lawrence, a New Zealand–Based Airbnb Host

Megan Lawrence lives in New Zealand but has had many of the same experiences as other travel hosts who use the Airbnb platform throughout the world. Prior to getting started with Airbnb, she had no hospitality experience.

Why did you initially decide to become an Airbnb host?

Megan Lawrence: "It's always been a dream of mine to own an accommodations business. We purchased a property that has two separate cottages that we use for short-term rentals."

What makes your property unique?

Megan Lawrence: "Our property is unique in our area for a couple of reasons. Firstly, our cottages are stand-alone structures. Our view is second to none, nestled in native bush above the Marlborough Sounds. It's a similar outlook to an island property, but we're only a 5.6-mile drive from the nearest town."

What would you say is the absolute best reason why someone should become an Airbnb host?

Megan Lawrence: "Personally, I love meeting people from around the world and am also extremely proud of New Zealand as a travel destination. I love sharing it with others. Airbnb is a great hosting platform, as they have great worldwide reach, but you also can qualify your guests, which helps limit any concerns over the quality of guests and our safety as hosts."

What are some strategies you discovered for creating an attention-getting profile and listing on Airbnb.com?

Megan Lawrence: "First and foremost, display the best photos you can get. Hire a professional photographer and stage your property so it looks its absolute best. Then, make sure that what the guests see when they arrive is exactly what's depicted within your photos. If it's not possible to hire a professional photographer in the beginning, use a smartphone with a wide-angle lens for some of the shots, make sure the lighting is good, and capture a range of different images."

NOTE

A single Airbnb property listing can include up to 100 different photos. Most Superhosts recommend showcasing at least 20 photos, if not more, that accurately showcase the inside and outside of your property in a way that creates realistic (and positive) expectations among potential guests.

How do you choose your nightly pricing?

Megan Lawrence: "We looked at our competitors to get a baseline indication. Our destination is quite seasonal, so we do charge a premium during the summer period."

Do you alter your pricing for weekends, holidays, or extended stays?

Megan Lawrence: "Yes, rather than using Airbnb smart pricing, we prefer to see what's happening in the area, and adjust our own pricing for holiday weekends, etc. We do also offer a 10 percent discount for stays of four nights or more."

How much interaction do you have with your guests, and what does this interaction entail?

Megan Lawrence: "Thanks to us offering stand-alone cottages with self-entry via smart locks, we can choose how much interaction we have with guests. If we're here, we'll always greet them personally, and try and gauge from there how much interaction they want. Some are keen to chat and pick our brains. Others make it clear that they want their privacy. We always let them know that they can contact us via text message at any stage and then we take it from there. I usually bake while they're here, so I will message them to let them know I've baked and ask if they'd like some. If they respond yes, I'll then deliver my baked goods to them."

Is it difficult or scary to invite strangers into your home, or has the experience been very positive, allowing you to make new friends?

Megan Lawrence: "We're lucky that we're not actually inviting guests into our home, so it's all been very positive."

How important are guest ratings/reviews, and what do you do to earn top-notch reviews?

Megan Lawrence: "Guest ratings and reviews are extremely important on Airbnb. I know as a traveler, I look first at a property's overall rating, and then read some of the reviews, as often they tell more of a story than you'll get from reading a property listing. This shows me as a host how important ratings are for converting 'looks' into bookings. One of the most important things as a host who is looking to earn top-notch reviews is to communicate to guests that you're looking to give them a five-star quality experience during their stay. This establishes straight up that you have a commitment to them."

How long did it take you to achieve Superhost status?

Megan Lawrence: "We started operating on October 22, 2022, and achieved Superhost status on January 1, 2023. Thankfully we started operating just before our summer and their busy period started, so we were able to get the required number of stays completed before the quarterly review period. It was easy of us to achieve the rest of their qualifications, as our guests have all given us five-star ratings.

"I believe there are two key benefits of being a Superhost. First is visibility. Airbnb gives Superhosts more visibility in their algorithm. Second, I believe it gives travelers extra peace of mind when booking, which I'm sure also increases bookings."

As an Airbnb host, what activities/tasks do you spend the most time dealing with each day or week?

Megan Lawrence: "Obviously cleaning is a huge part of our life as an Airbnb host. But communicating with guests requires another big chunk of our time. We have scheduled messages when confirming reservations, pre–check-in, etc., but some guests still ask for a lot of additional information beforehand. The most time-consuming part of that is when they're asking for local and personalized recommendations."

Do you charge an extra cleaning fee? If so, how much and what does this fee cover?

Megan Lawrence: "We do charge a $70 cleaning fee. We often use an external cleaner, whose charge is higher than this. It costs us around $100 for linen laundering, cleaning, and their travel."

Are there any other tips, strategies, pieces of advice, or warnings you'd like to share with potential Airbnb hosts?

Megan Lawrence: "When starting out, it's important to get your first three reviews as quickly as possible, as this will then give you a rating. Airbnb offers you the chance to offer your first three bookings at a discount. It's a good idea to utilize this, but while this mode is 'on,' limit the length of stay to just three to four nights. This way, you're not obligated to give away a huge discount for an extended period."

Managing Your Business Means Understanding Its Finances

Obviously, the purpose of any business is to earn a profit. Chances are, you want to be fairly compensated for your time, effort, and for the use of your property. To make the most profit possible while working as an Airbnb host, it's essential that you properly manage your finances. To maximize revenue potential, when necessary, invest or reinvest in your business.

The next chapter focuses on understanding the fees and expenses you'll likely encounter as an Airbnb host so you can set your operating budget accordingly. This will also put you in a better position to make accurate profit projections, and ultimately earn the most revenue possible as an Airbnb host.

CHAPTER 9

Managing Finances for an Airbnb Hosting Business

Many people decide to become an Airbnb host for the social interaction and the opportunity to make new friends. Others use this to help offset their monthly living expenses, or to generate extra income that can be used to improve their lifestyle or pay off their mortgage. The thing to remember, however, is that once you become an Airbnb host and begin inviting paying guests into your home or property, you immediately become an independent small business operator.

Thus, you need to handle your finances like a businessperson. Some of the additional responsibilities this entails include:

- Understanding the fees associated with being an Airbnb host. For example, for every guest booking that's processed through Airbnb, you're typically charged a 3 percent host service fee every time a reservation is completed. This fee is calculated based on the reservation subtotal, prior to other fees and taxes that apply to the reservation. This is the most common fee structure, although other options may be available, such as a host-only fee (which is higher and replaces the need for a guest to pay a guest fee to Airbnb for their booking).

- Choosing how Airbnb will transfer money to you via its Payout Preferences tools. For example, providing your bank account or PayPal account details, as required.

- Maintaining accurate and up-to-date financial records. Consider using bookkeeping (accounting) software such as Intuit's QuickBooks or QuickBooks for Rental Properties, plus keeping organized, paper-based, or scanned files related to all financial records and receipts from short-term rental-related purchases and expenses. Depending on your needs, the online edition of QuickBooks may be a less costly option to use.

 TIP

The benefit to using QuickBooks is that virtually all accounting services will accept these financial files, which makes filing your state and federal tax returns an easier process. Other popular accounting applications include NetSuite (www.netsuite.com), Zimplifi (https://ximplifi.com), Xero (www.xero.com), Wave (www.waveapps.com/accounting), and Sage Accounting (www.sage.com/en-gb/sage-business-cloud/accounting), many of which offer direct integration with Airbnb.

- Adhering to all local, state, and federal rules that apply to short-term renting your property (with the understanding that these ordinances, laws, and regulations are subject to change at any time in the future).

- Acquiring and maintaining a business license or permit, as required by your local government.

- Adhering to the rules outlined by your homeowner's association, co-op board, or apartment lease that pertain to using your house, condo, or apartment for short-term rentals.

NOTE

To help you understand Airbnb's current payout fees and policies, visit www.airbnb.com/help/article/459. Keep in mind, your payout can be affected by whether you charge a cleaning fee or other type(s) of fees and whether you activate a special offer or extended-stay discount to your guests. The breakdown of your earnings for each separate booking/reservation is displayed when you visit the Transaction History tool that's offered by Airbnb.

- Calculating and paying local, state, and federal taxes that apply to you personally, as well as your travel hosting business.

- Working with an accountant (CPA) to help you set up and manage the financial bookkeeping associated with your travel hosting business.

- Managing your additional and ongoing travel-hosting-related expenses so that they don't exceed your earnings.

- Understanding how to access and utilize the financial reporting tools provided by Airbnb, including the Transaction History information, which reports what you've earned and when you've earned it, as well as your gross earnings.

- Adhering to all of Airbnb's policies and guidelines (www.airbnb.com/help /feature/2), which are periodically updated.

Some of these tasks and added responsibilities may seem daunting at first. Once you understand what needs to be accomplished based on your personal situation, you can work with professionals—for example, an accountant, professional bookkeeper, or lawyer—to help you set everything up correctly right from the start and learn how to maintain the proper financial records.

Understanding your current bookkeeping and tax responsibilities may change once you become a travel host. Researching what local, state, and federal laws, ordinances, and regulations you may need to adhere to will require some effort on your part. Some of this will depend on the type of property you own or lease, where you live, where the short-term rental property is located, and your current financial and employment situation.

 NOTE

QuickBooks from Intuit (www.quickbooks.com) is the world's most popular bookkeeping and accounting software. Various versions of QuickBooks are available as Windows PC or Mac software applications. There's also an online version of QuickBooks that works with all internet-connected computers and mobile devices. Because several different versions of QuickBooks are available, consult with your accountant and/or Intuit to determine which version is best suited to meet your unique needs as a travel host.

Calculating Your Expenses

In addition to Airbnb's imposed host service fee and your tax-related obligations, becoming an Airbnb host will require that you cover a handful of onetime and recurring expenses so that you can provide clean, comfortable, and safe accommodations for your paying guests. Cleaning, property maintenance, landscaping, and amenities-related expenses are just part of what you'll need to cover.

Understand Your Tax Obligations

Depending on where you live, in addition to paying income taxes on your earnings (when applicable), you may be responsible for paying local taxes, federal taxes, and/or sales tax (for certain types of additional fees you charge to your guests).

The following Airbnb web page describes how some of these taxes work: https://www.airbnb.com/help/article/481. Rather than relying solely on the information provided by Airbnb, your best strategy is to consult with an accountant who understands the short-term rental business and the tax regulations in your town, city, state, or country (if you're outside of the United States).

For example, if you determine that you need to collect a tax from your guests, make sure Airbnb collects it on your behalf when a booking is made. If you're based in certain areas, the Airbnb service automatically offers a Collect and Remit feature. This helps hosts collect and pay region-specific occupancy taxes, when applicable.

Keep in mind, the Airbnb service does not handle any of the tasks associated with preparing state or federal tax returns if you're within the United States. Meeting these obligations is entirely the responsibility of the host, and failure to do so could lead to significant fines and/or legal problems.

Refer to the following figures to help you identify, calculate, track, and manage these various expenses:

- *Onetime (or Very Infrequent) Expenses* (Figure 8.1). This worksheet will help you take inventory of what furniture and amenities you already have within your property and determine what additional onetime (or very infrequent) purchases will be required to adequately host your guests. While some of the items listed within Figure 8.1 are mandatory, others are optional, which you can acquire right away, or wait until you've begun generating revenue as an Airbnb host before making the additional financial investment.

- *Weekly or Monthly Expenses* (Figure 8.2). These are expenses you'll need to pay on a weekly or monthly basis to maintain your property and keep it clean, for example. Some of these expenses you may already be paying, while others may be new once you start hosting guests.

- *Occasional Recurring Expenses* (Figure 8.3). These are expenses that you'll incur every few months, or once or twice per year. For example, while a bed frame and box spring could easily last for many years, the sheets, pillows, blankets, and towels will likely need to be replaced every few months.

TIP

Some hosts of more luxury-oriented short-term rentals make it a business practice to replace the sheets, pillows, blankets (or duvet covers), and towels every three to four months, whether it's needed or not, while other hosts wait until a sheet or towel shows too much wear and tear, gets damaged, or becomes stained in a way where it can't be properly cleaned. The more guests are paying for their accommodations, the higher their expectations will be when it comes to the freshness and new appearance of bedding and towels. Regardless of how often you opt to replace these items, it's necessary to always have extras on hand.

- *Frequently Recurring Expenses and Purchases* (Figure 8.4). These are expenses that you'll incur often and can relate to items you and your guests will use up and that will need to be replenished or replaced, such as toilet paper, paper towels, soap, coffee, bottled water, and shampoo. Cleaning products and cleaning service fees also fit into this category. To save money, consider buying items in bulk whenever possible.

Based on how you'll be handling your financial record keeping and bookkeeping, you may find it easier and more convenient to use bookkeeping software (such as Intuit's QuickBooks) to track all this information. If you're savvy using a spreadsheet application, such as Microsoft Excel, Google Sheets, or Apple's Numbers, you can create a custom spreadsheet to help organize and manage the financial aspects of your travel hosting business.

Many hosts find it extremely helpful to maintain detailed checklists, categorized by how often specific items need to be purchased or replaced. The checklist should include the make, model, and size of items, where you typically purchase them, and how often each needs to be purchased.

TIP

A sheet set for each bed should include an appropriately sized fitted bedsheet, flat sheet, and at least two pillowcases. Be sure to have an ample supply of sets on hand for each bed, because you may need to provide clean bedding multiple times per week based on guest turnover. Plus, you should always have one or two extra sets on hand for unexpected needs. The number of sets you will need to buy and keep on hand will depend on how many beds are within your property, how often you plan to offer clean bedding for long-term guests, how often you'll do laundry, and the number of new guests you anticipate checking in each week.

For example, if you have one bedroom that you rent out to different guests five to seven nights per week, this will require that you have at least eight to ten sheet sets on hand, especially if you only plan to do laundry once per week. Many hosts find it useful to use a duvet with a washable (and bleachable) duvet cover, as opposed to other types of blankets, because they're easier to launder.

Figure 8.1 Onetime (or Very Infrequent) Expenses

Description	Number Required	Already Acquired	Need to Purchase	Cost Each	Total Cost
Area Rug(s)				$	$
Bed Frame & Box Spring—King				$	$
Bed Frame & Box Spring—Twin				$	$
Bed Frame & Box Spring—Queen				$	$
Bedroom Door Lock(s)				$	$

Continued on next page

Description	Number Required	Already Acquired	Need to Purchase	Cost Each	Total Cost
Bedroom Dresser				$	$
Carbon Monoxide Detector(s)				$	$
Closet Hangers				$	$
Coffee Maker				$	$
Comforters or Duvets (One per bed)				$	$
Couch & Living Room Furniture Set				$	$
Curtains / Window Shades				$	$
Desk				$	$
Desk Chair				$	$
Dining Room / Kitchen Furniture (Tables, chairs, etc.)				$	$
Extra House Keys (Unless you're using locks with keyless entry options.)				$	$
Fans or Air Conditioners and Heaters				$	$
Fire Extinguisher(s)				$	$
First-Aid Kits				$	$
Guestroom Television Set & TV Stand				$	$
Home Security System (Including indoor and outdoor security cameras if you deem them necessary)				$	$
Iron & Ironing Board				$	$
Keyless-Entry (Smart) Door Lock for the Main Entrance				$	$
Lamps / Lighting Fixtures				$	$

Description	Number Required	Already Acquired	Need to Purchase	Cost Each	Total Cost
Laundry Hamper(s)				$	$
Living Room Television and Entertainment Center				$	$
Mattresses—King				$	$
Mattresses—Queen				$	$
Mattresses—Twin				$	$
Mini-Fridge (For each guestroom)				$	$
Mirror(s)				$	$
Nightstand(s)				$	$
Power Strips for Guestroom(s)				$	$
Smoke Detector(s)				$	$
Trash Cans				$	$
Washing Machine and Dryer				$	$
Wi-Fi Router and Internet Modem				$	$
Other:				$	$
Other:				$	$
Other:				$	$

Figure 8.2 Weekly or Monthly Expenses

Description	Payment Frequency	Total Cost
Additional Parking Passes		$
Cable TV or Streaming Service Fees		$
Homeowner's Association or Co-op Dues		$
Homeowner's/Renter's Insurance		$
Internet (Wi-Fi) Service		$

Continued on next page

Description	Payment Frequency	Total Cost
Landline Phone		$
Landscaping Services		$
Local/State Permit		$
Professional Cleaning Services or House Cleaner		$
Rent/Mortgage Payment		$
Short-Term Rental Insurance		$
Utilities—Electricity		$
Utilities—Gas		$
Other:		$
Other:		$
Other:		$

Figure 8.3 Occasional Recurring Expenses

Description	Number Required	How Often Purchase Is Required	Purchase Date	Cost Each	Total Cost
Bathmat(s)				$	$
Blankets				$	$
Comforter (Duvet) Covers (Washable)				$	$
Home and Kitchen Appliance Maintenance & Repair				$	$
Kitchen Supplies— Dishes, Glasses, Utensils, etc.				$	$

Description	Number Required	How Often Purchase Is Required	Purchase Date	Cost Each	Total Cost
New Towel Sets (Bath Towels, Hand Towels, Washcloths)				$	$
Pillows (Be sure to offer at least two or three options, such as down, cotton, latex, memory foam, or polyester fiber filled)				$	$
Sheet Sets—King				$	$
Sheet Sets—Queen				$	$
Sheet Sets—Twin				$	$
Shower Curtains				$	$
Waterproof Mattress Covers—King				$	$
Waterproof Mattress Covers—Queen				$	$
Waterproof Mattress Covers—Twin				$	$
Other:				$	$
Other:				$	$
Other:				$	$

Figure 8.4 Frequently Recurring Expenses and Purchases

Description	Number Required	How Often Purchase Is Required	Cost Each	Total Cost
Bottled Waters			$	$
Cleaning Supplies			$	$
Coffee			$	$
Dishwasher Detergent			$	$
Garbage Bags			$	$
Hand Sanitizer			$	$
Hand Soap			$	$
KN95 Masks (For yourself, cleaning crew, and guests)			$	$
Laundry Detergent			$	$
Light Bulbs			$	$
Paper Towels			$	$
Replacement Batteries			$	$
Snack Basket (Complimentary) for Guests Upon Their Arrival			$	$
Tissues			$	$
Toilet Paper—12 Pack			$	$
Travel-Size Toiletry Sets (Shampoo, conditioner, soap, etc.)			$	$
Other:			$	$
Other:			$	$
Other:			$	$

TIP

If you plan to send your laundry (linens, towels, blankets, etc.) out to a local dry cleaners or laundromat (as opposed to doing the laundry yourself or having your house cleaner do it), the ongoing expense of this service will also need to be calculated into your budget. When deciding whether this is a worthwhile expense, consider the amount of time out of your personal schedule doing the laundry will take or how much your house cleaner will charge to handle this responsibility. Also consider the additional wear and tear of using your own washer and dryer.

Additional Information about Setting Your Nightly Rate

By now, you should realize that many factors should be considered when setting your nightly rate. Strategies for setting a fair nightly rate have already been covered, but they do factor into your budget so let's quickly review some key points. As an Airbnb host, the primary way you'll generate income is by charging a nightly rate for guests to stay at your property.

You already know that Airbnb allows you to set your own nightly rate. To help offset your property cleaning and maintenance costs, you're also able to charge an additional cleaning fee, for example. Plus, based on other circumstances, you're able to charge extra guest fees or pet fees, or offer a discount to your guests who book a long-term stay.

More Considerations When Setting Your Nightly Rate

Start by setting a base nightly rate. This is the minimum nightly fee you plan to charge, regardless of other circumstances. This rate should cover your costs and allow you to earn a profit. Once this base nightly rate is set, you can increase or decrease it based on demand and other factors. However, you never want to decrease this rate if it means taking a financial loss.

If there's a major event (concert, sporting event, conference, or convention) coming to your area that will be attracting many more travelers into the region than normal, this is an opportunity for you to charge a premium nightly rate. The local hotels, motels, and B&Bs will likely be full, but additional travelers will still need accommodations.

Every city has a visitors and conventions bureau that can provide a listing of major events scheduled to be held in your area. You should also check the event calendars at concert venues, sports arenas, convention centers, and fairgrounds within a 25-mile radius, to determine what major events will be taking place in the weeks and months to come.

To recap, the nightly rate you charge should be based on the following:

- The type of accommodations you're offering (shared guestroom, private guestroom, or an entire apartment or house, for example)
- The collection of included amenities and value-added services you're offering on a complimentary basis
- Your geographic location and safety of the neighborhood, in addition to its appeal for tourists or visitors
- What nearby hotels, motels, and other Airbnb hosts are charging
- Local demand (and seasonal demand)
- The type of guests you're hoping to attract

Obviously, the nightly rate you opt to charge needs to cover the Airbnb host services fees you're required to pay, income taxes and other taxes you're responsible for, as well as the other expenses you'll incur as an Airbnb host. Plus, what you charge should allow you to generate a profit (above and beyond all of these expenses).

Guests probably won't be willing to pay a nightly fee to stay at your property that's higher than what it would cost them to stay at a nearby hotel, motel, or B&B unless you're offering special and unique accommodations, or an experience that goes along with the accommodations. Likewise, they probably won't pay a rate that's not competitive with another nearby Airbnb property that offers similar accommodations and amenities but for a lower nightly fee, especially if you're competing to offer budget accommodations.

 TIP

If your Airbnb property offers something truly unique, such as an upscale and premium location, ultra-posh or themed furnishings, luxury comfort, and/or you're including a collection of high-end amenities, then you will likely be able to charge a much higher nightly rate that your guests will be happy to pay. It will be your responsibility as the host, however, to clearly communicate what's unique or special about your property within your property listing, in a way that entices guests to want to stay with you and pay a premium rate. If you choose to charge a premium rate, keep in mind that guest expectations for cleanliness will be much higher.

Learning how to set the ideal nightly rate that covers your costs and that will allow you to consistently generate a profit is a skill, and one that gets easier with research and experience. Chances are, based on what you're offering, local demand (including midweek, weekend, holiday, or special event demand), and your location, it will take you time and some experimentation to determine the ideal nightly rate to charge.

While it's easy to turn on Airbnb's automated pricing (aka Smart Pricing) feature and allow Airbnb to set your nightly rates, many hosts have found that the rates calculated by Airbnb are often lower than what you could otherwise charge, especially if you're offering something special or unique that Airbnb's automated pricing formula does not consider.

According to the Airbnb website, "Smart Pricing is based on the type and location of your listing, along with season, demand, and other factors." These factors include: daily trends, seasonal shifts, and special events.

TIP

As a host, you're able to change your nightly rate at any time. (Rate changes will apply to all new reservations, not existing ones.) You're also able to manually set a different nightly rate for weeknights versus weekend nights (and/or holiday nights), or utilize Airbnb's Smart Pricing tool, which allows you to provide a base nightly price rate, and then allows Airbnb to set your actual nightly rate(s) based on local demand and other factors.

Independent Tools to Help You Generate the Highest Revenue Possible as a Travel Host

There are now many optional, online-based services you can rely on to help you enhance your hosting skills and manage your ongoing responsibilities. Some of these services provide you with proprietary research, and some even handle all aspects of setting and continuously updating your nightly rate for you. Here's just a sampling of the services worth looking into:

- *AirDNA* (*www.airdna.co*). Among other things, this service offers a dynamic pricing tool for Airbnb hosts, along with a wide range of location-based, data-driven insights and analysis. This is one of the most trusted and widely used services by Airbnb hosts around the world. According to the AirDNA website, "Powered by Vrbo and Airbnb data from over 10 million global properties in 120,000 global markets, MarketMinder is the number one leading platform for short-term rental intelligence. Use MarketMinder to discover the best places to invest in a vacation rental, set the perfect price every day, and stay two steps ahead of the competition."

- Beyond (*https://beyondpricing.com*). This site utilizes a data-driven pricing tool to help Airbnb hosts almost immediately increase their revenue by 10 to 40 percent. Once you turn on the Automated Pricing tool, the service will update your pricing daily, based on localized demand.

- *Guesty* (*www.guesty.com*). Among other things, this service offers a dynamic pricing tool for Airbnb hosts.

- *Hostaway*.com (*www.hostaway.com*). Provides a comprehensive software solution for handling reservations, guests, invoices, marketing, and reporting.

- *Mashvisor* (*www.mashvisor.com/air-bnb/analytics*). Provides Airbnb rental data to help hosts estimate Airbnb investment revenue.

- *PriceLabs* (*https://hello.pricelabs.co*). Offers a dynamic pricing tool and data-driven analysis for Airbnb hosts.

- *Wheelhouse* (*www.usewheelhouse.com*). This site is an independent online service that supports Airbnb hosts. It offers a collection of up-to-date, localized market research, as well as interactive tools that will quickly help you set your nightly rate and potentially generate up to 40 percent higher revenue as a travel host.

 TIP

While some of these independently operated pricing tools charge a flat monthly subscription rate, most charge a percentage of your booking revenue that's generated using the service's proprietary pricing tools. This fee is in addition to the 3 percent host service fee you're already paying to Airbnb. Most of these services offer a free 30-day trial and boast using them will increase your short-term rental revenue by between 10 and 40 percent. Take advantage of the free trial that's offered before making any financial commitments to any of these services.

Reasons to Reinvest Profits in Your Airbnb Hosting Business

You've read how important it is for a host to offer clean, comfortable, and safe accommodations for their guests. Assuming you do this, you'll be able to charge a nightly fee that's comparable with what other nearby Airbnb hosts charge for a stay at a similar property with similar amenities. Offering competitive pricing will typically earn favorable ratings and reviews from your guests, assuming your hospitality is also up to par.

Over time, however, you can improve upon your property by upgrading it with more luxurious furnishings, décor, and amenities. This will allow you to potentially charge a higher nightly rate that your guests will likely be willing to pay. This becomes much easier if you've already earned a collection of excellent reviews and five-star ratings, which gives you added credibility as a host.

While you can upgrade the furnishings and décor based on your personal taste, and what you think your future guests will like, consider the feedback you've received from past guests and your own experience as a traveler staying with other hosts to help you select the collection of amenities, décor updates, and new furnishings you'd like to offer.

Choose amenities that will be considered valuable or useful to most of your guests, who will appreciate them, and potentially be willing to pay a higher nightly rate to utilize them. After being an Airbnb host for an extended period, you'll develop a good understanding of the types of guests that most often stay with you, as well as what they like and don't like about your property and what you're offering. This is firsthand market research you should use to help you make intelligent decisions when it comes to upgrading your property and enhancing the collection of included amenities, furnishings, and even outdoor landscaping you'll be offering.

Depending on how often you host guests, how often you will need to perform significant (and potentially costly) maintenance and upkeep on your property and its major appliances will vary. However, these are future expenses you'll need to consider if you want to continue offering clean, comfortable, and safe accommodations for your guests over time.

Thus, long-term financial planning is required to ensure you'll have the funds on hand that are needed to pay for the timely maintenance, repair, and upkeep on the property, its furnishings, décor, landscaping, and appliances.

For example, once guests begin staying at your property, after a few years, if they start discovering the mattress is saggy, blankets smell moldy and have holes, the couch has tears in the upholstery, and the carpeting is ragged and stained, you'll begin earning poor ratings and reviews for not maintaining the property.

 **WARNING**

> If you're planning to sell your property sometime in the next few years, consider the impact (wear and tear) having paying guests (either periodically or continuously) will have on the property itself. Calculate how this will impact your property's resale value, especially if you don't handle ongoing maintenance in a proper and responsible manner.

Chances are, you'll need to repaint the walls every few years, replace the carpeting every few years, pay for the repair and upkeep of all appliances within the property, and cover a variety of other upkeep expenses that are a direct result of having guests utilizing your property. These are all long-term or future costs you'll likely need to calculate into your long-term operational budget.

Unfortunately, not all your guests will treat your property like it's their own, which will likely result in quicker wear and tear. You need to plan for this. While Airbnb's AirCover will help to protect you financially if someone damages your property or belongings, it will not cover problems related to normal wear and tear on your home or appliances.

Consider your long-term goals and objectives. Do you want to reinvest your profits as an Airbnb host into the property to ultimately be able to charge a higher nightly rate and/or increase the resale value of the property when you're ready to sell it? Or do you want to take the money you earn and use it to improve your lifestyle, pay off debts, or perhaps go on more extravagant vacations? These are among the financial decisions you'll need to make early on once you begin your travel hosting business.

Purchasing additional homes, apartments, or condos, for example, with the sole intent of using them as short-term rental properties is a viable business. However, if local or state laws or regulations change and prevent short-term rentals in the future, you'll need to have a backup plan in place to protect your investments. Choose additional properties wisely, and if applicable, make sure you fully understand the homeowner's association or co-op bylaws and rules that pertain to short-term rentals, before investing in the property. One of the focuses of Chapter 11, "Ways to Make Being an Airbnb Host Your Full-Time Career," is on investing in and managing multiple Airbnb properties.

Meet Airbnb Superhost Kirsten Schmidt

Like many Airbnb hosts, Kirsten Schmidt decided to use Airbnb to rent out extra bedrooms in her home once her kids grew up and moved out. She has since become a highly accomplished Superhost.

Why did you initially decide to become an Airbnb host?

Kirsten Schmidt: "After my oldest child left for college, we had an extra room in the home and needed a bit of extra income. I work in tourism and am a traveler myself, so this seemed to be something I would enjoy."

What makes your property unique?

Kirsten Schmidt: "It's a single-family home in the Hollywood Hills (a prime location in Los Angeles). It is in a convenient, very quiet, safe, and a friendly neighborhood. Plus, it's close to two major freeways."

What would you say is the absolute best reason why someone should become an Airbnb host?

Kirsten Schmidt: "I like generating extra income while having the chance to meet interesting people from all walks of life."

What are some strategies you discovered for creating an attention-getting profile and listing on Airbnb?

Kirsten Schmidt: "Good photography is key. Guests want to get a feel for the place and make sure it will serve their needs. Pricing is important, especially in the beginning when you need many bookings and five-star reviews."

Do you have any tips for creating attention-getting photos for your listing?

Kirsten Schmidt: "Highlight extras, add small design touches, and keep the place bright and super tidy."

How do you choose your nightly pricing?

Kirsten Schmidt: "I compare similar listings, look at Airbnb recommendations, and last but not least, know how much I need to earn to make it worthwhile."

Do you alter your pricing for weekends, holidays, or extended stays? If so, how?

Kirsten Schmidt: "I give weekly and monthly discounts for long-term bookings."

What special amenities do you offer that really appeal to your guests?

Kirsten Schmidt: "I usually leave bottled water and snacks in the room. Reliable internet is hugely important."

What are some of the absolute best and worst experiences you've had as an Airbnb host, and what did you learn from them?

Kirsten Schmidt: "The best part is chatting in the kitchen over coffee or wine, becoming friends, and having lovely guests booking my space repeatedly. The worst thing is having to deal with suspiciously behaving guests who never leave the room or who show no respect for my private spaces. The biggest lesson I have learned is to always check and read the prospective guest's reviews. Guests need to have several five-star reviews to be considered."

What are some of the mistakes you made early on, once you became an Airbnb host, and what did you do to fix them?

Kirsten Schmidt: "I was not comfortable turning down requests or asking questions. When you share your home with a stranger, you want to make absolutely sure that it's a good match."

How much interaction do you have with your guests, and what does this interaction entail?

Kirsten Schmidt: "Every guest is different. Some want to connect and share. Others want total privacy. It is extremely important to develop an intuition about how much privacy someone wants and act accordingly. I offer help with any questions a guest may have while they stay with me. I am always available to them throughout their stay via text or in person."

What House Rules have you established out of necessity?

Kirsten Schmidt: "No unregistered guests, no smoking, and quiet after 11 p.m. Use of the kitchen is upon request."

What House Rules do you recommend that all hosts require?

Kirsten Schmidt: "The nice thing about Airbnb is that you can always set your own rules. Decide what works for you and what doesn't, and then set your House Rules accordingly."

How important are guest ratings/reviews? What do you do to earn top-notch reviews?

Kirsten Schmidt: "Extremely important, as they influence your standing on the Airbnb platform. I am a Superhost, which means that my property gets listed high up and I have access to special customer service. I try to give the guests what they expect, which is a very clean, comfortable, relaxed place to stay in a safe neighborhood. My pictures are correct. I believe in total transparency. For example, I would always mention if there might be a problem while they are staying with me, like construction across the street or a malfunctioning air conditioner."

Day-to-day, what are the biggest challenges you face as an Airbnb host?

Kirsten Schmidt: "Being able to turn down requests. Airbnb flags hosts when they decline too many requests. I need to make sure I am comfortable with a booking request. I do not want to host any guests with questionable or no reviews, unreasonable requests, or an unconfirmed identity, for example."

What is the best part of becoming an Airbnb host?

Kirsten Schmidt: "Honestly, the income. Currently my rental income covers my mortgage."

What, if anything, have you done to maximize your revenue as an Airbnb host?

Kirsten Schmidt: "I created more rental spaces within my home by building an Accessory Dwelling Unit [ADU] on my property."

How has COVID-19 impacted your ability to earn money as an Airbnb host? Do you see this improving in 2023 and beyond?

Kirsten Schmidt: "Yes, of course it impacted the business, although I had a wonderful guest stay here during lockdown because he was not allowed to fly back to his home country. We are still friends. Business has vastly improved in 2022. Right now, I only accept long-term bookings for 30 nights or longer."

What extra precautions do you take resulting from COVID-19?

Kirsten Schmidt: "Extra cleaning and disinfecting, masks in all public spaces, and during the worst periods of the pandemic, I only allowed vaccinated guests."

In your opinion, has it become harder to make money as an Airbnb host in recent years? If so, why? How have you overcome this?

Kirsten Schmidt: "No. Rates for accommodations have gone up and guests are used to paying much more than they did only a few years ago."

These days, is it worth it financially for someone to become an Airbnb host, based on the time and effort that's required to become successful?

Kirsten Schmidt: "It is time consuming. Mostly the cleaning part and check-in coordination, but I have flexibility and like the extra income. For someone who enjoys hosting and interacting with people, it does not even seem like work."

Do you charge extra for pets or extra guests? If so, how much extra, and how do guests react to this? Have you lost potential bookings?

Kirsten Schmidt: "I have a no-pets-allowed policy. I do charge $20 per night extra for an additional person staying in my larger space. This fee is mentioned in my property listing, so it's no surprise."

Do you charge an extra cleaning fee? How much? What does this fee cover?

Kirsten Schmidt: "I used to, but not anymore, after the big public controversy and backlash against Airbnb due to hidden fees. Guests hate the extra fees."

Are there any other tips, strategies, pieces of advice, or warnings you'd like to share with potential Airbnb hosts?

Kirsten Schmidt: "Apply these golden rules: You should enjoy people and hospitality and be service-oriented. Do not accept instant bookings, but rather vet potential guests. Only accommodate guests you feel comfortable with. Be open, friendly, helpful, but leave your guests to their privacy when they want it."

10 Ways to Promote Your Airbnb Property

There are countless Airbnb hosts that simply create a property listing and profile, publish it on Airbnb, and then sit back and wait for the bookings to come in. They do nothing else to promote their property. Based on their location and the property's desirability, the host manages to maintain a 60 percent or higher occupancy rate. Unfortunately, this is not the case for many Airbnb hosts.

If you want to achieve an occupancy rate that's higher than average, want to attract a specific type of guest, or desire long-term guests (as opposed to guests that stay less than one week), chances are you'll need to take an active approach when it comes to promoting your short-term rental property. Obviously, start by telling your friends, family, coworkers, congregates from your house of worship, local PTA members, book club members, or fellow fitness class students that you have a short-term rental property available. Ask these people to keep it in mind if they have relatives coming to town to visit, or if they know people looking for accommodations in your area.

As you'll discover from this chapter, you can (and should) take this word-of-mouth promotion approach much further, by becoming active on social media, and encouraging your guests to tell their friend network about their experience staying at your property. While word-of-mouth will prove to be an invaluable tool for increasing your occupancy rate, you're about to discover nine other strategies you can adopt that will help increase your bookings and ultimately your revenue.

As you learn about these strategies, tap your own creativity to brainstorm ways you can use your network and resources to spread the word about your rental property—in the real world and online. Let's look at some of the low-cost (or free) promotional strategies you might choose to implement, depending on your available time, goals, and resources.

#1: Continuously Update and Tweak Your Airbnb Property Listing

The Airbnb platform keeps track of the ratings and reviews hosts receive, but at the same time, also tracks a host's response time to inquiries, and how often each property listing gets updated. In fact, more than 100 data points contribute to a property's visibility on the platform.

Many Airbnb hosts have discovered that by keeping their listing fresh (and maintaining high ratings), their search discoverability increases, especially if they're a Superhost. There are many ways a host can update and tweak a property listing once every few weeks. At the very least, plan on updating your listing a minimum of once per month. Some of the easy things you can do to update your property listing include:

- Add or change one or more property photographs. Especially if you're in a region that experiences the different seasons, show the exterior of the property during each season. Ideally, use landscape-oriented (horizontal) images that are bright, clear, high-quality, and visually attractive. They should accurately showcase your property in a way that grabs someone's attention.

- Anytime you add new furnishings or décor, be sure to mention this within the listing.

- Upgrade or add one or more in-demand amenities and promote it. For example, a laptop-friendly workspace, faster Wi-Fi, more cooking basics (pots, pans, etc.), a hot tub, a new washer/dryer, or a mini-fridge within each bedroom.

- If there are certain amenities or activities that your guests can only experience during a specific period or season, focus on these outdoor activities within the listing (for example, hiking, biking, skiing, or swimming).

- If you adapt your property to fit additional Airbnb categories, include this within the listing title, within the text-based description, and the relevant photos (with category-related captions).

- Anytime you choose to change your policies, such as becoming pet-friendly, this should be highlighted.

- Switch to Instant Booking. This helps your listing in Airbnb's Search algorithm, but many hosts prefer to be able to preapprove their guests and opt to keep this feature turned off.

- Pay attention to changes in the way property listings are displayed on the Airbnb platform and adapt your listing accordingly. For example, in mid-2022, Airbnb stopped displaying a property's title within the search results. It began only appearing after someone clicked on the listing. At the same time, Airbnb changed photo priority, based on the property's category (or categories). For example, a property listed in the Amazing Pools category would feature an image of the pool, not the image that the host added first to their listing.

- Update your property availability within the Calendar constantly, so it's always up to date and accurate.

- Focus on improving your booking rate percentage on the Airbnb platform. This is based on the number of people who view your property listing compared to the number of people who actually book a reservation. You want the booking rate (measured as a percentage) to be as high as possible, as this, too, is something Airbnb tracks and pays attention to.

- Temporarily lower your nightly rate, as this can help improve your property's search ranking.

- Add or update the host introduction within your property listing. Make sure it conveys a personal, warm, and welcoming tone that's catered to the type of guest you're looking to host.

TIP

Airbnb's Search algorithm is constantly changing, but a major emphasis is always placed on a listing's **price**, **quality**, and **popularity**. "Quality" refers to several things, from your property photos and guest reviews within the listing, to the property's size, location, and the collection of amenities being offered. If your property is being listed within the Beach, Beachfront, Lakefront, or Amazing Pools category, your professional-quality photos should showcase exactly what you're offering.

While you do not need to make extensive changes to your property listing every week, it's a good strategy to tweak, add, or improve at least one thing within the overall listing on a consistent basis. Not only does this keep the listing fresh, but doing this also demonstrates to Airbnb that you're an active host who is serious about landing new bookings. (Contrary to what many people believe is true, Airbnb does not reward hosts who simply sign into the service often. It does, however, reward hosts for responding quickly to inquiries and requests from prospective guests and booked guests.)

TIP

Becoming a Superhost offers you multiple benefits. For example, it automatically means your property will get preferential search result placement on the Airbnb platform, which will likely increase the number of bookings you receive. This potentially gives you an edge over your local competition. Again, because potential guests value this accreditation, they're typically willing to pay a higher nightly rate to stay at a property operated by a Superhost. Being labeled as a Superhost instantly boosts your credibility within the Airbnb community.

#2: Utilize Word-of-Mouth to Your Utmost Advantage

Word-of-mouth advertising is extremely beneficial, because when someone gives a friend, family member, or coworker, for example, a positive recommendation about your short-term rental property, it carries a lot more weight than someone stumbling upon and reading a generic listing when trying to find Airbnb accommodations. This is particularly true when the person giving the recommendation has stayed at your property firsthand and/or can vouch for you as being a friendly and accommodating host.

Once your Airbnb listing is created and published online, it will have its own website URL. When viewing the listing, someone can easily share it with other people by clicking on the Share option located near the top-right corner of their browser window, and then choose how they want to share the linking with others. Options include Copy Link, Email, Messages, WhatsApp, Facebook Messenger, Facebook, Twitter, Embed, or More Options.

To encourage past guests to promote your property to their friends, family, and online network, offer them and their referral a discount (such as 10 to 25 percent off) on their next stay, but limit the discount to a stay of up to five nights. You can offer this same discount to repeat guests.

You should also tap into your own network of friends, family, coworkers, and social media followers. Ask these people to recommend your Airbnb property to anyone they know. You can also extend this request to local business operators and people in your neighborhood you interact with at your salon, dry cleaners, fitness club, doctor's office, or house of worship, for example.

If you're specifically looking for long-term guests, reach out to the HR department at larger businesses in your area, local college housing departments, and the HR department and patient resources department of local hospitals. These last options will be useful for generating leads for potential long-term guests planning to relocate to your area for a few weeks or months and who need a more affordable and comfortable place to stay than a hotel or traditional furnished corporate apartment rental.

Register a Custom Domain Name for Your Property Listing

To make the word-of-mouth promotion process even easier, brainstorm a custom website address for your Airbnb property, register it with a domain registrar service, such as GoDaddy (www.godaddy.com) or Google Domains (https://domains.google), and then forward your newly acquired website address directly to your Airbnb listing URL.

Choose a custom domain name that's easy to spell, easy to remember, descriptive, and that ends with "dot-com." For example, an easy-to-promote domain name that's directed to your Airbnb listing might be "SmithVacationHome. com," "ComfortableOrlandoRoomRental.com," or "TropicalTreeHouseGetaway .com." Plan on spending between $10 and $20 per year to register and forward a custom domain name to your Airbnb listing.

This custom domain name can be displayed within the signature of your outgoing emails, on your business cards, within printed brochures, and within your various social media profiles. A simple domain name makes it easier for other people to help you spread the word about your short-term rental property.

#3: Become Active on Social Media

Chances are, you don't have time to become active on all the popular social media platforms, like Facebook, Twitter, Instagram, TikTok, SnapChat, Pinterest, and LinkedIn. So, once you determine the type of guests you're looking to attract, figure out which social media platforms are popular with that group of people and then create an account to promote yourself and your Airbnb property on just those services.

At the very least, you probably want to create a Facebook page for your Airbnb property, which can be linked to, but kept separate from, your personal Facebook account. This basically allows you to operate an online community for people interested in your Airbnb property, as well as past guests.

Directions for creating a free Facebook page for your business can be found at www.facebook.com/help/104002523024878; however, the process of creating the page begins by following these initial steps:

1. Launch your favorite web browser from your internet-connected computer and log into your preexisting Facebook account.

2. On the left side of the Facebook browser window, click on the Pages option.

3. Found below the Your Pages and profiles heading, click on Create New Page.

4. Enter the desired (and unique) Page Name and choose a Category. For an Airbnb property, the Local Business or Place category is most applicable.

5. Click on the Create Page option.

6. Once the page is created (which takes just a few minutes), you'll want to invest the necessary time to customize the page and populate it with your bio, contact information, location, profile photo, cover photo, and other content that includes a detailed description and photos of your Airbnb rental property, as well as information about the area where it's located.

7. Start by inviting your online-based Facebook friends to visit your newly created Facebook page and then start promoting it to the public, as well as any past or potential guests.

In addition to hosting a Facebook page, consider becoming active on various Facebook groups that are dedicated to Airbnb-related travel, general travel, vacationing, and short-term rentals. Also, join Facebook groups and other social media platforms that cater to the interests of your desired guests. If you cater to international travelers, setting up a free WhatsApp account and using the WhatsApp mobile app will make it easier to communicate with these people once they've booked a reservation.

Become Active on Airbnb and Travel-Related Facebook Groups

After logging into your personal Facebook account, within the Search Facebook field, it's easy to find Airbnb and travel-related groups to join and become active on, simply by entering keywords, like "Airbnb," "Vacation Rentals," "Short-Term Rentals," "Family Vacations," "Business Travel," or "Remote Work Locations." You can narrow down your search by adding the city, state, and country for the geographic area your Airbnb property is located. For example, "Orlando Vacation Rentals" or "Airbnb Orlando."

Along with attracting potential guests, you can also use Facebook Groups to interact with fellow hosts and find short-term rental-related services you need, such as cleaning services, property managers, or local maintenance people who specialize in working with Airbnb hosts.

Don't just limit yourself to Facebook, however. You can generate leads for Airbnb bookings using other social media services, too. For example, Instagram and Twitter are ideal for showcasing photos with text-based captions of your property. The captions should all include multiple related hashtags, such as: #Airbnb, #Airbnb[Your City Name], #[Your City Name]VacationRental, #AirbnbLife, #AirbnbTravel, and #AirbnbHome.

While you can invest as much or as little time as you'd like to utilize social media as a promotional tool for your Airbnb property, it requires an ongoing commitment to establish and continuously build your audience. Consider reading books or taking online courses that teach the ins and outs of social media marketing.

If you have the budget, advertising on Facebook, Instagram, and/or Twitter, as well as on Google, is a very easy and affordable way to quickly reach a highly targeted audience. And you can typically set up and launch an ad campaign for your Airbnb property for as little as $50 to $100 and begin seeing results within hours.

#4: Create a YouTube Channel

If you're a bit creative, have some extra time on your hands, and don't mind being in front of the camera, there are a bunch of benefits to creating a YouTube channel for your short-term rental property and then publishing a series of short videos that showcase the property itself and highlight some of the local attractions and activities in your area.

Not only will a series of two- to three-minute videos allow you to provide a video tour of your property and provide compelling reasons for people to stay there, each video will almost immediately generate an additional search result on Google (based on search terms and keywords you provide). Of course, each video you publish will include a direct link to your Airbnb listing for people to book their reservation.

 NOTE

> YouTube has more than two billion active users, so if you create videos with an attention-grabbing title and with informative content that's well produced, chances are you'll be able to target your most desired guests and entice them to book a stay at your property.

When producing YouTube videos (or any video content for social media), you'll want to shoot it in at least 1080p resolution (preferably 4K resolution) and make the content look and sound professional. This means that good quality lighting, sound, and overall production quality are as important as the information you're conveying within the videos. Yes, creating a YouTube channel with a series of short videos will require that you invest in some extra equipment, plus invest the necessary time to film, edit, and publish the videos. However, you may discover that, over time, your videos capture an audience of potential guests you might not have otherwise reached.

TIP

Once you produce your videos and publish them on YouTube, it's also possible to include links to them within your actual Airbnb property listing. According to research published by iGMS and HubSpot, "72 percent of customers would rather learn about a product or service by watching a video." You can discover useful tips for producing videos to promote your Airbnb property by visiting www.igms.com/airbnb-video.

As with any promotional or sales-oriented video that will be published on YouTube, social media, or within your Airbnb listing, the content should not be a blatant commercial. Instead, it's best to adopt a soft-sell approach with video content that offers information viewers will find valuable. Video topics might include: "How to Choose the Best Airbnb Accommodations in [insert your location]," "10 Fun Things to Do in [insert your location," "Why Stay at an Airbnb When Visiting [insert your location]," or "Discover a Cozy Airbnb Getaway in [insert your location]." You could also feature a narrated tour of your property and highlight the best reasons to stay there.

When creating the content for your videos, make sure what you include appeals directly to the intended guests. Also, be sure to include a call to action. This tells the viewer exactly what to do and when. For example, the call to action for an Airbnb property–related video might be, "Be sure to click on this link to learn more about our Airbnb property and book your reservation now, since space is limited." Another call to action might be, "If you book your reservation immediately and mention this video, receive a [insert percentage amount] discount on your stay."

Your videos should tell a compelling story, provide a complete walk-through of your property (inside and outside), discuss why people should stay with you, and explain the best things to see and do during their stay. Of course, you also want people to get to know you, their host. To achieve the best results, consider hiring a professional videographer who specializes in real estate and in producing marketing videos. However, you can also shoot good quality video using one of the latest Apple iPhones, Google Pixel smartphones, or Samsung Galaxy S series smartphones.

#5: Print and Distribute Business Cards and Brochures

You already know the power of word-of-mouth advertising. For people who network and share information in the real world, it's a good strategy to be able to distribute printed business cards or a full-color brochure that highlights your Airbnb property and that prominently displays the Airbnb URL (or a custom URL) that leads potential guests directly to your Airbnb listing.

On the front of your business cards, include important details, like your name, a few words that describe your property and who it's targeted to, the region where your Airbnb property is located (but not its exact address), and its Airbnb listing's URL. On the back of the business card, include a short list of bullet points that highlight amenities offered and key reasons why people should stay at your property. For example, if it's pet-friendly, suitable for business travelers, or offers a waterfront view. If you opt to have full-color, two-sided business cards printed, you can also feature one or two small photos of your property.

Creating a trifold, full-color brochure that you distribute to your network, guests when they stay with you, and local businesses in your community can provide a lot more detail about your Airbnb property and showcase additional photos.

A wide range of printers offer low-cost, full-color printing for business cards and brochures. Some even offer templates you can use to design and lay out your materials yourself on your computer. You can also use a service, like Canva (www.canva.com), to help you lay out and design printed promotional materials for your Airbnb property, even if you have no graphic design skill whatsoever.

Several business card and brochure printing services worth looking at include:

- 48HourPrint—www.48hourprint.com
- Costco Business Printing—www.costcobusinessprinting.com

- Local Staples office supply locations—www.staples.com
- Overnight Prints—www.overnightprints.com
- VistaPrint—www.vistaprint.com

#6: Publish a Website, Podcast, or Blog about Your Property and Region

Think of a website for your Airbnb property as being an online-based brochure and an extension of your Airbnb listing that you have 100 percent control over. Creating a basic website is relatively easy when you use a template and a drag-and-drop interface, like one offered by GoDaddy (www.godaddy.com/websites /website-builder), Wix (www.wix.com), or WordPress (https://wordpress.com /website-builder). No programming or website design skills are required.

By creating and registering an easy-to-remember website URL that leads to your website, this is yet another easy way you can promote your Airbnb property. To keep the website content fresh, consider incorporating a weekly or monthly blog into it. This will allow you to share more information about your property and surrounding area, while potentially attracting more guests. You can also adapt content you create for your Airbnb listing, guidebook, and house manual into the website.

A slightly more time-consuming promotional tool is to create a podcast about your Airbnb property and your local area. A podcast is like a free radio program that people can listen to via the internet using their computer, mobile device, smart speaker, or smart TV. If you opt to produce a podcast, plan to record at least 10 episodes that are between 5 and 15 minutes (no more than 30 minutes) each.

A few topics you can cover on your website, blog, or podcast include:

- 5 Reasons to Stay at Your Airbnb Property
- 10 Tips for Getting the Most Out of Your Airbnb Accommodations
- 5 Tips for Finding the Perfect Airbnb Accommodations for Your Best Vacation
- 5 Tips for Finding the Perfect Airbnb Accommodations for Business Travel
- Top 5 Things to See and Do in [Insert Your City or Geographic Area]

TIP

To learn how to produce and promote a podcast, be sure to pick up a copy of *Start Your Own Podcast Business* ($19.99, Jason R. Rich, Entrepreneur Press, www.entrepreneur.com/bookstore).

#7: Collaborate with Travel Journalists and Influencers

Instead of spending the time, money, and resources to build an online presence for your Airbnb property to capture the attention of travelers, consider working with already established travel journalists, podcasters, bloggers, and vloggers (YouTubers). With a little bit of research, you can discover the top travel-related journalists that cover your geographic area or that review accommodations and invite them to stay for two nights for free at your Airbnb property in exchange for a review or coverage within their printed or online-based publication.

Pinpoint the travel journalists who have the largest audience and influence, based on the type of people you want as guests to your Airbnb property, email them a one-page press release or brochure about your property, and then invite them for a complimentary stay.

You can find a directory of travel journalists using any of these databases, although some charge a fee to access them:

- Critical Mention—www.criticalmention.com/media-contact-database
- Everything Everywhere—https://everything-everywhere.com/list-of-professional-travel-journalism-organizations
- Intelligent Relations—https://intelligentrelations.com/insights/travel-writer-for-pr
- Jona—www.jonapr.co/lists/travel-journalists
- North American Travel Journalists Association—www.natja.org
- SATW Media Guide—www.officialmediaguide.com/satw

TIP

For tips on how to write an attention-getting, one-page press release about your Airbnb property, visit www.vistaprint.com/hub/how-to -write-press-release, www.prnewswire.com/resources/white-papers /guide-to-writing-a-great-press-release, or https://mailchimp.com /resources/writing-press-releases.

When sending a press release to a travel journalist, include a cover letter that contains a reason why they should be interested in reviewing or writing about your Airbnb property. Also, include an invitation to stay with you on a complimentary basis. Whether or not you choose to cover their transportation, food, and activities in conjunction with their stay is up to you (but this is encouraged for travel journalists who have a large audience).

#8: Add Your Accommodations Listing to Google Maps, Apple Maps, and Yelp!

If you choose to operate your Airbnb short-term rental property more like a tra-ditional bed-and-breakfast, and you have Instant Bookings turned on, you might want to add a listing for your Airbnb property to Google Maps and Apple Maps, so your information comes up when people are looking for last-minute accom-modations during their travels. Having a listing on Yelp! is also useful, since so many travelers rely on this service's reviews for accommodations-related advice.

To get your Airbnb short-term rental business listed on Yelp!, visit https://biz .yelp.com/claim. To add a listing on Apple Maps, visit https://register.apple .com/login, and to get listed on Google Maps, visit https://support.google.com /business/answer/2911778. When filling out the online forms for inclusion, be sure to provide all relevant information, including your Airbnb listing's URL. However, be careful about listing the exact address so people don't just randomly show up at your door looking for a place to sleep (unless this is something you don't mind happening).

#9: Connect with Your Local Tourism Office

Just about every region in the world has a local tourism office that travelers can contact for recommendations about accommodations, tourist attractions, activities, dining, and anything else having to do with their trip to a specific area. If you have brochures printed, be sure to provide a stack of them to your local tourism office. Also, make direct contact with that office to ask how you can start receiving referrals.

#10: Cross-Promote with Other Airbnb Hosts

Especially during peak travel periods, it's likely that nearby hotels, motels, B&Bs, and other Airbnb properties will sell out. With a little bit of networking, you could contact these local accommodation options and agree to refer guests to them when your property is totally filled, in exchange for them reciprocating the favor. Or, if your property is family-friendly, business travel–friendly, or pet-friendly, but other nearby Airbnb properties are not, ask those hosts to refer potential guests to your Airbnb listing, and agree to do the same when you encounter guests you cannot or do not wish to accommodate.

One of the easiest ways to meet and interact with other local Airbnb hosts is to join a local Airbnb Host Club. You can find a directory of these clubs at https://community.withairbnb.com/t5/Local-Host-Clubs/ct-p/en_clubs. In addition to providing a great networking opportunity, Airbnb Host Clubs are a great source for advice, guidance, and referrals for local services (like cleaning services, landscapers, handymen, plumbers, and electricians).

Join a Hosting Team or Become a Co-host

While an Airbnb Host Club is all about allowing Airbnb hosts to network, become friends, and share information, an Airbnb Hosting Team is different. This is when hosts team up to help manage each other's Airbnb properties either on a short-term or ongoing basis, in exchange for a commission on each booking.

In fact, becoming an Airbnb Team Host through this program does not require you to have your own Airbnb property. You can simply complete the necessary online training and certification, and then earn extra income by helping other nearby hosts manage their properties that you live close to.

Someone on an Airbnb Hosting Team can handle a wide range of tasks, like property preparation, listing management, guest interactions, writing guest reviews, coordinating reservations, and overseeing (or handling) cleaning and maintenance for a registered Airbnb property. To learn more about this opportunity, visit www.airbnb.com/help/article/970.

Meanwhile, an Airbnb Co-host is also something slightly different. It's a more informal relationship Airbnb hosts can establish to help manage each other's properties. A co-host can also be a nearby friend or family member who can serve as a host for your property when you're not available to do it yourself. To learn more about how Co-hosting works, visit www.airbnb.com/help/article/3153.

Registering as an Airbnb Team Host offers a formal income-generating opportunity—although it's less lucrative than making your own property a short-term rental. What you can earn as an Airbnb Co-host is dictated by the deal you make with each individual host on a more informal basis.

Ways to Transform Airbnb Hosting into a Full-Time Career

There are several ways to transform being an Airbnb host into a full-time career that earns you a respectable income. Some of the options that are explored in the next chapter include:

- Making additional individual rooms or spaces (such as a finished basement) within your existing property available as a short-term rental.
- Building additional stand-alone structures on your property, whether it's one or more tiny homes, a treehouse, cottages, cabins, deluxe tents, yurts, a barn, or campers that are set up with electricity and plumbing.
- Purchasing (or leasing) additional properties to be used exclusively for short-term or long-term rentals through Airbnb and other services.
- Becoming an Airbnb Team Host to supplement your income.

Whether you choose to pursue hosting full-time or part-time, as a side gig or as your primary career, being a host through Airbnb offers a handful of lucrative options, especially if you have the real estate knowledge and financial capital to invest in multiple properties and/or Airbnb-friendly apartments (www.airbnb .com/airbnb-friendly). Among the other topics covered in the next chapter is how to pinpoint the best investment properties to offer as Airbnb short-term or long-term rental properties.

CHAPTER 11

Ways to Make Being an Airbnb Host Your Full-Time Career

Over the years, Airbnb has evolved a lot as a service, platform, and online community. This continued evolution allows people just like you to generate income using short-term rentals in a lot of different ways. This chapter serves as a recap of ways you can utilize the Airbnb platform—based on your own goals and resources. It also explores ways you can transform your involvement with Airbnb and the short-term rental business into a potentially lucrative full-time career by investing in multiple properties to expand your offerings as an Airbnb host.

Increase Your Income as an Airbnb Co-host

In the previous chapter, the concept of becoming an "Airbnb Co-host" (also referred to as a short-term rental virtual assistant) was mentioned. This is an opportunity to manage other people's Airbnb properties in your local area in exchange for compensation.

As an Airbnb Co-host, your job is to help people who have a second home or multiple investment properties manage them as short-term or long-term rentals via Airbnb and handle most or all responsibilities associated with being an Airbnb host, without actually owning or leasing any property. In fact, if there are multiple property owners in your geographic area that want to generate some revenue by making their property available for short- or long-term rental via Airbnb, but they don't want to invest their own time and energy to become a host, that's where you can step in.

Airbnb Co-hosts are typically paid on a commission basis—receiving a percentage of the revenue generated by the Airbnb bookings they oversee and handle on behalf of the property owner(s) they work with. By taking on this role for several properties that wind up having an average to high occupancy rate, this can become an ongoing revenue-generating opportunity. Of course, if you already own or lease one or two properties of your own, you can continue serving as a host for them, while taking on the additional responsibility of being a host for other properties to earn extra revenue.

If becoming an Airbnb Co-host evolves into your part- or full-time job, consider setting yourself up as a legal business entity for the tax benefits and legal protections this offers, especially when your small business invests in the proper insurance policies. And, once you develop your network of trusted resources, such as reliable cleaning services, handymen, landscapers, plumbers, and other specialists that you have at your disposal when needed, you can hire additional people to work for you as part-time Airbnb Co-hosts or virtual assistants that will allow you to expand your clientele to include even more property owners in a larger geographic area. Again, this can all be done without owning or leasing any property.

The following three Airbnb web pages will help you become more familiar with the Airbnb Co-host problem and its current requirements.

- **Co-Hosts: An Introduction**—www.airbnb.com/help/article/1243
- **What Co-Hosts Can Do**—www.airbnb.com/help/article/1534
- **Co-Hosting Tips**—www.airbnb.com/help/article/1549

TIP

After agreeing to the financial terms for your co-hosting services with property owners, one way to ensure prompt payment is to set up a split-payment option for each property you manage through Airbnb. By doing this, as soon as each guest's payment is processed and collected by Airbnb, your percentage of that payment is automatically paid to you by Airbnb. This is a feature that must be set up by the property owner or property listing manager. Information about how to do this can be found at www.airbnb.com/help/article/1343.

According to the Hospitable website (https://hospitable.com/airbnb-co-host), there is no preset amount or percentage that a co-host gets paid. It's typically calculated based on their responsibilities, the size of the property, the location, and the amount of time spent managing each property. The website reports, "On average, Airbnb co-hosts charge 10 to 20 percent of the nightly rate, without cleaning the rental property. So, for example, if you co-host an Airbnb that earns $30,000 per year, you can expect to earn roughly $3,000-$6,000. But if you're supposed to take care of everything from check-in and check-out, to managing guest experiences and cleaning, you could charge up to 25 percent." So, if you're able to serve as a co-host for multiple properties, this can become a lucrative opportunity.

There are many ways to find Airbnb Co-hosting opportunities, including referrals, becoming active on Airbnb-related Facebook groups (such as The Host Nation, www.facebook.com/groups/283637939218027), or becoming active on the online-based Airbnb Community Center (https://community.withairbnb .com/t5/Community-Center/ct-p/community-center). You can also seek out online-based employment ads, on services like CohostMarket (www.cohostmarket .com) or the Airhosts Forum (https://airhostsforum.com). You can also find

Airbnb Co-host job listings on employment websites, like Simply Hired (www .simplyhired.com) or ZipRecruiter (www.ziprecruiter.com/Jobs/Airbnb-Host). There are also property management companies throughout the world looking to hire property managers with experience with short-term rentals and/or Airbnb.

Ways to Expand Your Existing Property

Once Airbnb hosts who rent out an individual room or space within their home become acquainted with the platform and start achieving some success, some opt to convert additional areas within their home into accommodations that can also be featured on Airbnb as separate listings. Doing this allows the host to potentially earn multiple incomes per night by making their property available to separate guests.

Ideally, you want all your guests to have access to their own full bathroom, but there is a vast group of Airbnb travelers looking for low-cost accommodations who are willing to share a bathroom or even a single room with multiple beds.

For a host to benefit from this, it might mean allocating another bedroom or spare room within your home, converting a finished basement into a rental property, creating an apartment or loft over a garage, building additional structures on your property (such as tiny homes or cabins), or offering some other type of alternative accommodations on your property (such as tents or campers). What's possible is limited by your own creativity and what type of accommodations Airbnb travelers to your geographic area are looking for.

Invest in Additional Properties

For short-term rental entrepreneurs, there's also the option of purchasing (or leasing) and managing multiple properties on Airbnb and other platforms. Obviously, this can be a riskier endeavor, especially if you're counting on short-term rental revenue to cover all costs associated with the additional properties (including mortgage or lease payments, property taxes, and upkeep).

If the world experiences another major pandemic (or a massive resurgence of COVID-19), or experiences a major recession, for example, your potential occupancy rate (and ultimately your income from the properties) could take a sudden and long-lasting nosedive.

Thus, if you don't have the financial means to cover the costs associated with the additional properties, you could find yourself in a foreclosure situation, in deep personal debt, or even bankruptcy if the investment properties were not purchased with guidance from an attorney and accountant who could show you how to protect yourself financially and legally.

There are proven ways, however, to mitigate this risk. For example, there are a wide range of online-based tools (such as investment rental income calculators) and services that will help you find and pre-analyze investment properties to determine their income potential as a short- or long-term rental property, before making the real estate purchase. Some of these services help you perform extensive research about a property, based on its location, number of bedrooms, number of guests that can be accommodated, local attractions and tourism, regional short-term rental occupancy rates, amenities you plan to offer, price, and many other factors, to help you pinpoint the best investment opportunities.

Some of these tools include:

- **AirDNA**—www.airdna.co/best-places-to-invest-in-vacation-rentals
- **Awning**—https://awning.com/airbnb-estimator
- **Mashvisor**—www.mashvisor.com
- **Evolve**—https://evolve.com/blog/homeowner-tips /vacation-rental-income-calculator

Once you've acquired investment properties, there are management companies and consultants that will handle furnishing and decorating the property on your behalf, and even manage all aspects of the property rental through Airbnb and other services.

According to the Awning website, "Owning an Airbnb can be very profitable, but like any investment it takes some research to get a good one. A profitable Airbnb needs to be in a desirable location with a solid daily rate. It also needs to offer great furnishing and amenities to have a high occupancy. Finally, hosts or property managers must work hard to ensure that guests leave plenty of positive reviews…. The best properties to compare a potential Airbnb investment to are ones that a guest would likely consider if looking at your property. Comparable properties should be in the same price range, have similar furnishings, offer the same amenities, and otherwise be in the same area or in proximity to the same destinations."

A few of the important factors to consider when seeking out the ideal investment properties to use for short-term rentals include:

- Geographic location
- Proximity to attractions and tourist destinations
- Local tourism in the area
- The size of the property and how many guests can be accommodated
- Accessibility to local restaurants, shopping, and activities
- Proximity to hospitals, colleges, or large companies where temporary employees (doctors, nurses, professors, interns, or contract workers) come to work for several months at a time
- What types of guests you're looking to attract, such as affluent travelers, people looking for bargain accommodations, families (with young kids or infants), honeymooners, business travelers, road trippers, people traveling with pets, solo travelers, people looking to stay near a particular attraction, etc.
- Proximity to local public transportation.

Even during the COVID-19 pandemic and lockdown, some Airbnb hosts wound up making more revenue than ever because their property was located close to a hospital, a college/university, or a major corporation that uses contracted employees or interns for just a few months at a time. This desirable proximity allowed the hosts to attract doctors, nurses, families with a close relative requiring long-term hospital care, students, professors, and workers who needed accommodations for several months at a time. These people often want a fully furnished, safe, and comfortable place to stay that does not offer the sterile environment of a costly hotel.

As a backup plan in case short-term rental demand slows down for whatever reason, make sure your investment property might appeal to long-term renters (30 nights or longer). Then, make your property available for booking through Airbnb (and similar services), a long-term rental management agency, and/or a realtor (or real estate rental agency).

 TIP

Before investing in one or more investment properties, do your due diligence and research related to its desirability and functionality as a rental property. And, most importantly, make sure that the town, city, state, or region where the property is located legally allows for short-term or long-term rentals. Seek out guidance from a real estate attorney, accountant, and local real estate agent (Realtor) who understand the short- and long-term rental business.

Lease Additional Properties

Instead of purchasing or financing real estate to be used for short-term rental, some Airbnb hosts have discovered that it's less risky and more lucrative to pinpoint ideal properties and then sign long-term leases for those properties with their existing owners. Once the property is leased, it's then managed as an Airbnb property by the lessee. Of course, the property owner must agree to this arrangement and short-term rentals must be legal in that geographic area.

Subletting a property that you then plan to manage as an Airbnb short-term rental can also be considered a corporate lease. And yes, it includes some risk, but not as much as purchasing (or financing) a property outright. This process is referred to as "rental arbitrage," which means you're renting out a property on a long-term basis for the sole purpose of listing it on Airbnb or a similar service, and then managing it as a short-term rental.

What About the Profit Potential of Rental Arbitrage?

Let's say you sign a long-term lease on a home or apartment that costs you $2,000 per month. You can then potentially sublet that property via Airbnb for $200 per night. Once you add your expenses, if you're able to maintain an occupancy rate that includes at least 12 to 15 paid nights per month, you'll probably wind up breaking even. Then, any additional nights you book via Airbnb will generate a profit for you. So, during a month with 30 days, your profit potential is around $2,000 (assuming 100 percent occupancy, which is rarely achievable on a consistent basis, unless you offer a superior property within an in-demand location and charge a competitive nightly rate compared to the competition, or you're able to consistently book long-term guests who reserve the property for one or more months at a time).

While these numbers are used for demonstration purposes only, don't even consider leasing a property that you're not extremely confident will have at least a 50 percent occupancy rate via bookings through Airbnb and similar services. Otherwise, the financial risk increases rather dramatically.

According to the Airbtics website (https://airbtics.com/how-to-find-rental -arbitrage-properties), "There are certainly various ways to find rental arbitrage properties, but it may take some time to figure out the best ones for you if you don't conduct the necessary research carefully."

Choosing this business model will require you to pay the property owner (lessor) a security deposit (which is typically two months' rent). You'll also need to hire an attorney to help broker the deal, acquire appropriate insurance, and then furnish the property—all of which must be calculated into your startup costs. You'll then incur all the usual fees associated with being an Airbnb host, including cleaning fees, landscaping fees, and potentially property maintenance fees.

Airbnb hosts who have chosen to pursue this business model for one or more properties must do careful number crunching to ensure that, based on the anticipated occupancy rate when offered as an Airbnb property, it will generate enough revenue to cover the lease and all related expenses, plus generate at least a 20 percent profit each month. A contingency plan must also be put in place to cover expenses when the Airbnb occupancy rate drops lower than expected, yet the property owner still expects their monthly lease payment and other expenses must also continue to be covered. Thus, you do not want to lease a property that will only generate Airbnb (or short-term rentals) seasonally, unless the profit you're able to generate during the peak season will cover your leasing and operating expenses for the entire year.

According to the iGMS website (www.igms.com/corporate-lease-airbnb), "Once you have gotten the hang of how a corporate lease on Airbnb works, you can basically apply the same strategy to get a second property. This way you can grow your property portfolio and ultimately your business much faster. As you will be using others' properties, you can start a short-term rental business without owning any of your own rental properties."

If you choose to adopt a rental arbitrage business model, seriously consider forming and operating as an LLC (Limited Liability Corporation), which provides you with some added legal protections. Again, consult with an attorney before pursuing this type of short-term rental opportunity.

Once you become fully acquainted with the corporate leasing strategy and have one unit successfully up and running (and profitable), you can grow your business by leasing additional properties that you'll also operate as short-term rentals via Airbnb.

 **WARNING**

If you're thinking about subletting an apartment or home that you already lease or rent, the Nolo website (www.nolo.com/legal -encyclopedia/how-sublet-rental-unit.html) offers this advice: "Before you spread the word or post an ad on Craigslist for a subletter (also known as a subtenant), check to see whether your lease or rental agreement prohibits sublets (called subleases). Be sure to get your landlord's permission before allowing someone else to move into your rental on a temporary basis. Finally, get all sublet-related agreements with your landlord and new subtenant in writing."

There are many real estate websites that can help you find investment properties to lease that would be ideally suited to manage as an Airbnb short-term rental property using rental arbitrage. Once you understand exactly the type of property you're looking for, you can browse through many available property listings by region quickly using services like:

- Apartments.com—www.apartments.com
- Realtor.com—www.realtor.com
- Trulia—www.trulia.com
- Zillow—www.zillow.com
- Zumper—www.zumper.com

 TIP

You can learn more about the ins and outs of Airbnb rental arbitrage from information provided on AirDNA's website (www.airdna.co/blog /airbnb-rental-arbitrage) and Hostfully's website (www.hostfully.com /blog/airbnb-rental-arbitrage).

Become an Airbnb Consultant

Once you've proven yourself as a successful Airbnb host (and potentially have earned the Superhost classification), yet another revenue opportunity is to market yourself as an Airbnb Consultant. This is someone who shares their experience and knowledge with a prospective or first-time Airbnb host and who charges a fee for their consultations and time.

You can market your services online via Airbnb-related Facebook groups and by joining Airbnb Host Clubs (https://community.withairbnb.com/t5/Local -Host-Clubs/ct-p/en_clubs). How much you can charge for your consulting services will depend on what you're offering and the time you spend with clients.

Consider Hiring an Airbnb Consultant to Help You Get Started

If you're looking for more expert advice as you initially get started, you can learn a lot from the Airbnb Superhosts interviewed within this book, but if you want more personalized, one-on-one guidance—based on your specific property—consider hiring an Airbnb Consultant to help you get started successfully.

While there are many short-term rental consulting businesses, like BuildYourBnb (www.buildyourbnb.com/product/airbnb-consulting), you may find it more helpful to hire an already established Airbnb host (or Superhost) in your geographic area who will meet with you in person and offer you guidance as you get your short-term rental business of the ground.

Meet Superhost Anna Schiller

Based in Del Rio, Texas, Anna Schiller is an expert in the short-term rental industry. She's also the founder and CEO of Capri Temporary Housing, a provider of furnished, short-term rental apartments between Texas and California. In this interview, Schiller shares her advice about what it takes to be a superior Airbnb host and ultimately expand your own short-term rental business to include multiple properties.

How did you get involved with short-term rentals and Airbnb?

Anna Schiller: "Back in the early-2000s, a friend of mine gave us a book that explained the value of building assets through real estate. We started by getting involved with rental homes by purchasing a four-plex. Shortly after that, a perspective tenant approached us by asking what we'd charge for a fully furnished apartment. After doing some research, I determined there was a need for furnished short-term rentals in my local area [Del Rio, Texas]. When some of our apartments went empty, I furnished and decorated them, but then waited for potential short-term bookings. At the time, Airbnb did not exist, and I had no clue how to promote our property.

"Our first guest was someone who came to our area to pursue alternative cancer treatments and needed a place to stay. After that, word started to get around about what we were offering. Over time, I then learned about subleasing apartments [rental arbitrage] and began to expand our offerings. When Airbnb came along, I created property listings for several of the properties we then owned. In the times when our regular, long-term leases didn't provide us with full occupancy, we were able to fill our properties using short-term rentals. This became a very profitable revenue source for me and my husband, because Airbnb did all the marketing.

"If you're doing rental arbitrage in apartment communities, it's essential that you build strong relationships with those communities, as well as the apartment owners, because there's way too much potential for things to go wrong. Many apartment communities do not permit short-term rentals, so it's important to follow the rules."

As of early-2023, how many properties do you own, lease, or manage?

Anna Schiller: "My company now operates more than 50 short-term and long-term rental units, although not all of them are on Airbnb. One thing I don't like about Airbnb is that, aside from determining if they've been verified with Airbnb, you can't do too much research about potential renters. Not all the Airbnb short-term guests are as conscientious about keeping a property they're staying at clean, for example, as long-term renters who the landlord has done a background check on. For someone first getting started with Airbnb, I recommend working with properties that they own in regions that allow for short-term rentals."

What would you say makes the perfect short-term rental property?

Anna Schiller: "I look for something that is in a good location. Airbnb travelers always want to stay in a safe location, so that's my first criteria for identifying a potential Airbnb property. I then retrofit the property with quality locks, peep-holes in the doors, and outside lighting, if appropriate. Some of my locations are located near a lake that people like to go boating on. As a result, I chose properties that offer ample space for guests to park their car and a trailer for their boat. However, if your plan is to host business travelers, you want a space that's close to work centers, malls, and restaurants. If you want to target traveling medical professionals, you'll want a property that's close to a hospital or nursing home, for example. I start by picking a target audience and then choosing a property in a location that attracts those types of guests."

In terms of security, how do you feel about using security cameras inside and outside of the property?

Anna Schiller: "Personally, I do not install cameras in or around our properties. If you're going to do this, you must be up front and honest about the presence of the cameras with all your guests. Never even consider installing a security camera within a bedroom or bathroom. That's a hotbed of liability. If you insist on using security cameras inside your property, they should only be present in the common areas. Travelers who book accommodations through Airbnb want their privacy."

What are some of the strategies you discovered for creating attention-grabbing property listings on Airbnb?

Anna Schiller: "I started looking on the internet to see how nearby hotels and apartment complexes were talking about their properties and what amenities they were offering. I then created listings for my properties based on what I saw was drawing people to those nearby hotels and apartments. I looked at the kinds of photos hotels were using on their respective websites, and then created photos for my properties using those for inspiration and that I felt would be appealing to me as a traveler. For example, in my Airbnb property listings, I would never feature a photo of a toilet, unless I was also showcasing a hot tub located in that bathroom.

"I also browsed through many Airbnb listings and paid attention to what I believed made those listings successful, and then mimicked those approaches in my property listing text and photos, always without plagiarizing those other listings. I also write my property listings geared toward the type of guests I am looking to attract."

What tips do you have for creating property photos that will appear within an Airbnb listing?

Anna Schiller: "I take my own photography using the cameras built into my iPhone. Start by preparing the property and staging it in a way that will look exactly how a guest will see it when they first arrive. For example, in all the bedrooms, I always feature all white linens. In photos, the beds are nicely made. The cleanliness of the rooms and linens is always displayed, and I often place a tray with a tea set on the bed, because I feel that's very enticing and makes the bedroom look more welcoming and cozier."

As an owner or manager of many properties, how do you maintain quality consistency?

Anna Schiller: "I rely on multiple checklists. I have a list for everything that belongs in each property and where it goes, and another checklist for all the cleaning and arranging that needs to be done in between guests. I also have a checklist I use for inspecting the property before a guest arrives. If I can't inspect the property myself, I insist the cleaning crew send me photos of every room to make sure they've cleaned and prepared the property perfectly. For me checklists are essential for maintaining the cleanliness and quality standards I want maintained for my guests. If a vendor, such as a cleaning service, does not follow my checklists exactly, they will not continue working for me. It's that simple."

Do you find it challenging to find quality and reliable cleaning and maintenance people that live up to your standards?

Anna Schiller: "This is probably the biggest challenge I face. When I am reviewing potential applicants for a cleaning position, for example, I determine if I think they're teachable. In other words, will they follow my guidelines and checklists to maintain the quality and cleanliness I insist on. If I don't feel an applicant will take direction well, I will not hire them. It's all about building relationships, finding people you trust, and clearly communicating exactly what you expect. People who work for me need to understand what my expectations are and be willing to do that work for the fee we agree upon."

What strategies do you use to set your nightly rates?

Anna Schiller: "I start by figuring out exactly how much money I need to earn per night to cover all my expenses for that property and make it profitable based on the property itself and the level of amenities I offer. Since I am operating a company, I have more overhead than someone who manages just one Airbnb property, so my nightly fee must be higher. For example, I have a cleaning service and property maintenance service that needs to be paid. I created a formula that covers my expenses and allows me to earn a profit, but that helps me stay competitive in the area where each property is located.

"I do not use Airbnb's Smart Pricing tool. I have found that the nightly pricing it comes up with is often significantly lower than what I can charge for that property. If I can get close to that price, I will, but I rely on my own formula. Part of this formula involves considering depreciation of the furniture and appliances within the property, so there is money set aside to periodically replace that furniture and the appliances every few years when it becomes necessary. I also consider ongoing cleaning and maintenance costs, as well as the Airbnb fees. If you're not making a profit from your short-term rental business, being a host will not be fun. If you're going to be a host, you want to have fun and enjoy meeting people."

How much interaction do you have with your guests once they check in?

Anna Schiller: "I make it clear that I am available anytime if a guest has a question or problem, but I try to leave them alone as much as possible and respect their privacy. I also found that the best and safest way to interact with guests, especially short-term guests, is through the Airbnb messaging service. Most Airbnb travelers are not wanting to hang out with their host. They just want a place to stay that's better than a hotel."

What amenities do your properties offer that you found to be the most in demand and important?

Anna Schiller: "All of my properties have washers and dryers within them. I found that's a big deal. I also leave snacks and bottles of water for people for their arrival. Another thing I do is make sure that every property, even if they're in proximity or there are multiple apartments within the same building, has its own internet and that separate guests never need to share an internet connection. I also try to offer parking right outside of the door of each property. I come from an Italian background, so I try to offer some Italian décor and amenities within each short-term rental property. This helps to set my properties apart and share my heritage. For example, within each kitchen, I will leave spaghetti and spaghetti sauce that guests can make for themselves."

What House Rules have you discovered are the most important to list and enforce?

Anna Schiller: "I have quiet hours in each of my properties. I also do not permit guests to host parties. I do not allow smoking inside, period. Keeping a property clean that allows smoking is extremely costly. If someone smokes, I charge a $500 cleaning fee, and that does not even cover my cost. I do charge a refundable deposit, but I have only needed to keep this deposit a few times. Most of the time, I found that guests follow the House Rules and are respectful of the property."

What other tips or strategies do you have for Airbnb hosts?

Anna Schiller: "Once you set a nightly rate that you believe is fair, stick to it. Don't be willing to negotiate. While you can offer a discount for a weekly or monthly stay, for example, don't allow short-term guests to try to wheedle you down on your nightly rate. I have found that it's often the people who try to pay less than the nightly rate that cause the most damage, are the messiest, and that show the least respect for the property. For example, I had a woman who asked for a lower rate, which I agreed to, but then she wound up bringing a pet to the property where I do not allow pets and insisted on staying longer at the discounted rate than her original booking. After trying to accommodate her and make her happy, she wound up leaving a poor review. As a host, love yourself enough to stick to your pricing. Be confident in the product you're providing and be consistent in what you're offering."

Final Thoughts...

By now, you should understand that Airbnb is a constantly evolving short-term rental platform and community comprised of travelers, hosts, and experience providers. Becoming a host offers tremendous opportunity for making money and meeting new people.

Becoming successful will require you to provide clean, comfortable, and affordable accommodations that travelers want to stay at. It will also require you to invest the time, money, and effort to maintain your property, keep it clean, manage your Airbnb listing, and interact with travelers (potentially online and in person). The people who achieve the most success on a part-time or full-time basis have an outgoing and social personality, believe in the importance of hospitality, and are willing to take those extra steps needed to make all their guests feel as welcome and comfortable as possible during their stay.

As a host, you'll always need to be friendly, professional, patient, detail-oriented, honest, a good communicator (and listener), and have a thorough understanding of how Airbnb works. You also need to be a bit creative and have at least a basic level of aptitude for running a small business. Remember, becoming an Airbnb host is not a get-rich-quick opportunity, but over time, it does offer you the ability to potentially expand your offerings to include operating multiple short-term rental properties that you own, lease, or manage on another property owner's behalf.

After reading this book, you now have the basic understanding of what's required to become a successful Airbnb host. You should now know how to prepare your accommodations to appeal to your guests in a way that'll help you generate consistently positive ratings and reviews, as well as a steady income. Pay attention to the advice and information shared by the Superhosts and hosts interviewed within this book, as they have extensive advice and experience you can learn from.

However, before you get started, do some additional research and networking to make sure you acquire the skills, knowledge, and resources you'll need to achieve long-term success as an Airbnb host. Most importantly, remember to have fun and avoid taking shortcuts as you get your short-term property up and running.

Index

Printed in the USA
CPSIA information can be obtained
at www.ICGtesting.com
JSHW052026161023
50286JS00007B/7

9 781642 011616